a Lousã

Serra da Gardun

Proença-a-Ve

Serra de Alvéos

Idanha-a-Nova .

Velha

Salvaterra
do Extremo .

Segura .

Castelo Branco
.

Rio Ponsul

Rio Erjes

Piedras
Albas

Rio Ocreza

Vila Velha de Ródão

Rio Salor

Alcántara

Cedillo

Herrera de Alcántara

. Santiago de

Alcántara
Los Perales

Tagus

. Nisa

Rio Sever

Membrio .

cia
antes

Belver
.

Rio Sever

Rio Salor

Rossio ao Sul do Tejo

. Pego

al

Alpalhão

. Castelo de Vide .

. Marrão

Valencia de Alcántara

SPAIN

Serra de São Mamede

Portalegre .

Bilbao

. Valladolid

. Salamanca

MADRID .

cantara

Toledo

. Valencia

dajoz

Elvas

lla

Granada

Mediterranean

BADAJOZ

MOROCCO

Rio GUADIANA

. Olivenza

. ÉVORA

BACKWARDS OUT OF THE BIG WORLD

By the same author

BACKWARDS OUT OF THE
BIG WORLD

A VOYAGE INTO
PORTUGAL

Paul Hyland

HarperCollins*Publishers*

HarperCollins*Publishers*
77–85 Fulham Palace Road,
Hammersmith, London W6 8JB

Published by HarperCollins*Publishers* 1996

Copyright © Paul Hyland 1996

Paul Hyland asserts the moral right to be
identified as the author of this work
A catalogue record for this book is available
from the British Library

ISBN 0 00 255556 5

Set in Garamond No. 3 by
Rowland Phototypesetting Limited
Bury St Edmunds, Suffolk

Printed and bound in Great Britain by
Caledonian International
Book Manufacturing Ltd, Glasgow

CONTENTS

ILLUSTRATIONS

King Sebastião in his niche on the mock-Manueline façade of Lisbon's Rossio Station.

A glimpse of the dictator Salazar's New State: mighty *Cristo Rei* and the Monument to the Discoveries on either side of the River Tagus.

A small world within the paved compass or 'rose of the winds' at the foot of the Monument to the Discoveries.

In the miraculous cloister of Jerónimos, the monastery built to celebrate Vasco da Gama's discovery of India.

Eça de Queirós: 'Upon the strong nakedness of truth the diaphanous cloak of fancy.'

Chiado's stage-set. Resurrection after the Lisbon fire of August 1988.

The Tower of Belém. A serious fortress, an icon of *saudade*.

The steps of Montijo's packed womb church during mass on the feast of São Pedro.

Fishing boats that escorted São Pedro across the water.

Campinos on the day of the *Colete Encarnado* (red waistcoat) festival at Vila Franca de Xira.

Bull-running in the streets.

At dawn, the Tagus bridge below Santarém.

A beggar at the heart of Santarém.

Tending the first-floor garden, Santarém.

A barefoot *avieiro* in a street of houses on stilts at Caneiras.

Riders and Lusitano mounts at the National Agricultural Fair.

The hilltop fastness of Marvão, supervising Spain.

Fonte de Vila, the oldest medicinal spring in Castelo de Vide.

About seven in the evening I got into a chaise on shore, and was driven through the nastiest city in the world, though at the same time one of the most populous, to a kind of coffee-house, which is very pleasantly situated on the brow of a hill, about a mile from the city, and hath a very fine prospect of the River Tajo from Lisbon to the sea.

HENRY FIELDING, *The Journal of a Voyage to Lisbon* (1754)

I myself, on these stifling summer nights, often travel as far as my window to get a sight of the snippet of the Tagus at the end of the street . . . My pen was always ambitious: poor yet presumptuous, it needs a broader theme. That is just what I shall give it. I shall go to Santarém, no less, and I swear that everything I see and hear, everything I think and feel, shall be chronicled.

ALMEIDA GARRETT, *Travels in my Homeland* (1846)

In the plausible intimacy of approaching evening, as I stand waiting for the stars to begin at the window of this fourth-floor room that looks out on the infinite, my dreams move to the rhythm required by long journeys to countries as yet unknown, or to countries that are simply hypothetical or impossible.

FERNANDO PESSOA, *The Book of Disquiet* (1912–35)

ACKNOWLEDGEMENTS

Researching this book was made a pleasure by the warmth and generosity of the people who helped me, notably Michael Collins and Portugal 600, José Abilio, the Anglo-Portuguese Society and Canning House library, Eileen Barnard, Graça Batista and Centro Municipal de Cultura e Desenvolvimento de Vila Velha de Ródão, Margaret Jull Costa, Joaquim Duarte, Augustín Egurrola, Ana Luísa Faria, Célia Ferreira, Helder Ferreira, Maria Salomé Ferro, Mike Gerrard, Kathleen Griffin, Pedro Tamen and José Blanco at Fundação Calouste Gulbenkian, Julian Hale and BBC Radio 3, Lala Isla, Ray Keenoy of Boulevard Books, Eric Lane, Eugénio Lisboa, Thomas McCarthy, Bernard McGuirk, Carla Alexander Maestre, Luísa Mesquita, Peter Miles, Maria Lucília Moita, António Morgado, the staff of the North Devon Record Office, Helder Ferreira de Oliveira, Célia Penteado, Miguel Serras Pereira, Pilar S. Pereira, José Reinaldo, Anthony Rudolf, Emilia Saunders and TAP, Phyllis Scott, Fernanda de Sousa, Mike Spring of Hyperion Records, Sir Hugh Stucley, L.C. 'Kim' Taylor, AbdoolKarim Vakil, Manuel Vaz Vicente and Maggie Ware.

A number of quotations are attributed in the text, but here I gratefully acknowledge those from David Ferry's rendering of *Gilgamesh* (Bloodaxe Books, 1993) and from *fados* (in my English versions) by, in order of appearance, in Chapter 17: David Mourão Ferreira, Aníbal Nazaré, António Corrêa d'Oliveira, Alberto Jerónimo, Silva Nunes, José André and Frederico de Brito; in Chapter 18: Frederico de Brito, Francisco Radamanto, Sousa do 'Casacão', Domingos Gonçalves Costa, Augusto Martins and, again, Frederico de Brito; in Chapter 19: Guilherme Pereira da Rosa and Azinhal Abelho.

Special thanks go to the writers Luísa Costa Gomes, Almeida Faria, Ernesto Manuel de Melo e Castro, Helder Macedo, Isabel Allegro de Magalhães, Fernando Martinho and Lídia Jorge; to the President of the Instituto da Biblioteca Naçional e do Livro, Maria Leonor Machado de Sousa, and to Dom Duarte Pio, the Duke of Bragança, all of whom recorded interviews with me for two BBC Radio 3 programmes, *Crick in the Neck* and *Once-and-Future Portugal*, from which I have quoted here.

PROLOGUE

After journeys in Africa and India, I've decided to come home to
Europe. Everyone's been tripping around Eastern Europe recently,
but I want to arrive at the western edge and go in from there. The
edge is Portugal, a country underestimated out of ignorance, a
history that amnesia has wiped clean, a dictatorship which lasted
almost forty years, a revolution we hardly noticed. When I was a
kid I made myself sick on *marmelada*, Portuguese quince jelly. Two
boys who lived with us for a few years, like older brothers to
me, had brought it as a gift from home. Once, I sneaked a gulp
of port too. I thought I'd die; it tasted like bad medicine. My
tastes have changed, but ever after that I wanted perversely to be
Portuguese.

I can't fully explain that enchantment. It's not Portugal's charm
that draws me, it's deeper and darker than that. It's also more
luminous than I could have imagined before meeting the people.
Of all the European powers they took the world in their hands the
earliest, and hung onto it the longest. Today, however, they are
turning their backs on that edge, the world's brink, and talking
about being Europeans, forgetting that their great modernist poet
Fernando Pessoa spoke of 'the Others, Others by birth, Europeans
who aren't truly European because they are not Portuguese'. His
people alone, he believed, were destined to understand that 'the
future is to be universal'. Perhaps it's in this sense that I want to
be Portuguese.

I'd like to find out, to journey in a country which adds up to
somewhere much bigger than the sum of its parts. I want to discover
the discoverers now, at the moment they are turning away from
the temptation of the sea. I want to do it before corporate Europe
exorcises, if it ever can, the primitive spirit for good. And ill. In
the words of the courageous poet and storyteller Miguel Torga

(1907–95), 'I'm going to tell you about a wonderful kingdom – mine, but also belonging to all those who deserve it . . .'

1

THE BRIDGE

Alcântara

THE TAGUS divides Europe from Africa. It's a trick of more than the light. At a thousand kilometres, from its high Spanish birth to its sluggish death in the Atlantic Ocean, the Rio Tejo is the longest river in the Iberian peninsula. As it nears Lisbon and the sea, flowing east to west across mid-Portugal, it disengages continents.

But then, Portugal's destiny always was to refashion our notion of the world. It did it in caravels with compass and astrolabe. Its navigators edged down land masses and struck across great waters, losing sight of the sky marks they knew, and of the Pole Star that kept them sane, until they feared they would sail out of the known through a door into chaos, those black seas conjured by imagination and ridden with monsters and devils. There's a saying with which they confronted and exorcised such perils: *Não se vence perigo sem perigo*, 'Danger's not vanquished without danger.'

The small cargo boat I'm aboard is bringing me south in relative comfort. Treacherous Biscay merely hinted at its old tricks, but somewhere between the galley and the engine room, where metallic high-energy voices echo in the diesel-laden atmosphere and the sound of kitchen knives cuts to the quick before seeping out and dwindling to zero in salt air above a slabby sea, storms brew amongst the Filipino crew. I don't know what to expect for dinner from a frail but apoplectic cook, now breathless and bruised and wrung out with ghastly passion. With impatient regard for each crew member's 'face', German officers separate combatants and quell the dying squalls with abrupt commands.

I'm embarrassed by the accuracy of racial stereotypes. West meets

East. Portuguese sailed out of the river mouth we're approaching to make it happen. The smart Herr Capitain and his smarter First Officer, at whose table I am a guest, grunt with something like satisfaction over a dinner no bloodier than usual. I'm excited, now mutiny has abated, with the prospect of entering the mouth of the Tagus. *'Prost!'* we toast destinations in general. *'Saúde!'* I toast mine in particular. I'll disembark at Lisbon, only to embark on a new journey upriver into Spain. It will be a short trip, a marvellously long voyage into once-and-future Portugal.

North of the Tagus, the country is made of the green hills, valleys and snowy mountains of northern Christian Europe, pale-skinned and pious, conservative and consecrated to the work ethic, or as devout and dedicated as can be in the real world. To the south lies the Alentejo, from *para além do Tejo*, meaning 'beyond the Tagus', free-thinking people in towns of white houses on hot plains, lives shifting between light and deep shadow, bowing to the harsh sensuousness of sun and soil but untroubled by too much religion, as relaxed about church as the Moors mostly were about Islam.

What do these two small continents, north and south, have in common, apart from a long seaboard and an equally long border with, or against, Spain? They combine to shape a country whose frontiers have remained virtually identical, squabbles and pained intermissions excepted, since 1249. These two Portugals have been one, and the same, for the best part of eight centuries. Only island nations can compete with that. Portugal has one tenth of the United Kingdom's population in a little more than a third of the UK's size; or, to put it in perspective, in a little less than 1 per cent of the area of the United States. But the sum of Portugal's parts is greater than its boundaries can possibly embrace. And much greater than the flimsy idea – the port and golf, beach and sardines, poor-man-of-Europe caricature – that's carried in most non-Portuguese heads.

We can't help but carry baggage into other people's countries. I'm gravid with a containerised cargo of information and uncertainties, strong feelings and prejudices, memories of earlier journeys here. I'll try to dump most of it on Alcântara's quay and travel light. I'll take the country as it comes, as it offers itself to me. In any case I suspect that my Portugal, the country in my head, is

2

too grandiose. Maybe I'll come to agree with those proud, self-deprecating natives who turn their backs on the ocean horizon and say, in a sing-song chant, with a nod and a wink towards Brussels, 'Once we were so great, but now we are so small.'

The bump of Cabo Raso is just a thicker sort of darkness until its lighthouse shafts the night. I sharpen my ears, fruitlessly, for the detonating boom of swell in the caverns and blow-holes christened *Bôca do Inferno*, or Mouth of Hell. Lights of the resort of Cascais and the casino and palaces of Estoril glitter thinly like baubles, diamanté clusters and strings of paste pearls. All that luminescence to the north of our pale wake is the playground called Costa do Sol, but known simply to locals as the Marginal. It would be uncharitable to point out that *marginal* means 'delinquent' as well as, of course, 'on the edge' or 'barely there at all'. Some say Portugal itself is Europe's *marginal*. To the south of us is nothing but night.

But after the island fortress of Bugio, there's a trickle of lights there too, running out into darkness down the long beach called Praia da Caparica, the lazy bow bend that ends with the lighthouse at Cabo Espichel, a fitful spark in the mist. All at once these romantic, vague distances shrink and we're within the Tagus's gullet. To starboard, oil-tanks loom and phalanxes of pipes climb and dive in unison as only the most refined plumbing can; then, to port, appears the floodlit genius of Belém where Vasco da Gama came and went to India, with its dainty but in-dead-earnest fortress tower and its mighty monument to the discoveries. Still ahead, high overhead, the bridge of 1966 glints like an erratic ballrace as headlights chase across it. These visions appear in quick succession, but it seems an age before we pass in slow motion beneath the bridge, manoeuvre our way in under the steeply banked lights of Lisbon's hills and make fast, opposite giant *Cristo Rei* on his towering plinth, at the dock called Alcântara.

Alcântara, from Arabic *al-kantara*, means 'the bridge'. A bridge changes the meaning of a river. The Tagus separates continents. This bridge, or that glittering chain of vehicles, links them. A bridge's meaning may change too. In honour of the dictator who ruled here for almost forty years, this American-built single-span two-and-a-half-kilometre suspension bridge – longer than San

Francisco's Golden Gate – was inaugurated as the Salazar Bridge. But it soon changed its name following the day in 1974 when an almost bloodless military coup restored democracy to Portugal: *Ponte Vinte e Cinco de Abril*, 25 April Bridge. It's an endless argument, whether the coup was a real revolution, or could have become one. The young don't even care to argue the toss any more. The revolution's name belongs to a bridge. On hot days it's just a traffic jam, a jam with a view, between the city and the beach.

After April the infamous commander of the old regime's riot police crept to the new rulers and offered himself as traffic controller for the capital. Recently the Foreign Minister, in a sales-pitch for his country at a London dinner, announced that two cars had just crashed on the bridge, causing a jam several kilometres long and making the lead on all TV bulletins. 'Fortunate is the country,' he said, with only a trace of irony, 'where a minor traffic accident is the main news of the day!'

Twenty years after the revolution, vehicles up there jammed with a vengeance. On a Monday in June 1994 drivers began to protest at a 50 per cent overnight rise in the toll. Commuters who'd been paying 100 escudos had to find 150 escudos each day, lorry drivers much more. They didn't refuse to pay but they paid with one-escudo coins, or with 20,000-escudo notes, and leant on their horns.

On Tuesday more people got the idea, oddly exhilarated by slow-moving chaos and a crescendo of discordant sound across the Tagus.

All day Wednesday I worried, over-elaborately, for the inhabitants of Alcântara: whether *en masse* car-horn harmonics would unhinge the girders high overhead.

Thursday, my friend António, with his tragic sense, said in English, 'Pity the poor fish above the bridge.'

'Below,' said José, the English teacher.

For an instant I had seen flying fish, huge ones like silver submarines that metamorphosed into barrage balloons.

On Friday six lorries blocked the Ponte Vinte e Cinco de Abril from morning until late afternoon. The police broke up the jam with batons. I saw it on the news: a lorry driver, covered in blood, on his way to prison. Later I heard that the GNR – National Republican Guard, or the kind of police who are trained to 'shoot into the air' – fired at, rather than above, the head of a young biker and paralysed him.

Luísa, who lives on the south side of the bridge, told me how she'd taken the kids for a day out in town; she had to abandon her car, cross the Tagus by overloaded ferry and get home by taxi. Then she discovered she'd lost her house keys.

'Not such a bad day,' she sighed. 'I mean, there were families on that bridge in that heat for seven hours. Can you imagine?'

'Grief, I can imagine.'

'But the police action,' she almost spat, eyes burning with defiant shame, 'that's real Third World stuff.'

'Old habits die hard,' I said.

Government spokesmen had repeatedly protested the need to raise revenue, but that evening the then Prime Minister, Cavaco Silva, came on TV to talk about the bridge.

'I am always right,' begins one of his choicer sayings, roughly translated, 'I am always right, and seldom mistaken.'

He said a lot more that night. But he cut the toll.

Tonight the Filipinos and the Germans seem happy to be in Lisbon. And sad to see me disembark for good. What is this sentimental loyalty that I feel, this foolish sense of shipboard community, this nonsensical identity that a steel hull, or boundaries on a map, give us? Anything to insulate us from the anarchy of the waters, the bigness of the world. Though my head understands this, as I step from the gangplank on to the Cais de Alcântara and process through official landing procedures, my sea-legs are unreliable and I feel guilty of betrayal, of deserting ship. But behind me the dark tide flows away under the vertiginous bridge and down to the ocean.

I shall swim against the current, like some blindly homing fish. A river is a journey: from the sea towards its source in the Sierra de Albarracin, and downstream again to its mouth and the life of the ocean. The Tagus ignores human frontiers, even the oldest one in Europe, and once launched discoverers on voyages beyond imagined horizons. Spanish kings vainly hoped to make it navigable for trade as far as Toledo. Not so long ago, in a small craft, I could have ascended it to Spain. Now, between the Montes de Toledo and the northern *sierras*, the Tagus steps down from the Iberian *meseta*, sluice by sluice, dam by hydroelectric dam. Spain has the power to hold waters back or to spill them into Portugal, exaggerating treacherous extremes of drought and flood. Dams have turned the river into an impossible obstacle race for boats, or for fish driven by instinct. However I travel – afloat, on road and rail, or on foot – the river will be my reason. My journey will be the Tagus, up it and many a metaphorical tributary. I am travelling inwards from the edge, backwards out of the big world. A river runs one way, like time itself, but I am going with a different flow, feeling for the river beneath the river, *o rio por baixo do rio*, the deep one that runs back into the heart.

The stone statue of Christ, a replica of the Redeemer on the Corcovado above Rio de Janeiro, rises in floodlit majesty above the far bank, arms spread wide. To one priest he was a benefactor, they say; the father is supposed to have embezzled a fortune from moneys raised to erect him and run off to South America. To irreverent drivers heading south across the bridge he is *o sinhaleiro*, the traffic cop. He stands high on his attenuated pyramid, like an angel on the blunt metaphysical point of a pin that pierces small-town Almada on its hill and disrupts the old proportions: those of the monastery, church and white houses that, until they were dwarfed, stood proud against a sea of pine trees. *Cristo Rei* casts his reflection, like a bleached shadow, on the black river. He is poised on the far bank, sure enough, *além do Tejo*, but his arms are outstretched to embrace Lisbon and the north. His back is turned upon the south and its Moorish manners.

I turn my back on the dock, the river, the southern sky and make my unsteady way behind a supermarket up a side street called Rua da Cozinha Economica – 'Thrifty Cuisine Road' – searching for the Alcântara Mar nightspot. I'm looking for the wrong thing, because I'm looking for what I expect. At last I find an anonymous building, once some sort of warehouse or depot, that's been open since midnight. Yes, this is Alcântara Mar. *Mar* means 'sea'. Its exterior's blank, its interior sounds wild. Maybe I can get a drink here and set my sea-legs dancing.

I am still treading that *terra infirma* between salt and soil and, as I make an undramatic entrance into Alcântara Mar, I find myself adrift. Inside, the club is larger than its walls. I step into a darkness where my eye roams towards infinity when it's not caught and enthralled by gilt and glitz that shimmers and gleams in shocking close-up or disarticulated middle distance. Shifting lights glance off the stage-set of which all things visible consist, then are sucked into nothingness – the invisible matt-black paint and fabrics which comprise the limits of inner space. Faces ride the darkness, groomed and painted masks, beneath gel-sculpted hair and above the expensive black clothes of opulent postmodern existentialists and bourgeois bohemians.

I'm glad I dressed up for this, though my sage linen suit isn't the right uniform. Figures in dress suits and velvet gowns gaze impassively from heavy gilt frames, and heads that are more flesh than paint strike attitudes, nod, grimace, laugh, spin above tailored rags in the dark glitter of many mirrors hanging on what might be walls. Pillars, marbled and lacquered, seem substantial but stand in space and bear no weight. Chandeliers' storeys shimmer with the music's beat, the pulsing membranes of so many luminescent jellyfish. The bar's like a boat, with a brilliantly-lit superstructure, cruising the night. I say 'like a boat' with a dry tongue in my cheek. For a week of nights I've been on the deck of the real thing, part of the transient sparkle, watching pale froth fold from the bow like grey matter solidified in the churning, only to bubble and thin and evaporate like a lifetime's lost memories.

I've never been in Alcântara Mar before, but I have good memories of this city. Lost memories, good memories, I'll drink to them. The barman serves me an *aguardente velha* – 'old fire water' – with delicate superciliousness. *Lembranças!* Good memories are half-lost anyhow. There is no mind, and no simulator yet invented, that can re-enact experience, no hologram that can hoax all the senses. Once dismembered, even the perfect moment cannot be remembered. The perfect flavour, or sunset, or orgasm demands to be repeated. We must move on: to something new or something old, but always on. We travel to remember, or to rewrite memory. Nostalgia moves us. We travel to forget too, of course, not out of despair – despair is stationary – but out of at least a little hope, or nostalgia for the future. Most peoples are pretty good at it, but the Portuguese are artists of nostalgia and of yearning: they have a word for it, *saudade*, which, with arcane pride, they always say is untranslatable.

7

This *aguardente* is good. *Saudades!* And before we get too senti-mental, let's toast my landfall at the Cais de Alcântara, and landfall here in postmodernist Alcântara Mar. Here's to memory without reason, sentimentality without feeling. Here's to fashion waifs. Here's to *fin-de-siècle* chic. To now! But with my tongue out of my cheek I want, not glossy-journal, music-business 'now', I want real-time, real-world now. Now is what the past adds up to, without justification or explanation; it's not a whimsically-whipped-up con-fection. I want what happens, just before what happens next.

Here anything can happen, fact or fiction, past or present. Any-body can turn up, in period costume, drag, high fashion or DMs in this warehouse of dreams. Inês de Castro is here, holding her face up to the light and her hand out to be kissed, all pale and new, covered with babysoft flesh. It's six centuries since her corpse was crowned and courtiers filed past to kiss her knucklebones. Behind her, Dr Ricardo Reis sits in a corner behind the newspaper *Diário de Notícias* with a small brandy. The newsprint of a distant day dances before his eyes. At the start of José Saramago's novel *The Year of the Death of Ricardo Reis* the doctor completes his voyage from Rio de Janeiro on board the *Highland Brigade* and disembarks at the Cais de Alcântara in 1936. So why shouldn't he turn up here at Alcântara Mar tonight? He's a persona of the poet Fernando Pessoa who died in 1935. Hasn't Pessoa himself just walked through the door, sixty years late, after meeting the narrator of Antonio Tabucchi's *Requiem* on the quay? Now in the restaurant they are enjoying *nouvelle cuisine*, a bottle of chilled Colares Chita and delicate post-mortem discussion.

In the cloakroom I'm surprised to find Alexandre Herculano vigorously scrubbing his hands. The venerated historian died upriver at Santarém in 1877. Now when he turns his romantic, austere gaze in my direction I feel compelled to explain myself.

'I'm a writer, you see,' I stammer stupidly.

'So I feared. In England there's no fool who doesn't write a travel book, no archfool who doesn't write it about Portugal.'

He thrusts his hands beneath the dryer and the roar of hot breath mercifully drowns any possibility of conversation.

My eye's still open for Portuguese celebrities, but also for the English who turn up in Lisbon looking for something. There's

Henry Fielding for instance, the great magistrate and novelist with a glass of port wine in his paw. 'Great' is a quantitative description for he's bloated with dropsy, heaving with asthma and splenetic with rage at his last home's shortcomings. He sailed here for his health's sake and died a year before the great Lisbon earthquake. He was forty-seven years old. Pessoa died at that age too. I'm forty-seven now. The thought makes me shiver a little in these small hours amidst mirrors and faces and the deep space of the present moment, but I'm intent on ascending the Tagus, not crossing Lethe.

One man I'm pleased to find sitting here drinking too much red wine is Tom Stucley, a near-neighbour of mine in Devon, who's not outshone by all this glitter. He's rumoured to have English royal blood in him, but I know he's a con-man and it's probably his fault, as well as Alcântara Mar's, that I've slipped so easily into fantasy. They say he's a 'bubble of emptiness and meteor of ostentation'. It's his ambition to rule all Ireland, but for now it seems he's stepped off a leaky boat at anchor in the Tagus and taken on protective coloration here.

'Hi, Tom.'

'Greetings,' he slurs. He's in his rugged but elegant fifties and struggling to keep his style, cool and macho. 'So what brings you to this place?'

'Just travelling.'

'What the hell for?'

It's a good question, but he doesn't expect me to answer it, unless it's with a question of my own.

'You?'

'I'm waiting to see King Sebastian.'

'You're not the only one,' I laugh.

El-Rei Dom Sebastião died in battle in Morocco in 1578. Or so they say. Others say he did not die. And some say he's coming back, if you can believe it. Like Britain's King Arthur, asleep under the hill, Sebastião's dozing under a desert dune. I'm not going to get into this sore subject so early in the morning, I'm going to take a taxi to the centre of town, find a bed and maybe get up tomorrow with land-legs.

In the morning I'll ask myself why the hell I travel. Cheers,

Tom! Then I'll start searching. I want to find out how Portugal – discoverer of most of the world, founder of the first modern empire and, once, the richest country on earth – gets on with being not-great any more. Not-greatness is a habit Great Britain can't quite learn, and the United States soon must. Left on the shelf at Europe's edge, Portugal has had to shift its gaze from the ever-seductive horizon, turn its back on the ocean and flutter its eyelashes at Brussels. I'm going upriver in that direction, as far as Alcántara in Spain, to find out where Portugal begins and ends. If it's lost its role and its riches, at least it can be not-Spain.

It was not not-Spain for sixty years as a direct consequence of its traumatic defeat under Dom Sebastião. It became a part of Spain, that supreme humiliation. So why is Sebastião a metaphor, if not a synonym, for hope? Travel is hope on wheels, and I'm travelling in search of Sebastião. Whether I want to dissect or resurrect the cadaver, I'm not sure.

'You waiting for him?' Tom nudges, not me, but the young woman at the next table with her back to him. He knows she's been listening. She turns. Below cropped hair her face is ashen and stylishly pinched. Her breasts, under a skin-tight black top, are small and conical. Her eyelids and lashes are heavy but they lift to Tom's face. The eyes light.

'Yeah, sure,' she says with a TV-American taint, 'I wait.'

Tom shifts his gaze to her friend, who has swivelled to confront him too. Her coiled hair holds ruby shimmerings. Her big breasts quiver above a masochistically buckled black belt.

'*Sim*,' she says. Yes. That's all. Perhaps that North African sand-hill really is just across the bridge.

'*Boa noite, senhoras*,' I straighten up. '*Boa noite, doces senhoras, boa noite, boa noite*.'

It's too early to say *Bom dia*. I slap Tom on the back.

'See, you're not the only one.'

2

A LONG SLEEP

Buenos Ayres and Bethlehem

A LONG SLEEP was what I wanted. A sleep in a bed that stayed still. The taxi driver seemed sleepier than I was. He grunted and sped me through town, a silent movie of eerily-lit landmarks heavy with memories. But my heart grew lighter as we went. When I lied to Tom Stucley and said I was just travelling, it was because in a postmodern nightclub you can get laughed at for mentioning anything that might be misconstrued as Odyssey, Quest, Pilgrimage or Mission Impossible. They've all got such big capital letters. 'Travelling' doesn't sound pretentious because, with its inverted commas around it, it's still a fashionable delusion, one that's survived from the sixties and been tarted up in nineties colour supps. The chicken crosses the road. Tom's question – 'What the hell for?' – was good. I'd answer it in my own time. I knew as well as anyone that nowhere was exotic any more, and even when it was it was in someone else's back yard. He, 'Lusty' Stucley, had his own sad, bad reasons for turning up here, in his time, by accident. I cross the road to find things out. My quest with a small q was to question 'Quest', and travel itself. Are they crude antidotes to death? Are they forlorn attempts to bring life to life? Portugal, so great, so small, is the place where upper and lower case collide most vividly, where mundane continually rubs up against Myth. If you want an exotic back yard you can't do better than Lisbon. I love it. By the time the taxi driver dropped me in Praça da Figueira, Fig Tree Square, the city felt like home.

I rang the bell of a *pensão* and waited. High on horseback upon a fat plinth in the middle of the square sat the shape of King João

I. His most famous victory, won with the help of English bowmen, kept Spain (or rather Castile) at bay for almost two centuries until Sebastião's little African adventure brought Portugal to its knees. João I had signed the Treaty of Windsor in 1386 and sealed it by marrying Philippa of Lancaster, John of Gaunt's daughter. It was not the first treaty between England and Portugal, but it's the one that's always invoked when either describes the other as 'our oldest ally'.

Those times were messy and inglorious, the alliance was pretentious and often frail, but tonight João I's resolute statue was unambiguously silhouetted against the floodlit Moorish-then-Christian castle which crowned the heap of houses riddled with alleys and steep steps that amounted to the ancient quarter called Alfama, the dim lights and shifting shadows of real life.

The entry-phone rasped incomprehensibly in my ear and, before I could answer, the latch shot back with a chime like a ricocheting bullet. I staggered up three floors, six flights. At the top, bleary and ready to be grumpy, was Nuno, one of my oldest allies. His big face uncreased and he took my hand.

'Ah, my friend, it is you. You stay long?'

'Not long this time. I'm off up the Tejo.'

'Not long, but you are welcome. And my cousin, he has a very good hotel in Castelo Branco.'

Having played a walk-on part in Nuno's sweet dreams I hoped to enjoy my own. In a typical Lisbon night there is one hour between midnight and dawn when the city seems to pause for breath. This was it. The noise was deafening. My window at the far side of the building overlooked the Rossio, the busiest of Lisbon's squares. I have slept in quieter hotels, only to be woken irregularly by street banter, by trams' clang and wheeze, by taxis' squealing. I chose this place because the continuous rush of traffic, like the roar of a river, was as good as silence. I knew I could float on it and be swept towards daylight.

But it was louder than usual. Between two French rococo fountains, one playing, one bone dry, the Rossio's reptilian skin of setts – not cobbles, but rough-cut cubes of white and black stones laid in mosaic patterns – had been peeled back. Inside a barricade of yellow boards, the earth was flayed and heaped and puddled by machines. Sifted gravel dribbled on to conveyor belts. Blue light spat and sparks spewed as small masked figures welded airy piers from reinforcing rods. A concrete mixer spun like a hungry globe. Diggers shifted recalcitrant matter under arc lights. A crane lowered a pair of mighty mandibles towards a slot in the ground. Little men tottered forward and back as they fought to steady the mouthparts and fit them to the waterlogged hole. Cables sang, mud gushed like a geyser, the eating machine sank out of sight. It was a surgical instrument probing a neat, deep, disturbing incision.

This nightmarish drop into the underworld was one end of a European-funded scheme to extend the underground, the Lisbon Metro. Beside it, and growing out of the same dishevelled ground, a second bronze king stood erect and aloof on top of a marble column as tall as the crane. Rossio is the square's democratic name – *o rossio* is 'the public square' in any town or village – but its royal, seldom-used title is Praça Dom Pedro IV.

You'd expect Dom Pedro IV to be perched high above it. After all, the inscription on the column's pedestal praises him: liberal Dom Pedro who came from Brazil via the Açores to liberate Portugal from his absolutist brother Miguel in 1834. But it's not the victor of the War of Two Brothers on the column. It's Emperor Maximilian of Mexico, or was when it was cast. Well, Maximilian's statue happened to be passing through, *en route* for Mexico from France, when his execution made it suddenly superfluous. Someone in authority thought it a shame to waste it. Perch it up high enough and the features wouldn't matter even to those who had known Dom Pedro well.

Bathed in sound and fury I lay down. To wear Maximilian's face in death was, I felt sure, no problem to Pedro who, in life, had been compelled to fight a brother wearing Sebastião's mantle. I pondered our pathetic need to raise kings and heroes from their graves and place them high for immortality's sake. I thought of the long sleep under the hill, that Celtic dream that's hardly more than a fairy story to us now, and woke refreshed.

On these hills – seven of them, to be poetically correct – Ulysses founded his city of Olisippi. It was the 'calm haven', Alisubbo, of the Phoenicians. It became the Romans' Felicitas Julia, then a

Visigoth stronghold. The Moors took it and gave it the name Lishbuna, until savage English Crusaders helped Portugal's first king to drive them south. The Lisbon of the English. For ever Lisboa, *Lisboa para sempre*, whose relationship to the Tagus rivals that of Istanbul to the Bosphorus.

You can be lifted to the city's upper storey by the Elevador Santa Justa. Everyone says it's by Eiffel because he's the French engineer we remember, but at the top I saluted Raoul Mesnier who really designed it. One minute you're deep in the Baixa, the next the city is at your feet. A catwalk leads to Carmo church, a ribby ruin left over from the great earthquake. From the catwalk I gazed into the chasm of the Rua do Carmo, heaped with builders' sand and gravel. This was the scene of the traumatic Chiado fire of August 1988. It started in the nineteenth-century Grandela department store only hours after one of the company's directors had been arrested and released on bail, charged with arson and insurance fraud in connection with an earlier fire in another store. Eight hundred firemen fought this one for ten hours. Smoke hung over the Tagus. A man died as he fell from a burning balcony. Of the businesses burnt out, one was Casa Batalha, Portugal's oldest shop, run by the same family since the middle ages. The fire touched a collective nerve raw since the earthquake of 1755, which, the way *Lisboetas* talk, might have been yesterday. Many wept. Shells of five- and six-storey buildings threatened to crumble. Now a smart young woman stood on the fourth-floor balcony of an immaculately restored block on the right side of the street and stared through the empty window-sockets of a gutted one on the left, nothing more than a façade propped up like scenery. Deep within it men and machinery gouged out new footings with a sound like the furies of hell.

Rua Garrett, officially named after the writer Almeida Garrett but better known as Chiado, runs up from Rua do Carmo to the Largo do Chiado. This is Lisbon's Bond Street. Its famous Bertrand bookshop was founded in 1732, and the writers' café A Brasileira existed, at least in literary legend, to pamper poets and philosophers. Now it patronises tourists. Outside it I found Fernando Pessoa, unlikely colossus of twentieth-century Portuguese culture, sitting at a table with an empty chair beside him. The poet was slight of build, almost asexual in a clerk's neat clothes, bow-tie, fedora. His face arranged around a trim moustache, myopic eyes set behind gold-rimmed spectacles, he sat quite still, waiting for whom?

Was it for Ophélia Queiros, the young secretary who captivated him but whom he could not allow to come too close? His frigidity and genius kept her at bay. *Pessoa* means 'person', singular, but Fernando Pessoa assumed *alter egos* he called heteronyms. Perhaps we should say that his pen was assumed by some of the multiple personalities of which he, and every other *pessoa*, was made. This person, and the table and chairs, were cast in bronze. If we could melt Pessoa he'd order another *aguardente*, light maybe his seventy-fifth cigarette of the day and, if he was comfortable, snap at the world and dazzle us with his cool, original mind. They say he was fun to be with. He was a visionary patriot, a nostalgic modernist. He wrote mind-stunning poetry and prose and a dull English-language guidebook glorifying Lisbon. He published mostly in journals. His book *Mensagem* (Message), a re-vision of Portugal's destiny, found its focus in the myth of Dom Sebastião. Published in 1934, the only book of his poems in Portuguese to appear in his lifetime, it won a special prize in a competition run by Salazar's Propaganda Ministry. Pessoa despised Salazar but took the prize. 'I am, in point of fact, a mystical nationalist, a rational Sebastianist.' In 1935 he thought he had two years to live. The horoscope he'd cast said so. His friend Raul Leal saw that he'd miscast it, but kept quiet. Pessoa died that November of cirrhosis of the liver. The previous day he'd written his very last words, in English: 'I know not what tomorrow will bring.' Perhaps the empty bronze chair beside him waits for a dutiful tourist or for any *pessoa* willing to lift an eyebrow at destiny. Or for Ophélia. Or for the king, Dom Sebastião.

As I reached the Largo do Chiado a yellow tram ground around the corner. Number 28. On cue. Its destination was Prazeres, the cemetery where Pessoa was buried. I boarded it. A boy I recognised, who sold flowers at night in every restaurant in the Bairro Alto, stepped up casually at the rear and hung on for a free ride. It was a lazy switchback affair, the driver spinning wheels madly to take tight corners with panache and clanging his bell to shift illegally-parked vans from our path. There were steep squints to the bright Tagus as we nudged our way down tight streets where a jeweller's full of yellow Brazilian gold was neighbour to an exotic fruiterer's and a cobbler's dark cave. We clambered across the open space before the São Bento palace, where Parliament sits, and I alighted at the high point called Estrêla ('star'), marked by the clock towers and miraculous pale dome of the Basilica of the Sacred Heart.

The hill used to be called Buenos Ayres. Because of its 'good airs' the district was graced by many expatriates. There's much to tell about the hill and the church which is also the tomb of its foundress, half-mad Queen Maria. There's much to describe in Estrêla Gardens where crazies walk beneath palms and jacarandas and banyans as if they shuffled across the continents of the world, where old men hunch over cards by the bandstand or lob metal discs at wooden pegs in a game of *jogo de malhas*, and where black swans on a green lake circle a sculpture of the King's Daughter Keeping Ducks . . . But I could tell you far too much. Didn't Henry Fielding write, 'To make a traveller an agreeable companion to a man of sense, it is necessary, not only that he should have seen much, but that he should have overlooked much of what he hath seen'?

That, and many other wise things about travelling and writing, he set down in his *Journal of a Voyage to Lisbon*. He came to Lisbon in 1754 to die. He hoped for a cure not a grave, but feared the worst, in what he called 'the nastiest city in the world'. Nasty or not, Lisbon was at its richest, gorged on Brazilian gold and diamonds. João V had spent the first half of the century earning his title 'the Magnanimous' by patronising education and the arts and by commissioning baroque palaces, churches and monasteries. Nor did his good works stop there: he transformed convents into high-class, that is aristocratic, brothels in which nuns bore him royal bastards, for whom of his charity he built yet more gilded palaces.

Prodigious wealth and political stability give a ruler, and a ruling class, scope for pleasure. I do not speak of fishwives or slaves. Church and state enjoyed the most intimate intercourse, but any moralist might have told João V or José, his opera-obsessed successor, that Lisbon was riding for a fall, without first bothering with decline. Though no one could have prophesied that the crash would come so cataclysmically. Just before it came Henry Fielding arrived.

When he embarked for Lisbon, Fielding was a jaundiced, asthmatic bag of lard heavy with slops, limbs bandaged tight against the gout. From a small boat he was winched up in a chair, and lowered aboard the *Queen of Portugal* at Rotherhithe. He was 'dying of a complication of disorders' and had several times had his dropsical belly tapped of ten or twelve or fourteen quarts of fluid at once. With fair winds the voyage should have taken two weeks. With contrary weather it took six. Fielding's daughter Harriet, and Mary, his second wife, were prostrate with seasickness. To distract himself from melancholy he set about composing his *Journal*, of which 'some of the most amusing pages . . . were possibly the production of the most disagreeable hours which ever haunted the author'.

By the time he'd been lugged ashore on 7 August he had witnessed a fair sample of the vices that beset ports and customs houses: corruption, officiousness, avarice and lethargy. It was not a good introduction. The city was unlike any other that he'd seen. Its large white-stone buildings arose 'one above another, and that in so steep and almost perpendicular a manner, that they all seem to have but one foundation'. They looked 'very beautiful at a distance; but as you approach nearer, and find them to want every kind of ornament, all idea of beauty vanishes at once'. He was sick and tired and crammed into a chaise, making for a coffee-house on the brow of a hill where, with mixed feelings, 'we regaled ourselves with a good supper, for which we were as well charged as if the bill had been made on the Bath Road, between Newbury and London'.

Prices here worried him badly, though he resolved to cure his finances by writing a mighty, money-making history of Portugal. Servants caused frustration and alarm. Wife and daughter ganged up against him. In order to prove a point about Harriet's pet parrot, 'I condescended so low as to take the opinion of my black, for these blacks being the countrymen of the parrots are really good judges in them, but, so the devil ordained, my honest black knowing who was master' agreed with the women. The *Public Advertiser* of 16 October told friends at home that Fielding was 'surprisingly recovered since his Arrival in that Climate'. In fact he had already died on the eighth.

At the far side of the Estrêla Garden I crossed the road and pressed the bell at a door in a wall. There was no reply. The English burial ground, held in common with the Dutch, had been walled and camouflaged by cypress trees in compliance with the Inquisition's order 'to hide the graves of the heretics from the eyes of the faithful'. When at last I was let in I found Fielding's grave easily, for it was marked by a big monument with a long Latin inscription. But was it? His bones lay unmarked for so long that the French Consul tried to put up a marble tombstone to spite the philistine English. Dom João of Bragança tried too. The elaborate memorial on which I rested was not erected until 1830. Mrs Quillinan, Wordsworth's daughter, got it right when she wrote that Fielding's 'monument, a huge ungainly thing, is on a spot selected by *guess*. The bones it covers may possibly have belonged to an idiot.'

The hidden graveyard beside the English church of St George was a village of the Protestant dead. At the end of the tram line, Prazeres cemetery was a city. On Sundays gypsies set up stalls at its gates selling shirts and T-shirts, socks and shoes, so that you can enter the world beyond in new clothes. *Prazeres* means 'pleasures'. It is a city of houses among cypress trees, streets of them with classical pediments or Dutch gables, the occasional gothick castle, the usual columns and urns and sometimes the romantic trunk of a stone tree felled in life's storm. Names of occupants are inscribed on house fronts, and if you peer through wrought-iron-and-glass doors you can see their photographs, faded artificial flowers, yellowing lace, purple and black silks and velvets covering coffins in varying states of grandeur and decay. It's like looking in the windows of antique shops in Rua Dom Pedro V. I was looking for Pessoa's bones.

I'd found the house he lived in for the last fifteen years of his life, at first with his mother on her return from South Africa and later alone. It wasn't far away, in Rua Coelho da Rocha. It's called the *Casa Pessoa* now, though his spirit has been exorcised by the literary industry. Here in Prazeres I couldn't find him either. In a painting of 1980 by Mário Botas, *Map of Pessoa's Tomb*, a line leads the eye down this funereal crag along a path between cypresses to a plot, beside a grave with an anchor, marked with an X. I knew he'd been interred in the vault of his grandmother Dionísia on 2 December 1935. In his journal the late Miguel Torga wrote of hearing the news. He shut up his surgery and fled into his beloved mountains. 'There, with the pines and the rocks, I wept for the death of the greatest poet of our times, whom Portugal watched pass by in his coffin, on his way to immortality, without even asking who he was.'

At the city of the dead's west end soldiers are buried under humble stones on the brink of a precipice. Among the perfumes and the rotting flowers I looked towards Belém. I overlooked the Alcântara valley, down to the 25 April Bridge and up to the great Aqueduct of Free Waters whose thirty-five pointed arches, finished not long before Henry Fielding arrived, are an engineering master-piece. If Fielding overlooked the aqueduct, or never saw it, Hans Christian Andersen admired it a century later and wrote of a bandit who had terrorised the district in the 1840s. Once, this man threw a mother and child down from the aqueduct. The child thought he was playing when he tossed it in the air. It laughed and stretched out its arms. The bandit forgot his many victims' cries of anguish, but never that laughter, never the carefree, haunting smile.

At the cemetery office a glum official looked up from his coffee and came into the sunlight wiping his fat hands.

'I'm looking for Fernando Pessoa,' I said.

'He is not here.'

Miracle! I thought, but said, 'He was buried here?'

'He's been moved.'

'Moved?'

'Belém.'

'Really?'

'Jerónimos.'

The Tower of Belém is an icon. Pessoa calls it 'one of the most expressive memories of Portuguese military and naval power'. It's the logo on Lisbon's visiting card. 'God gave the Portuguese a small country as cradle but all the world as their grave,' wrote Padre António Vieira, the seventeenth-century Jesuit maestro of prose. Belém is Bethlehem. The quintessential cradle. The royal village. From here the navigators set sail to midwife new worlds for God. Not all came back. Set spaciously on the riverbank as on a stage, Belém is the theatre of national *saudade*. From here Sebastião cast off on his fatal expedition. Off here each spring lay the cod-fishing fleet of schooners bound for the waters of Greenland and New-foundland.

When mariners saw Belém Tower again they knew they were home. Off the beach where discoverers embarked, it was built in 1515–21 by Francisco Arruda, an architect who restored Portuguese fortresses in Morocco and returned home with Moorish inspiration and courage to eschew European fashion. Because Dom Manuel I ordered it, its style is called Manueline. It may seem a trinket standing in the water, a flight of fancy topped with Byzantine cupolas and encrusted with emblems, but it was constructed with exquisite seriousness. Arruda's stone lace gives an illusion of light-ness belied by the thickness of the walls. Winding gear and hefty chains lifted its drawbridge. Its cannon defended Lisbon's approaches. I climbed down to the arsenal's grim cells and up to the whispering gallery where a little girl and I said *Bom dia!* to one another from opposite corners, very quietly and distinctly. One of the grotesques on the terrace above the gun-ports is playing a violin.

Across Avenida Brasilia and Avenida da Índia, with the Marginal railway between them, stands the Belém Cultural Centre, nick-named 'The Bunker' or 'The Chunk'. It's built of blocks of crystal-line rock, roseate and pale ochre. Sun beats into its inner spaces and hot wind sweeps through its canyons. It's a Foreign Legion desert fortress, but one intended to be stuffed full of high culture, low culture, very postmodern, but in fact a façade concealing not much. It's a pyramid, a grandiose tomb. I saw an exhibition of animated Lego there.

'EU funding encourages façade,' said a writer I met in the bar. 'The taps in the toilets run automatically for two minutes. They can't afford the water bill, let alone art.'

Gnarled olive trees have been transplanted into the brand-new first-floor garden. From there, across beds of subtropical vegetation, I could see *Cristo Rei* on the far bank, the 25 April Bridge and, this side, the Monument to the Discoveries set beside the Tagus like one of the *padrãos*, or stone ensigns emblazoned with shields of Portugal, that the navigators used to plant at the mouths of newly discovered rivers. It was designed in 1940 and erected twenty years later. Some say it's boring Fascist Realism, but they're half-blind. New State architecture or not, it's a brilliant marriage of abstract symbolism and classical realism. Seen from the north it's a mighty cross that is also a sword. From east or west it's a massive *padrão*, and a steep prow. Sail-shapes belly above a line of pioneers and priests who, with the poet Camões, queue up behind Henry the Navigator standing proud on the bow with a caravel in his hand.

Once we were so great. I entered beneath the point of the sword. Appropriately, in the basement, there was an exhibition of photographs of present-day native life in Latin America.

'This *padrão*,' said the man in the lift, 'is the equivalent of twenty or twenty-five storeys high.'

He confided this, as though it was for my ears only. From the top I could see the city, the palaces, the ocean beyond Belém Tower, the world. Down on the Tagus the aircraft carrier USS *Eisenhower* landed sailors, rigged out in tasteless civvies, off the ship's boat *Ike 8*. It was as if a town from another planet had tied up at the front gate. The wide world, or a map of it, lay below me at the heart of a paved compass set in a wavy sea of mosaic. This new *rosa dos ventos* ('rose of the winds') was modelled on the great compass attributed to Henry the Navigator at Sagres, close by the *fim do mundo*, 'end of the world'. Up here a Portuguese could overdose on self-esteem.

Due north, beyond a geometrical garden laid out around a concentric fountain in the Praça do Império, stood the monastery called Jerónimos, masterpiece of Manueline architecture, whose cornerstone was laid by Dom Manuel I himself in 1502 to thank God for Vasco da Gama's return from India. Even Henry Fielding called it 'one of the most beautiful piles of building in all Portugal'. Lads hosed down the paving in front of the extravagant south doorway, under the cross of the Knights Templar, and supervised by Our Lady of Bethlehem. I made for the cloisters, a miracle of engineering and stone-carving. On two fan-vaulted storeys the precise elaboration of multiple arches has the flexibility of rope and the swell of ocean, the sense of an enclosed submarine world, of coral-laced caverns where saint-sprites shelter beneath scallops. With wonderful irony it was here, where Portugal sealed its pact with global destiny at the turn of the sixteenth century, that on New Year's Day

1986 President Mário Soares signed the membership treaty of the European Economic Community.

I looked into the doleful eyes of a once-proud lion dribbling water into a basin. In the shadows I found a restrained memorial standing aloof in a voluptuous niche. It was a square column of pink marble and stainless steel. So this was where they'd put the poet. 'Fernando Pessoa 1888–1935' was engraved on steel, and verses of his four poetic heteronyms were cut into marble, one to each face. The date at the base, of the unveiling on 13 June 1985, was a few months short of the fiftieth anniversary of his death. It was smart enough, but somehow shabby, out of keeping. I'd last walked these glorious cloisters in 1984. I wished I'd taken the trouble then to go up to Prazeres and find Pessoa before the body-snatchers got him.

He's in the pantheon now. Officially. Above the monastery church's west door disconsolate pigeons ruffled their feathers beside a nativity scene supported by the wings of angels. A man on scaffolding was researching weathering, the effect of the microclimate and efflorescence on the local limestones used in the doorway's construction. It was reassuring and unnerving to see such scientific fervour applied to the house of God. Inside, sung mass was filling all the building's spaces and interstices. On the left, Vasco da Gama lay with hands clasped on a sarcophagus borne by six lions. Amongst carved cabling and acanthus, cartouches framed the Templar cross, a caravel and an armillary sphere, that Manueline symbol found everywhere in Portugal. It's not a globe, for the bands around it represent sun, moon and stars. It's a skeleton of the heavens and an article of faith inherited, via the Moors, from Arab astronomers.

Their knowledge enabled the discoverers to sail and got Vasco da Gama to India, an achievement celebrated in this building. Its fan vaulting over three naves is sustained by six richly ornamented but delicate octagonal columns. If stone eyes opened, they'd see pillars like palm trunks, tracery like fronds, great spans opening spaces beneath in which exotics might flower, in which we can meditate on destiny. In here, Reynaldo dos Santos points out, we are far from the gothic, whose proportions stress both man's smallness and his aspiring spirit; in here we inhabit the atmosphere of a cave, as though the sea might suddenly rush in. When Vasco da

Gama's remains were sent back from Cochin in 1539 they were entombed, not in the convent he inspired, but at Vidigueira, near Beja. His bones were not moved to this vast cavern until the 1890s when Portugal was desperate for glory.

Luís Vaz de Camões, the poet whose epic *The Lusiads* defines the Portuguese and extols Vasco da Gama's exploits, lies opposite on a matching tomb under crusty tracery, softly lit by an arched window. His supposed ashes were brought here at the same time as da Gama's. He was buried first in a plague pit. Then what someone guessed was his corpse was interred in a church beneath a stone which read: 'Here lies Luís de Camões, prince of the poets of his age. He lived as he died, miserably and in poverty.' That resting-place was razed by the Lisbon earthquake. Now, pomp at last. For poets, especially passionate ones like him, it's no more than the accredited route to the pantheon. If there's anything of him here at all.

Camões died in 1580, two years after Dom Sebastião's defeat in Morocco. They say that Sebastião's loss and Spain's assumption of the Portuguese throne broke the poet's heart. 'Everyone will see that my country was so dear to me that I was content to die not only in it but with it.' He died of an outbreak of plague that superstitious souls took to mark the end of Portugal's Golden Age.

Bronze escutcheons from caravels that went to India and Brazil are mounted in the vault high above the crossing. The image of St Gabriel that Vasco da Gama took to India in his own vessel stands in a niche in the south transept. I made my way there when mass finished. The devout left the echoing cave clutching the blessing about them like a coat.

I was searching, as you know, for Dom Sebastião. And there he was. On the backs of two marble elephants, tusks fitted by a cheapjack dentist, rested a tomb of porphyry and Estremoz marble. This was the sarcophagus of the young king whom many supposed, some still suppose, not to have died. The inscription began, *Conditur hoc tumulo, si vera est fama, Sebastus* . . . 'This tomb preserves Sebastião if rumour is true . . .' and went on to say that he'd died of his wounds in North Africa. The Spanish king who'd taken Sebastião's throne paid the Moors a fortune – 100,000 *escus* – for the corpse, and staged a royal funeral in its honour to convince the credulous that their king was dead. Why then borrow Virgil's phrase, *si vera est fama*? If rumour is true. The bones within this tomb are almost certainly not his. If rumour is true Sebastião never died. The king who lost his realm to Spain and made Camões despair quickly became a metaphor for hope. He was *o encoberto*, 'the hidden one', the once-and-future king who would return and restore Portugal to greatness. Some said he reappeared twenty years after his 'death'. Some say he's still to come.

I might have found Pessoa's remains, but not Sebastião's. Jerónimos's lofty interior felt cramped and close. I escaped to the river and the great *padrão* on its brink. A breeze had blown up. On the huge rose of the winds a young man was sailing a radio-controlled land-yacht to and fro, tacking across the map of the world. Ah, now we are so small.

3

POSSIBLE WORLDS

Candide, Carcavelos and Cascais

AT THE MOUTH of the Tagus a captain and his crew watched with rising panic as just prior to ten o'clock one autumn morning the sea lifted their vessel some sixteen feet in five minutes, before it sunk them in much the same time into an unnatural trough, and then rose up and fell and rose again. On land people felt an appalling shock and couldn't believe their eyes as the river, with its great estuary the Sea of Straw, emptied itself into the ocean and at once refilled behind a wall of water. It was 1 November 1755, All Saints' Day. Multitudes of candles flickered in churches packed with congregations ready to celebrate mass.

Lisbon was no stranger to tremors and earthquakes. One in the spring of 1531 is said to have killed twenty thousand. They say that another big one is overdue. But this one was different. It was bigger. It cleft rocks on Lundy Island off North Devon. It shook France. Its tidal wave lapped Scotland and Jamaica. It was more profound, hitting the edge of Europe just at the moment when an alloy of rationalism and deism, admixed with wealth plundered from other continents, had combined to forge a historical moment of maximum optimism.

'This is the Enlightenment, for God's sake. Such things can't happen.'

Stones and whole buildings ground one against another. The first shock lasted three or five minutes, the second came after fifteen minutes, the third half an hour after that, the fourth about noon. Ten thousand buildings, more than half the city, toppled. Fires, kindled by shivered hearths and upset candles, were fanned by

25

unearthly winds. People ran into the open and towards the river where they faced a tumbling, building, rolling hill of water. It chucked its flotsam of wreckage and corpses about, then sucked most of it out to sea. What the tidal wave didn't flatten, fire consumed. Men and women fled with what they could carry. Air already heavy with dust thickened with smoke, cinders, steam. Crowds congealed around priests and friars, begging absolution. Many are the tales of lucky escapes and agonising deaths. Riverside palaces, the Inquisition and the convent of São Domingos were swept away. Public papers, libraries of books and all the music of the Royal Chapel were expunged. It was as if a culture had been erased.

Shocks continued. A large tremor at midnight on the second revived the terror. Prisoners were set free. Jews, whose deaths at the stake had been postponed because the *auto-da-fé* scheduled for All Saints' Day had been superseded by something more dramatic, were tied onto horses and driven under guard to Coimbra. At five in the morning of the eighth a quake, shuddering and guttural, lasted half an hour and turned the bowels of many to water. Still shocks came, with news from the south that whole towns had been swallowed up. Fifteen thousand were supposed to be buried in Lisbon's ruins. Perhaps thirty thousand died here all told. It was a long story, of salutary thought and superstition, of refugees and opportunists. Looters and arsonists were summarily hung. Sister Kitty Witham, one of the nuns of ruined Syon House who had moved into a temporary wooden house in the garden, wrote home about 'shakes and trembles' as late as 27 January 1756: 'last night we had a vere sharp one which renewd our fright vere much,' and to her aunt, 'tis thought this World will not last long so itt behoves us to prepair for the Other.'

A Brazilian gold rush had marked the years immediately before and after 1700. Though the flow was slackening by the time of the earthquake, Lisbon had never had it so good in this world, and could prepare for the other in some style. Mafra's vast and overbearing convent palace, Portugal's answer to the Escorial, was not many years old, and the pink rococo palace of Queluz, a little Versailles, had only been finished in 1752. Behind the austere façade of the Jesuit church of São Roque in the Bairro Alto – where the allegedly uncorrupted body of the exiled Cornish saint Francis Tregian is interred, 'a martyr of chastity' for refusing Queen Elizabeth's advances – a brand-new chapel had just been installed, beside others of exquisite vulgarity. This chapel of St John the Baptist was made of choice marbles, alabaster, green porphyry, amethyst, jade, agate and lapis lazuli together with gilded bronze and 'paintings' of fine mosaic. Built in Rome, it was blessed by the Pope, dismantled, shipped to Lisbon and painstakingly reconstructed. It cost £250,000 *then*.

The earthquake shattered Faith's solid rock. It made humanist hearts miss a beat. It filled them with metaphysical terror. There was nowhere to run. Earth, air, fire and water conspired against God and man. Lisbon laughed at the Enlightenment, at Leibniz's contention that 'all is for the best in the best of all possible worlds.' He had more faith in nature than in man: 'one Caligula alone, one Nero, has caused more evil than an earthquake.' Alexander Pope put it this way:

> All nature is but art unknown to thee,
> All chance, direction which thou canst not see;
> All discord, harmony not understood;
> All partial evil, universal good . . .

He summed up his belief:

> One truth is clear,
> Whatever is, is right.

This was the comfortable ground on which Europeans stood. The Lisbon earthquake pulled it from beneath their feet.

The poet Faria Cordeiro scripted a bleak debate between three shepherds who learn that whatever is, is not necessarily right at all. There is evil in the world. All they can do, and it's enough, is 'to look after sheep, and live in the village'. In his poem on the earthquake Voltaire viciously attacked Pope's optimism. In *Candide* he sent Leibniz up rotten. Shipwreck lands Candide and the philosopher Pangloss near Lisbon just in time for a great, bitterly comic quake. All Pangloss's cant, that finds good reasons for everything, is venomously ironic. At the end, he still insists that 'there is a concatenation of events in the best of all possible worlds', and that the catalogue of tragedies they have suffered is all for the best. 'Excellently observed,' answers Candide, 'but let us take care of our garden.'

Somehow, and it seems miraculous, the real marvels of Lisbon – Belém tower, Jerónimos monastery and the Aqueduct of Free Waters – withstood the trauma. But King Dom José's latest pride, the opera house, collapsed in an instant, and the royal family camped out in palace grounds. The prime minister, Sebastião José de Carvalho e Melo, moved into a hut. He is better known by his later title, Marquês de Pombal, the name history has given to his rebuilding of the Baixa, *Lisboa pombalina*. He rebuilt the economy too, reordered commerce with Brazil, restructured the wine trade, reformed the army and the education system, expelled the Jesuits, abolished slavery and put the nobility in its place with exemplary executions at Belém. Liberal minds applaud his achievements, forgetting all too easily that in Portugal, as in most of Europe, the Enlightenment fostered not constitutionalism but absolute power. Pombal was the paradigmatic exponent of the humanist *auto-da-fé*.

His first name was Sebastião, and it is for the rebirth of Lisbon that he is popularly remembered. He was over six feet tall, handsome and charming. But he had, said Dom João, hair in his heart. He despatched enemies with ruthless barbarity. A one-time supporter said that he 'wanted to civilise the nation and at the same time to enslave it. He wanted to spread the light of the philosophical sciences and at the same time elevate the royal power of despotism.' Nevertheless, he picked Lisbon up and put it back in a possible world. His is the city's most massive memorial. He stands, surveying his work, high above the Rotunda at the head of the Avenida da Liberdade, even though liberty was emphatically not his middle name.

Mercifully, Henry Fielding died a year before the quake struck. He would have recognised the cant that followed it. When London had experienced tremors in the spring of 1750, churchmen found degeneracy enough to justify God's anger. Among other immoral influences, they'd blamed the earth's unsteadiness on books such as Fielding's *Tom Jones*. In the Lisbon of 1755, before Pombal sent them packing, the Jesuits preached that the sinful Portuguese deserved God's awful judgement. Significantly, the Portuguese made their own judgements upon God. Instead of him, they found a terrible judge, and a saviour, in Sebastião, Marquês de Pombal.

Among the exotic presents – melons, monkeys, parrots, onions – that Henry Fielding sent home in 1754 was a half-hogshead of 'calcavella' for his publisher Andrew Millar. Carcavelos is a dry or medium-sweet fortified wine the colour of topaz with a nutty nose and an almond flavour. It is still produced west of Lisbon, though development behind the Marginal resorts has gobbled up all but one of the *quintas* that grew it. In 1752 King Dom José despatched a gift of Carcavelos's finest wine to Emperor Ch'ien-lung's court in Peking.

Carcavelos lies beyond the fortress of São Julião da Barra, just outside the mouth of the Tagus. It boasts a wide beach ideal for inverse snobs glad not to be at Estoril, a malodorous subway beneath the Marginal road through which one must run the gauntlet of tacky stalls, and a walk into town between family hotels and jolly schoolkids' murals. Why are resorts like this so stultifyingly frantic? Bronzed boys in big shorts and billowing T-shirts cut a path through slow-moving matrons and madonnas. How is it that here even the innocent pleasures reek indelibly of sex? Deep within the busy tiled oasis of the Café São Jorge a waiter with the mobile face of a born clown and a born misanthrope's capacity for disdain served me a *bica* (small, startlingly strong coffee), a *pastei de nata* (egg-custard tart) and, before I'd asked, which is as it should be, cinnamon to sprinkle on it from a miniature J&B whisky bottle with a perforated cap. Vasco da Gama brought cinnamon back from Calicut. One boatload of it paid for a whole expedition to India. The coffee was delicious. The *pastei* was succulent within crisp pastry, just a touch caramelised, the spice heady. Perfection. The waiter blessed me with the hint of a smile.

Outside, a man sat in a wheelchair with concertina'd black rubber waders instead of legs, and an outstretched hat. It was a Thursday. Between noble trees, avenues of awnings sheltered trestles and boxes, racks and ropes heaped and hung with clothes. This weekly event is called a gypsy fair, and it's true that a man stood about beneath a bunch of helium-filled balloons. Aside from him, it was about as fair as a bear market, with each transaction handled like a hostile bid. The stallholders' eyes were hard and everywhere at once. If you like your gypsies romantic, don't come. Police patrolled as if they were necessary. They looked like guardian angels.

Like the Spanish, the Portuguese kings repeatedly legislated against gypsies. In hard times all gypsies in the kingdom were identified with roaming brigands and condemned to the galleys. More liberal legislation, like the edict of Dom João IV, ordered their arrest if they lived and moved in the wrong places, that is, close to the royal court or to the frontiers. They were prohibited from practising *jeringonza* (magic arts) or teaching them to their children. Gypsy costume was forbidden, proper work was obligatory and begging only permitted where they lived, and only by those who were old or sick, so long as trickery or *buena dicha* (soothsaying) was never employed.

An old beggar woman, cowled in a scarf, sat at the edge of the clothes fair on a little plinth. A young woman stuffed the teat of a feed bottle into the noisiest of her infants' mouths and pumped an asthmatic tune out of her small accordion. Wary-looking gypsies manned handcarts of bananas, carnations and cherries. There was a low whistle and high drama. The carts were pushed, fast, up a cul-de-sac and out of sight. In the rush a pair of scales and a bunch of bananas fell into the street. But for those, there'd have been nothing there. As it was, a policeman made his entrance, sedately. He patted his pistol holster, stared at the offending articles and indulged in whimsical badinage with the girl left behind to distract him. She was already flushed from her part in the disappearing act but let fly at the officer with an indignant torrent of abuse and managed a little extra flush of injured innocence, just for him.

On 3 August 1968 Prime Minister Salazar fell. Not from power but from his director's chair. He had been sitting in the Santo António fort, his summer residence in Estoril, waiting to have his bunions attended to. His chiropodist was washing, as he always did before taking the dictator's feet in his hands, when he heard a noise. He, of course, described it retrospectively as a 'crash', but whether it was the crack of splintering wood when the canvas chair collapsed, or the thud, of a kind that must be qualified by the word 'sickening', when Dr António de Oliveira Salazar's skull struck the tiles, that alerted him, I don't know.

Life without Salazar was unimaginable for those who loved or loathed him. He'd come in as national saviour when installed as finance minister, on his own terms, forty years before. He became prime minister in 1932 and unveiled his New State the next year. His initial was S, and he used it. He was no populist, but he let the aura of Sebastianism envelop him. Like Sebastião he never married, though he adopted two children. He cultivated modesty, austerity, the Franciscan virtues, and avoided the histrionics of German or Italian Fascism. He never went abroad except to meet Franco. Born in the same month as Adolf Hitler, Salazar was Portugal's hidden king.

At the end of the Spanish Civil War he recognised Franco's government, but only after Britain had done so. In 1939 he concluded a friendship and non-aggression treaty with Spain. During the Second World War neutral Lisbon had a secret life as a haunt of spies, a drop, a rendezvous and a cauldron of intrigue. It was a city tense, too, with inexpressible and hidden hopes. On 3 May 1945 all official flags were flown at half-mast until noon next day in mourning for Hitler. The day after that, on VE night, half a million people streamed into Pombal's Praça do Comércio to celebrate victory over fascism. Many believed it was Salazar's death-knell too.

In the mid-fifties Salazar thought he might turn the clock back. He considered a possible world with a king as head of state once more. Of the two pretenders to the throne, one turned up in Lisbon, Dom Duarte Nuno Fernando Maria Miguel Rafael Francisco Xavier Raimundo António, Duke of Bragança. He couldn't speak Portuguese. It didn't work out.

'I know quite well what I want and where I am going,' Salazar had announced when he first came to power. 'For the rest, let the country study, let it suggest, let it object, and let it discuss, but when the time comes for me to give orders I shall expect it to obey.' And thirty years later, in an interview with *Le Figaro*, he said, 'I do not believe in universal suffrage, because the individual vote does not take into account human differentiation. I do not believe in equality but in hierarchy.'

The cult of the leader, of saviour, demands such faith. It also demands inspiration. But Salazar's talent was accountancy. His was a parochial vision of Portugal's universal greatness, a sentimental yearning after implacable destiny. His genius was for mediocrity. As Peter Fryer and Patricia McGowan Pinheiro wrote in 1961, Salazar 'handed the direction of intellectual life over to tenth-raters, time-servers, obscurantists and hacks'. When asked whether fascism was ever stimulating, the poet Sophia de Mello Breyner Andresen replied, 'Yes, but it lasted so long and made us all so tired.'

I walked in beautiful gardens at Estoril with people not so much dressed as framed by clothes and jewellery and hair, alarmingly pressed and primped and permed, alarmingly well-preserved. The gardens belonged to the casino where those with nothing better to do with their lives but think about money go to pass the time, to win some, to lose more. Russian roulette, I thought, would be as just, and more honest. Estoril used to be the graveyard of superannuated royalty, the deposed with nothing left to be but themselves. The past had once been stacked beneath their feet like gold bars in a vault. Then it was hollow, an echoing memory. I thought of Dom Sebastião's sense of destiny, his gamble on an illusory certainty. His impulsiveness, his passion and crazy courage were Portuguese qualities which Salazar conspicuously lacked.

The dictator's one-time colleague, long-time enemy Henrique Galvão had them. In January 1961 he hijacked the cruise liner *Santa Maria* off Venezuela, flew a banner '*Santa Liberdade*', turned the ship into the directorate for the Iberian revolution and sailed to foment the struggle in Portuguese Angola. The next month rebellion broke out there. Two years earlier, Galvão had escaped from secret police custody by leaving a bolster under his hospital bedclothes. I thought of a relative of mine, arrested for allegedly smuggling politically active Angolan students out of Portugal. Imprisoned in Lisbon's Aljube gaol, he was interrogated for days and nights. Bright lights. No sleep. His cell door was left open, and the door at the end of the corridor, but he resisted that bait. Finally deported, he returned to England. He had aged years in seven weeks.

He was one of thousands of victims of the International and State Defence Police, PIDE, to which one in ninety Portuguese was recruited. The midnight knock on anyone's door could mean three months in gaol without charge, then another ninety days with Ministry of Interior authorisation, then indefinite detention, life, which 'permits it to be said to the prisoner that it is in his hands to be free' (Decree-law no. 40,550, 1956). PIDE *embirros* (bailiffs) were well schooled by the Gestapo and by Mussolini's skilled operatives in the intricate catalogue of torture. Psychological seduction. Beating. Cold and hot water alternately poured into ears until the suspect was stone deaf. 'The statue'. The cell called 'the refrigerator'. Genitals nailed to the wall, defenestration, deportation to the colonies, hard labour, blessed death. A PIDE witness was once asked what he'd do if someone wrote 'Peace on earth to men of good will' on a wall. He told the court, 'I'd arrest him.'

Towards the end of August 1968 Salazar, the benevolent father-figure, suffered bad headaches. A borehole in his skull relieved the pressure of the haematoma occasioned by his fall. Halfway through September he screamed out loud. A new haemorrhage had caused a stroke and last rites were hurriedly administered. But he made a remarkable recovery. He died at last on 27 July 1970 with the reins of power still in his hands, or so he believed. No one had had the courage to tell him that Marcel Caetano had been prime minister for almost two years.

Graffiti was everywhere when I first came to Lisbon after the coup of 1974. It was published and republished on walls with revisions, amendments, refutations and glosses, a spray-paint history of intoxi-cating times when the pendulum swung far left and right, left, right. Soon staid citizens had *saudades* for a dull economy that ran on time and a solid edifice of state that was never overwritten. Twenty years on, most walls are blank ones, though I saw a black man on scaffolding at Alcântara laboriously chipping away at a huge hammer-and-sickle. Not the kind of thing you want nowadays on a gentrified waterfront.

At Cascais though, there is lots of graffiti. Skins' words, No Name Boys, disaffection with democracy, the affectation of anarchy.

In the centre of town Camões's face is sprayed green. The poet would have understood the youths' thinly-disguised despair, if not their nihilism. He was a bohemian at home in palace, bar or brothel, a wild and sorry man in his time.

Wild man Tom Stucley put his troops ashore here from a leaky ship in 1578 *en route* from Rome to Ireland. Camões would have also understood the crazy English Catholic's determination to relieve Bad Queen Bess of the Emerald Isle. They may have met. Stucley enjoyed an immediate audience with Dom Sebastião and looked forward to aid and fresh ships.

Cascais is a place for aristocrats and fishermen. King Dom Luís made the seventeenth-century citadel his summer residence in the days when the Praia do Peixe (Fish Beach) was more business than pleasure. Now the children of the rich no longer play with poor fishermen's families, and all fifteen boats that dock at the new wharf today land between them what one boat alone would have brought in twenty-five years ago. Though they bemoan the small catch, men like João Parracho, head of the fish auction, smile at current prices. In the 1960s there were five hundred boats, but prices were low and the fishermen poor. 'It was slavery,' they say, 'exploitation and slavery.'

They are proud men though. Didn't I know that a Cascais fisherman, Afonso Sanches, discovered America in 1482, ten years before Columbus? And wasn't St Anthony himself honorary colonel of the Cascais regiment? Aside from the fish auction, the palaces and hotels, Cascais is middle class and full of the middle-class obsession, shops. A pony minces out of town between the shafts of an open landau full of tourists. A van wallpapered with bullfight posters drives round and round all afternoon, its loudspeaker blaring *Viva Espanha!* The bullring is the largest in the country, they say, but built on a site better suited to a windmill.

The real natives are friendly, but many in the tourist business here have lost the art of hospitality, as they have in the Algarve. To them, we're members of a migratory species that will always flock to their watering holes. They should remember the saying, *Cascais, Uma vez e nunca mais*, 'Cascais once but never again'. At a beachside bar a surly waiter serves me a beer at an absurd mark-up. I'm so mad I shout at the boss. There's a machine above the toilet designed to serve hygienic paper seat-covers. I press the handle idly. Nothing happens. There are no covers. But then, there's no lavatory seat. And no flush.

Water churns, sucks and blows deep in the rock's plumbing down at the Mouth of Hell. Here, beyond town, the Atlantic swell floods caverns beneath the headland. The *Bôca do Inferno* gulps, throbs, sounds airy bass notes, spews water from blow-holes and, when the sea withdraws, sighs spookily and takes a panicky breath. Here, with admirable dramatic judgement, the magus Aleister Crowley staged his own disappearance.

The son of a brewer-turned-Plymouth Brother, Crowley had joined W.B. Yeats and others in the Order of the Golden Dawn, theosophists fascinated by cabalistic magic. Fernando Pessoa, the occultist, translated Crowley's 'Hymn to Pan' and drew up the magician's astrological chart. He addressed Crowley, by letter, as *Carissime Frater*, 'dearest brother'. Even as his marriage dissolved, Crowley brought his German scarlet woman, nineteen-year-old Hanni Jaeger, to Lisbon in September 1930. She was cast as 'the Monster' in their drama, he as 'the Beast of Revelation'. His pet name for Hanni was 'Anu', from *anus*, the part of her he liked best. As they landed from the steamship *Alcântara*, the poet was waiting. 'Pessoa met us: a very *nice* man.' But an encounter in the flesh may have been a disappointment after meetings in spirit, and on paper.

'God once tried to wake up Lisbon – with an earthquake,' the Beast told the Monster. 'He gave it up as a bad job.'

The Monster gave up the Beast as a bad job. Rites of sexual magic made her weep hysterically. Crowley's aura was stifling and she escaped to Berlin. Her betrayal might have shattered Crowley but he fed, as only the most noxious egotists can, on rejection and depression. He vanished, leaving a suicide note weighted down with his cigarette case above the *Bôca do Inferno*: 'I cannot live without you. The other "Boca do Inferno" will get me – it will not be as hot as yours! Hjsos! Tu Li Yu.' As arranged, Pessoa primed the newspapers. They whipped the affair into a sensation that should have satisfied any magician's vanity. The World's Wickedest Man had killed himself at the very Mouth of Hell. I'd like to know what Fernando Pessoa thought of the vengeful stunt he was party to.

And of Crowley's resurrection – after a decent interval – at an exhibition of his own paintings in Berlin.

If Portugal knows how to suffer God's wrath and Salazar's stranglehold, it also hopes for resurrection in the marrow of its bones. The Church gave it Jesus, and gives him at every mass. History gave it the king that it once longed for. It still longs.

'You can't know the country,' writes the American diplomat Datus Proper, 'without knowing *sebastianismo*.'

Portuguese intellectuals I'd spoken to in both London and Lisbon looked sideways when I mentioned it. Or they laughed too loudly. It embarrassed them to have to think about it, so I knew I was on promising, perhaps holy, ground. It embarrassed them that their greatest, maybe the greatest, twentieth-century poet was obsessed with it. They were suspicious of foreigners like me peeking in and finding Portugal with its trousers down. They despised it as they despised the opiates of Salazar's time, *salazarismo*'s F words: Fado, Fátima and Football. They wanted *sebastianismo* like they wanted a lobotomy. And they didn't want me meddling with their frontal lobes.

In *Salazar Blinks* David Slavitt notes acerbically how tourist writers or Portuguese hacks inevitably latch on to a shortlist of key words in attempting to define national character. He was mostly thinking of the S words: *siso* (good sense) versus *loucura* (madness), *saudade* (nostalgia), *sebastianismo* and *salazarismo*. Yes, he says, those are the words, and the terrible thing is that the hacks are right, because that is the character of our people.

It's only sensible to look at the clichés again, crazy not to, though everyone knows *saudade*'s not what it used to be. As for *sebastianismo*, is there life in the old cadaver yet? Careful now. Portuguese intellectuals make fun of these things, but naturally they don't like foreigners doing it.

'Joking apart,' a journalist told me at dinner in the Bairro Alto, 'if you want to talk about *sebastianismo*, you should really talk to Dom Duarte.'

Dom Duarte, current Duke of Bragança, is the most serious claimant to the vacant, or non-existent, throne of Portugal.

'How can I contact him?'

'That I don't know.'

Later that evening, on a crazy whim, I looked him up in the phone book, knowing that he must be ex-directory. But he wasn't. I rang. He said yes, please let us meet tomorrow afternoon. It was the easiest appointment I made all trip.

4

HISTORY OF THE FUTURE

Rua Duques de Bragança

NEBUCHADNEZZAR the King of Babylon challenged Daniel the prophet of Israel to do what his own wise men could not do and reveal his dream. So that Nebuchadnezzar might know the thoughts of his own mind, Daniel put into words the bright and frightening image which the king had seen in his sleep: head of gold, breast and arms of silver, belly and thighs of bronze, legs of iron, and feet of iron mixed with potter's clay. It stood firm. Then a rock, hacked from the mountain by an inhuman hand, smashed the feet of the image and shattered all its metals to glittering scurf that flew like chaff from the threshing floor. But the rock grew to be a mountain that filled the earth.

Daniel took a breath and interpreted the dream like this: Nebuchadnezzar was the head of gold, whose high kingdom would be followed by inferior kingdoms of silver and bronze. Then a fourth kingdom strong as iron would crush all things, but, like the image's feet, it would stand divided. Partly strong and partly brittle, it was destined to be broken in pieces by the rock which is the sovereignty of God, the fifth kingdom which is never to be destroyed.

I called at Number Ten on a hot April afternoon. Number Ten in the Rua Duques de Bragança, that is. From a corner of the Largo de São Carlos, where Fernando Pessoa was born in a fourth-floor flat opposite the National Opera, the steepening street ran away riverwards, or would have done if the ground hadn't dropped precipitately to the square far below called Corpo Santo, 'holy body'. In the row of dour grey façades Number Ten was a small house washed with ox-blood distemper. It might have been plucked up from a provincial town and dropped here. A gate in a high wrought-iron fence opened on to a tiny paved yard; three steps, flanked by potted geraniums, led up to a dark green door modestly furnished with brass fittings and shaded by a vine. There was no name, but this, I was sure, was the Fundação Bragança. The door was slowly opened by an aged retainer in a rig of funereal shabbiness. His air of dignified servitude was abruptly blown away by a small man who loomed first behind, then in front of him and ushered me jovially into an anteroom. His late father, he told me, had been secretary to the Duke of Bragança for many years. He himself, name of Fred, had been born in Moçambique, worked in South Africa, moved to Holland with his Dutch wife.

'I'm ex-Rank Xerox,' Fred sighed, 'and now I'm in Portugal where the climate is good.'

On the wall hung foxed engravings of members of the House of Bragança. They had ruled Portugal and its empire from 1640 to 1910, from the victory of João IV 'the restorer' to the abdication of Manuel 'the unfortunate'. A tall wardrobe was surmounted by Portugal's coat of arms in bronze. A dingy display of feather flowers in a glass case sprung from a piece of cork-oak bark. Bad cracks ran in walls and ceiling. The paintwork was patched with grey and white and an apology for azure. It was as if someone knew how the house should look and had hopefully touched it up: a metaphor for the ruling class perhaps. Fred gossiped about Africa. When I mentioned Kinshasa, he used its colonial name, Léopoldville, and placed it on the Zambian border. I'm not sure how accurate his nostalgia was.

'Those blacks,' he told me, 'can be nice people.'

I don't think he was with me in this room where kings stared from battered frames. There was a big formal photograph of Dom Carlos 'the martyr' with his sons the Crown Prince Luís Filipe and Prince Manuel. On 1 February 1908, as the royal family drove in an open landau through the Terreiro do Paço, the king was felled by two bullets and a second assassin mortally wounded his heir. Young Manuel II, 'the unfortunate', ascended the throne but couldn't hold things together.

He'd been born in the same year as Salazar and Hitler, and on the very day, 15 November 1889, that Brazil lost its last Bragança emperor and became a republic. When the revolutionaries of 1910 declared Portugal a republic too, fishermen ferried Manuel and his family out from the beach at Ericeira to the royal yacht *Dona Amélia*. The unfortunate king died in Twickenham in 1932. At Wimbledon the tennis-club flag was flown at half-mast. In the photograph here the royal family was stiff but still alive. In a glass case beside them perched a stuffed partridge assassinated by Dom Carlos. The big fridge that stood beside my chair shuddered and stopped humming.

Kingdoms come and go. Ourique in the Alentejo is Portugal's birthplace. There, as Dom Afonso Henriques was preparing to fight the Moors in 1139, he was visited by a sign of Christ foretelling that if he won the battle the Portuguese would rule the fifth empire which would grow to fill all the earth.

Five centuries later a famous shoemaker lived in the walled town of Trancoso, north of the Serra da Estrela. Gonçalo Eanes Bandarra was more famous for prophecy than for shoes. Popular amongst the Jews of his home town, he was investigated by the Inquisition for that reason. *Bandarra* means 'idler' but he was busy writing doggerel verses, *trovas*, anticipating the *Quinto Império* or fifth empire and celebrating the redeemer-king who would bring it into being. This saviour was biding his time somewhere, so Bandarra said, until the time was ripe. Then *o Encoberto*, the hidden one, would appear.

Fred recognised a hand on the front door and a soft footfall on the stair. Hurriedly he showed me into a further room. The plaster was cracked and the paint was patchy there too, but it was furnished with red plush and gilt furniture salvaged perhaps from a derelict palace or an opera-house prop store. Fred's master entered and greeted me warmly.

'I apologise for my lateness,' he said. 'I don't want to sound snobbish, but I have been delayed by talking with the king of the Zulus. Please.'

I sat down.

'Will you take port?'

He called for glasses. Like a court usher Fred echoed the cry.

'Chief Buthelezi has, it seems, a rather more constructive attitude than the ANC. And coffee?' the duke said without pausing. 'Yes, coffee.'

At a nod from his master, Fred rushed off in search of coffee. Dom Duarte adjusted the mustard-and-green cravat at the neck of his red-and-white-check shirt and grey tweed jacket. I asked how he would describe himself.

'I am Dom Duarte, the Duke of Bragança, the actual heir of the Portuguese throne, descendant by male line from the first king of Portugal and from almost all the kings of Portugal, except Dom Sebastião because he didn't have sons.'

He crossed his legs: brown suede shoes, grey socks, marmoreal calves, navy-blue trousers. For years, those who cared had been almost resigned to Dom Duarte remaining single like Dom Sebastião. Even though he is descended from Dom Miguel, whose line was excluded from the throne in 1834 when he lost the war for succession to his elder brother, latter-day monarchists and would-be consorts always hoped for a marriage as near royal as could be in a republic. Smart magazines like *O Quê?* habitually pictured Dom Duarte – always referred to as *Sua Alteza Real*, 'His Royal Highness' – with beautiful women at high-society functions.

'The dukes of Bragança were a side line of the royal family,' he continued, 'so when Dom Sebastião died in Morocco in 1578 we were under Spanish rule for three kings, until a coup overthrew the Spaniards and its leaders persuaded Dom Sebastião's cousin, the Duke of Bragança, to be king. He became João IV, 'the restorer' of 1640, and the father of Catherine of Bragança who married your Charles II and started, with Bombay as her dowry, the British empire in India.'

What better match for a Restoration king than a restorer's daughter?

'She brought you tea and orange marmalade, as well as china and the use of forks for eating.' He chuckled. 'She had a very strong civilising influence in England.'

We talked of how her father's court had come under the spell of an extraordinary Jesuit, Father António Vieira (1608–97). The priest, so the king believed, was the greatest man in the world. He championed, among other causes, freedom for Brazilian Indians and toleration for Portuguese crypto-Jews. In the early 1900s he was hailed by Fernando Pessoa as the greatest of all Portuguese writers, the master of prose. But this sophisticated scholar and diplomat took inspiration from the cobbler-prophet Bandarra who peddled his vision of a Portuguese millennium drawn, via the writings of the Calabrian hermit Joachim de Fiore, from the Book of Daniel. António Vieira refined Bandarra's crude poetry and from it forged with critical rigour and impeccable logic his most celebrated work, the *History of the Future*.

'But,' I said, 'Vieira applied these notions to João IV, not to Sebastião at all.'

From Sebastião's grave João IV had brought Portugal back to life. Vieira projected an epoch of spiritual empire under his beloved king.

'Portugal was still under threat from Spain,' said Dom Duarte. 'All kinds of myths and popular beliefs would help to strengthen the king, help him hold on to the throne.'

But in 1656, after just sixteen years, João IV died. So, in a kind of wild hallucination, a most un-Jesuitical high fever, Vieira found himself proposing the late king's resurrection.

Fred held the door for the aged retainer and his tray of coffee, milk, cups and saucers and glasses. He made it to an unsteady-looking round table between Dom Duarte and me. Dom Duarte reached for a bottle of Ferreira's old Porto Duques de Bragança which had been standing like a prop on the sideboard. The cork came out with a small deep sound like a man discreetly clearing his throat. Dom Duarte began to pour port into glasses at the far side of the tray, just as the aged retainer began pouring coffee. Their arms crossed and they tangled for a moment. Nothing was said or spilt. The retainer paused.

I thanked Dom Duarte for my port. The belief that his ancestor, the first Bragança on the throne, would come back to life was what really started Sebastianism off, seventy years after Sebastião, 'the one so longed for', had died in the desert. Immediately after the event people began to believe that Sebastião had not died. Several pseudo-Sebastiãos put in appearances. These kinds of folk beliefs, bastards born of the potent coupling of nostalgia with hope, are common to peoples who want better times. But Vieira gave long life to the big idea. The resurrected redeemer-king and Portuguese destiny converged in a new notion of nationality that would grow, like Daniel's rock, to fill the whole world.

I thanked the retainer for coffee. The cup hardly shook in the saucer. I was talking myth that wasn't folksy like King Arthur. I was talking sleeping lords with a would-be king who longed for his country to wake up to him. He wasn't playing at it.

'The whole story,' he began again, 'has to be integrated with older myths which started with King Dinis, that the duty of Portugal was to prepare the third epoch of humanity, the Empire of the Holy Spirit.'

Here I was, in a shabby-genteel, no, a shabby-noble room, listening to a late-twentieth-century pretender to the throne talking in a twelfth-century voice. I shivered. Dom Duarte spoke the language of Joachim of Fiore who divided time not by five but by three. It was an ascent through three successive ages: the Age of the Father, characterised by law; the Age of the Son, characterised by faith and grace; and the Age of the Holy Spirit, in which the eternal gospel would supersede the forms of religion. Joachim, and the early Joachites, believed human history was to culminate in about 1260 when a new leader would draw mankind towards the things of the Spirit. Antichrist would hold sway over the earth just prior to this, and would chastise and destroy the corrupt Church. Joachim's language, though not necessarily his spirit, informed all later radical movements – all flagellants, ranters, anarchic millenarians and their brethren – up to and including Marxists.

Dom Duarte was not hoping for the fruits of dialectical materialism, but fervently looked forward to spiritual synthesis.

'The Discoveries were done following this idea. The Brazilian Indians were considered to have escaped original sin, because they were naked. They would be one of the bases for the third epoch. The secret teaching of the Empire of the Holy Spirit was the driving force behind the Discoveries.'

Dom Duarte smiled broadly, knowing that what was to him a commonplace was likely to be a revelation to me. I had the irreverent thought that a tooth or two, if not his head, would have benefited from a crown. Beneath a neat moustache his lower lip stood proud. His eyes were somewhat uncoordinated. He smoothed his soft thatch of hair before expanding on his vision of the past.

43

'Evidently the Discoveries had to be paid for, so commerce was necessary. Local people in Africa and so on would not always readily accept the Portuguese. The Muslims were always fighting because they had been expelled from Portugal and the peninsula not very long ago, so they still were at war with Europe; they were trying to conquer Vienna. When the Portuguese rounded Africa and arrived at India, we made alliances with the Hindu kings against the Muslims, attacking them from the back. This was the strategic side of the Discoveries. We needed a reason for doing it and the basic reason why we believed we had the right to do it was this: that you have to unify the world so that it would be possible for God to establish the rule of the Holy Spirit around the world.'

'How,' I wanted to know, 'can we align that spiritual but, given the assumptions of the time, pragmatic view with messianic dreams about Sebastião himself?'

'This is easy, in the sense that when Dom Sebastião was invited by a Moroccan king – a king who'd promised that if he won he would give liberty of religion in Morocco – to come to his aid against his nephew, Dom Sebastião decided he had to do it. But it was badly prepared, the military operation, it was a defeat, a tragedy. This is easy to understand. The main problem was how to deal with practical circumstances.'

He digressed into questions of slavery. How the Portuguese had never redefined slaves as animals; the British did that, so that they could treat them inhumanely with a good conscience. I appreciated this because I knew how, before they shipped them from Africa to the New World, Portuguese traders often branded their human cargo with *IHS*, Christ's monogram. Like animals maybe, but animals with immortal souls. He compared the morality and legality – or their opposites – of slavery then with those of prostitution now. It was an interesting view, if remote from North African sand dunes and Renaissance Lisbon.

'I'd like to revert to Sebastião,' I said.

'Ah, yes,' he changed tack instantly. 'Many of our people believed that Dom Sebastião did not die. The Spanish tried to say yes, the body's found, here he is in this coffin, but it was not him, even the coffin that is now here in Lisbon, the bones of the king, they are not his real size, they are not him.'

'They have been examined, have they?'

'Yes. And then somebody appeared in Venice saying he was King Sebastião, and the doctors came and declared he was the king, but I don't know. Politically it was impossible to admit it because then the Spanish would have to give back the throne of Portugal to him. If he had been alive he would have been killed, just as probably happened. After a certain number of years everybody of normal common sense admitted that he must be dead, but the common people kept the belief alive, hoping first for the restoration of Portuguese independence, but also for the restoration of the spiritual size of Portugal.'

So, size was important. So small, so great. With a mission, with God on your side, with God on every side, lines on maps could be transcended.

'Much later on in Brazil, there was a popular uprising, after the republicans took over; they still expected the return of Dom Sebastião, but from heaven not a Moroccan grave, to liberate the oppressed population of northern Brazil. There are some areas of the world where they still expect him. Even in Morocco there are certain groups who secretly wait for him.'

'Are there still people in Portugal who hope for Sebastião's return?'

'I hope,' Dom Duarte laughed.

'You hope?'

'Yes, I hope. If we don't believe that we have a spiritual duty, if we think that our role in the world is just to be a brave little European country with enough money to have all the luxuries of life, then it's a life without perspective, without a future. But if we believe our country has a duty, a mission, a mission to work with the Portuguese-speaking countries – Angola, Moçambique, Timor, Brazil – to create a fraternity and develop our spiritual dimension, then . . . We have many Portuguese working in Africa, not for money but because they believe they have to be there. We need to believe in something higher than the day-to-day life.'

'It's as though monarchists and Communists have a common vocabulary,' I put in.

'That's true,' Dom Duarte laughed again. 'It's the deep feeling of the majority, even if most people are not conscious of it. Opinion polls show that people are more concerned for peace and liberty in Timor and Angola than for conditions here at home. We have the duty to do something for them.'

'So the Portuguese are still looking towards the horizon?'

'Yes, our vision is not of a Europe looking inside, centred on its stomach, but of Europe looking outside. Like England, we are divided between the Continental vision of Europe and the Atlantic vision. Though we don't see any short-term profit in looking outside, because Angola and Moçambique are destroyed, Timor is under Indonesian occupation and the people are in total misery. It's a moral not an economic proposition.'

'If you were able to assume the crown of Portugal, would you be willing to take on the mantle of Sebastião?'

'Well, I don't want to be misunderstood in answering this. There are many points in *sebastianismo* that are totally mythic, its mentality can be passive, something for nothing, waiting and hoping for something to arrive without working for it. But *sebastianismo* is also positive. We have to fight for what we believe. As they said in medieval times, the fight is your duty, the victory is the business of God. In this sense, yes.'

'Isn't there a great danger in looking over your shoulder, hoping that somehow one can replay the past and create a different world which is a dream?'

'On the other hand, if you try to learn the lessons of the past, correct the mistakes, then it is useful to know the *real* history of the past. For instance, the fight with Islam, it was a fact of the time. Nowadays I am very much in favour of working together with the Muslims; I was living with them in Moçambique and in Guiné Bissau, and I am trying to work with the government of Moçambique now to make them understand how to deal with our Islamic problem. They behave like we did, the bourgeois of Maputu, looking with great suspicion to the north and to the Islamic population. Now they are changing, they are much more open-minded. The president has even now a very clever Indian guru who is teaching him meditation and some spiritual values. For a former Marxist it's very useful I think.'

'You are a Sebastianist yourself,' I ventured.

'I am,' Dom Duarte cut in, 'in a very special way.'

'In a very special way,' I had to agree. 'How can you translate that into practical politics now?'

'We must not surrender ethical values to the dogma of free trade. If you sacrifice everything to this, it will drive Europe to disaster. The weakest areas of Europe, including ours, will be ruined by the north. All developments should be subject to one criterion, the happiness of the population now and in the future. You cannot sacrifice the future for today, this is why green issues are so important; what we are doing now in Europe and North America is suicide.'

'St Sebastian, after whom the king was named, survived the emperor Diocletian's firing squad, all those arrows,' I said, 'but he was cudgelled to death in the end. A lot of people feel very strongly that *sebastianismo* is a distraction which should finally be killed off. How do you counter that feeling?'

'It *was* a distraction in certain epochs, the negative side of it. Not so today. It's an issue which interests Communists, Jews, Freemasons, Catholics. There are philosphers and poets and pop groups who are Sebastianistas. The people who think it's a waste of time are business people only interested in profit, of a nineteenth-century mentality which doesn't consider the future. Poets have an important duty; they open eyes to long-term matters. Monarchies also, they give a sense of continuity while republics are short-term with short-term priorities.'

By republics I think he meant democracies in general.

'Most European republics, like ours, are frustrated monarchies. Peoples want father figures. Our presidents try to behave like kings, and they do it very well.'

Portugal's father figure, President Mario Soares, is nicknamed *a Rainha da Inglaterra*, the Queen of England, because of his powerlessness. I was wondering what sort of absolute monarch Dom Duarte would make. Would he let his people eat cake while he nurtured a global Empire of the Holy Spirit?

'The rest of the world can't understand Portugal,' he said with no pleasure at all. 'For example, why are we so interested in the Timor issue? We don't understand why our neighbours won't help. They don't help because Indonesia is such good business. We are trying to get the countries of Europe to join us in a fight to liberate this little little island whose people are more Portuguese than we are.'

He was being charitable. Europe understood all too well. The United States had perverted the processes of the United Nations. Britain had supplied arms to Indonesia. Australia had stolen East Timor's oil, all in the knowledge that repression and unspeakable torture filled the vacuum there following the Portuguese revolution. The world's power-brokers colluded with a squalid but rich dictatorship. They blatantly encouraged what Mario Soares has called by its name: genocide.

'Do you feel it your duty to go to them in Sebastianic mode?'

'Well, yes,' he said. 'Only a few days ago I was in Macau, meeting Timorese people. Some were working with the Indonesian government as functionaries, I cannot say more; others were from the guerrilla movement who are fighting the Indonesians in the mountains. They all said to me, You must go to Timor, you must visit the traditional chiefs and tell them that you don't forget them, that the Portuguese are with them. They don't expect military intervention but they do expect moral support. Our ancestors gave their loyalty to your ancestors, and vice versa, so you have the duty to do it.'

I felt as though we'd been talking in medieval fancy dress, and suddenly walked out into the real world still wearing it. Dom Duarte was quite comfortable.

'And the same thing happens in other places,' he added. 'The chiefs of Cabinda just came to me and asked me to act. Tribal leaders in Africa want my support because they feel that I am the person who has the duty to give it, because their ancestors signed those treaties with my ancestors. I hope I can do something useful. But I must do it, even if it's not useful.'

Here was a man resisting the small-mindedness of the Eurocracy by responding to a weighty sense of duty in the service of a large destiny, a destiny conceived in medieval times and still to be fulfilled. On the day Dom Duarte, 'the eloquent', was to ascend the throne in 1433 his astrologer warned him that the stars were ill disposed. That Dom Duarte replied, 'I'll do it because I must.' This Dom Duarte echoed him, knowing that today's politicians could never take on destiny as he could. Dom Sebastião had done it; he'd put his country's money where his mouth was. He'd left Renaissance Portugal for Morocco with a medieval army and the pope's blessing. He'd carried powerful weapons: a sacred banner, one of the Roman arrows that had pierced St Sebastian, and the sword carried by the first king of Portugal. Could Dom Duarte do more than talk?

'Will you go to East Timor?'

'Yes. I don't want the Portuguese government to be too much offended, so I will try to do it in agreement with our president. The Indonesians will of course use it as propaganda. The question is, how not to abuse their hospitality but, on the other hand, help the ordinary Timorese to have hope.'

'You really do feel, in a practical sense, the heir to Sebastião?'

'Yes, in a sense, yes, but evidently I have to avoid the mistakes, like making an expedition that was badly prepared and was a disaster. But the idea behind it I agree with.'

I could not think beyond the tragic waste. Blood on the sand. But Dom Duarte could still contemplate a glorious mission.

'Probably I would have done the same thing at the time,' he added, 'if the Moroccans had asked my help.'

5

ADAMASTOR AND THE DOCTOR

Lisbon Viewpoints

I WALKED UP the steps of the Hotel Bragança. I was going to see the rooms where Ricardo Reis stayed in 1936. A phone call from the duke had opened the doors to me. The whole Rua Duques de Bragança, with the hotel that backed on to it, belonged to the family before the revolution and is now owned by the duke's foundation. The janitor showed me up the steep and endless stairs that Dr Reis climbed to register on the first floor. I glanced through half-open doors into rooms that looked like school. The Bragança is not a hotel today, it's a drab university building. We climbed onwards to the second floor where Dr Reis lived for some weeks before finding himself an apartment. The janitor had no idea which rooms I wanted. They looked down to the river, I knew that, and here they were on the corridor's right side. The chambermaid Lydia had knocked on this door with Dr Reis's breakfast balanced on one arm; she'd opened it silently every night and slithered into his bed. There was no bed and breakfast now. The rooms were quite empty. That is, they were littered with educational detritus, but scoured of the significance for which I was looking. Students scurried between rooms with miraculous self-possession. The janitor urged me upwards. At last I climbed out on to the roof. Undulating pantiles of weathered terracotta tipped into a broad gutter bridged by a series of heavy iron sheets that tilted and clanged as I walked, or jumped where there were gaps, around the building's edge. Dr Reis never trod this vertiginous path, but from up here I could survey the changed, barely-changed, homeland he rediscovered in Salazar's secretive repressive present: the same parched roofscape, the dim chasms between buildings, the crumbling cliffs of stucco, the shimmering river. But had I been able to find the pre-war hotel registers, with marbled covers and leather corners, stacked far below on a basement shelf under a filmy shroud of cobwebs, I'd have turned up the entry for 28 December 1935 in vain. Dr Reis's signature is a fiction.

It is remarkable that a novel as intensely Portuguese as José Saramago's *The Year of the Death of Ricardo Reis* should have made such an impact abroad. Saramago himself has implied that you have to be Portuguese to savour it fully. Its hero is a doctor-poet with monarchist sympathies who returns from Brazil to Lisbon in the last days of 1935. But Ricardo Reis is one of Fernando Pessoa's heteronyms, a poet invented by the poet, one of his many multi-faceted personalities. What's more, in Saramago's novel he outlives his creator. He arrives here soon after Pessoa's death and, once he has settled back in Lisbon, his creator comes to haunt him benignly. Mind you, those who believe that the dead are anything but dead are reproved early in Saramago's next novel: 'if anyone ever said otherwise, or suggested, for example, that Fernando Pessoa visited Ricardo Reis, the one being dead and the other alive, it was their foolish imagination and nothing else.'

Ricardo Reis was in the habit of walking to the viewpoint of Alto da Santa Catarina by way of the Praça Luís de Camões; it's a dogleg of calm gradients, up then down. If you cut straight across to it, as the gull flies, the city grows stormy, streets on steep peaks, steps down into deep troughs and out again, houses gasping *de profundis* for the sun or standing proud, gilded with light. Today I left the ex-Hotel Bragança and opted for the gentle swell, past bronze Pessoa sitting in wait for someone outside Brasileira. A few steps downhill stood the nineteenth-century novelist Eça de Queirós, whom Zola acknowledged to be 'far greater than my own dear master, Flaubert'. He had no need to wait; overdressed in the manner of his time he was looking deep into the eyes of a woman who leant back against him, arms wide, her only covering a gauze draped over her lower belly and legs.

Just after the white marble statue was unveiled in 1903, Eça's manservant remarked that it was a good likeness of his late master, but not so much like the *senhora*, his wife. This *senhora* is Truth. The line from Eça that inspired the sculptor is carved on the base: 'Upon the strong nakedness of truth the diaphanous cloak of fancy.' Veil or no veil, as soon as the monument was recently cleaned, some artist or literary critic with a black felt-tip pen fancied some pubic hair. But it was Lisbon's year as Europe's cultural capital and Truth was quickly scrubbed clean.

Bronze Camões stood eleven metres high above his square, grasping sword and book, half-blinded by Moors and half by pigeon shit, supported by stone scholars and lesser poets, all surrounded by elm trees where, as Pessoa whimsically wrote in his English guidebook, 'a legion of feathered visitors does duty for the leaves in winter'.

In January 1890 men climbed a long ladder, scrambled on to Camões's plinth and threw black drapes over the poet. The square was the rallying point for patriots angered by Britain over the affair of the Pink-Coloured Map. The scramble on their minds was the scramble for Africa. The *Mapa Cor-de-Rosa* proposed a Portuguese corridor across Africa from Angola to Moçambique, but Britain, with Cecil Rhodes's Cape-to-Cairo ambitions in mind, colluded with Germany and Belgium to sabotage its oldest ally's plans. The two thrusts, east—west and north—south, collided. A British ultimatum forced an outraged, betrayed Portugal to withdraw from territories in the middle. It so happened that my great-uncle Dan Crawford, later renowned for his book *Thinking Black* (1912), was walking into Central Africa at that time of terrifying flux, on the way to being enslaved by the emperor-chief M'siri in present-day Shaba, Zaïre; *en route* he met the explorer (and slave-trader) Silva Porto in the ruins of his house at Bié, Angola, only days before the famous old man, disillusioned and unable to broker peace, retired to his private chapel and settled himself on a bed of powder kegs spread with the Portuguese flag. He lit a match. Here in a chill Lisbon, the trees were bare then and Camões was shrouded in mourning. Now there was plenty of foliage, plenty of shade in which to doze. In sun, a small black girl bopped to a tune from a snack stall and at intervals charged pigeons, sending them flying.

On Rua do Loreto I passed a shop's awning made of a yellow VW beetle's bonnet and bumper. I paused at a restaurant for its name's sake: Casa da Índia. From his high viewpoint, Camões could

see as far as both Africa and India. He'd fought there, loved there,
suffered there. In his lifetime the Portuguese trade corporation,
Casa da Índia by name, went bankrupt; a factor in the rapidly
tarnishing Golden Age that young King Sebastião inherited, a
Golden Age for ever regilded by *saudade*. Through plate glass the
restaurant looked large and solvent. A serious young waiter served
beer and snacks to an old man wearing an olive-green houndstooth
jacket and a broad tie, red-blue-yellow splattered on white, held in
place with a pearl clip. The pearl, the tie and the jacket were of
different generations and the white-haired woman in shrunken black
facing them must have been the old man's mother. A drunk pushed
the door open with both hands and came out talking. The waiters
within bent double, exploding with laughter, except for the one
who didn't even smile. The drunk turned back, argued with the
door, re-entered crying *'Faz favor!'* The staff threw up their hands.
Please. Do me a favour. The man fell over. I decided to return to
the Casa da Índia for a meal.

The big house that overlooked Alto de Santa Catarina was being
gutted like so many others, as if EU money is dedicated to organ
transplants, new hearts in old bodies. It was a hollow stage-set for
builders, diggers and cement mixers. Washed by their tumult, old
people sat gazing across the river. Between the seats and the belvedere's railing small boys and a ragged girl played football. The
game was controlled by a not-so-small boy with an incipient beard,
a sad mouth and dazed eyes who'd cast himself in the role of striker,
referee and executioner; a blundering king whose subjects squawked
with delight, fawned, or howled and clutched their balls with both
hands. The palm trees' shredded fronds hung still, somewhere
between limp and stiff. Reis stares over the edge, waiting for a
lover. Beside him stands Pessoa wearing a sardonic smile and a
black overcoat, hands gripping the railing. Now a middle-aged
couple climbed steps to the viewpoint. They did not hold hands,
but touched one another glancingly now and then by accident.
Nor did they look at anything but the stairway underfoot and the
panorama falling and spreading from their feet to the horizon from
which and beyond which half-remembered ships threaded evan-
escent wake through large unknowns. The lovers gained the Alto,
this high place. They stood, blithely separate, looking and not

looking, held within their feral aura as between moist sheets, but released into the world, scenting it, tasting it, being in it.

Up here the Alexandrian virgin Santa Catarina might have lit her beacon for sailors, might have spun unharmed on her splintering Catherine wheel, or let her head fall from her shoulders with a gush of milk not blood. Nothing of her nourished the place now. Far below, to the left, lay Cais do Sodré station and a dishevelled quayside where a giant tunnel-borer glinted, waiting to get its teeth into the earth. Ribeira market's pierced dome shone like an inverted rice bowl topped with a spiky lantern. To the right, the 25 April Bridge sieved a still-high sun's light through its cables. Ahead, ferry boats plied to and from Cacilhas. Behind, at the back of watchers on seats – who keep vigil at every viewpoint and public place in Portugal – water trickled almost unheard into a fountain dominated by the craggy, disquieting mass of Adamastor.

Adamastor is one of the Titans, children of Uranus and Gæa, who declared war on Heaven. Camões cunningly cadged him from the Greeks and placed him beyond their imagination: at the southern tip of Africa, and at the midpoint of his epic *Os Lusiadas*. Vasco da Gama's vessel approached the Cape, then known by the name the discoverer Bartolomeu Dias gave it, the Cape of Storms. An intimidating cloud mass blackened the sky and, with the deep roars of something vainly battering at reefs, instilled dread into da Gama's heart . . .

> Oh Power – I said – sublime,
> What divine threat or mystery
> Does this weather and this sea reveal
> Looking like something bigger than a gale?
>
> I hadn't finished, when a figure
> Showed itself in the air, hale, able-bodied
> But of misshapen and gigantic stature,
> Its face threatening, the beard squalid,
> The eyes hollow, and its posture
> Frightful and vile, its colour earthy and pallid,
> Its hair clotted with soil and frizzled so,
> Its mouth black, its teeth yellow.

Adamastor's colossal size and huge voice made the sailors' flesh creep, their hair stand. His words were no more reassuring, for he promised vengeance upon discoverers and fixed penalties for all impudent Portuguese who dared to navigate unploughed waters and to cross forbidden boundaries. Presumption was punishable. Camões erected a mythic warning at the corner of the world where they turned east. Da Gama had been lucky; he got back from India. The Cape of Storms was renamed Cape of Good Hope but, as the grizzled shape predicted, later voyagers discovered that hopes, good or bad, too often are ill-founded. Da Gama died in India at last. Adamastor is the bogeyman who haunts all dreams of empire.

It was a ship named *Adamastor* that gave the signal, from the Tagus below, for revolution on 4 October 1910. On that day Camões's giant was a republican. Now his sculpture glowers over gentle waters in the fountain up here on what should be renamed Alto de Adamastor, though the rumour runs that the Titan himself has shaved, put on a suit and moved to Brussels.

I moved across town to see the doctor. Warmed by a visit to the sumptuous, surly Port Wine Institute I crossed the road to one of Lisbon's best-known viewpoints, the terraced garden of São Pedro de Alcântara, for a glimpse across the centre – I picked out my shuttered window down in the Baixa – to the Moorish castle and the fortress-like cathedral. I ran for the Elevador da Gloria, and jumped on one of two funicular trams, counterweights on cables that grind and clang up and down an alarming gradient, which dropped me all the way to Praça dos Restauradores. I scuttled across wide spaces on the city floor and found the Elevador do Lavra waiting, quite empty, at the bottom of its steep, narrow ascent. I'd assumed it would shuttle up and down with Gloria's dignified frequency, but the driver was in a phonebox, deeply engaged in a conversation copiously illustrated by wasted gestures. I wanted to see the doctor at the top before the light failed. Slowly the tram filled up. Two men got off again and climbed. A woman followed the driver in and, with a filthy look, told the black man next to me to move along. She muttered imprecations all the way up. At the top she bent to fondle and cajole a scabby pye-dog lying in the road.

Men in black crowded round a red transistor radio on a park bench arguing football. Under trees a carp pond quivered, in the bushes old kids played doctors and nurses. Below, in a round pool on a terrace, a mermaid rode a dolphin. A pale young woman in a yellow T-shirt and purple trousers sang past me, looking sideways. I looked outwards: the terrace was a tiled roof level with other roofs and chimneys, backs of apartments above small streets and a shrunken Avenida de Liberdade with all the ancient and postmodern clutter of the western heights beyond; it was a new perspective. Turning I saw, on the terrace in a cave-like shelter, the woman without her purple trousers, squatting. I stared at ornamental palms and the pink, white and cream villas that overlooked me. Invisible to them, she stood and danced a slight gyrating dance, breasts, large white belly and black pubic hair.

She might have done this in the bald shadow of a suburban block of flats, in some corner of Santo Marters, one of Lisbon's many *bairros de lata*, 'tin-can quarters', or in one of the real caves where some of the poor still live. I doubt it. Up above the city, where grand houses and the palace of the cardinal look down from on high, she chose to hide herself, expose herself.

A well-groomed, white-haired man sat in the public garden filing his fingernails. A silver-handled Malacca cane was propped beside him. He turned a benign face on me and, though it was growing late to see the doctor, I felt compelled to stop and chat.

'The heat!' I said.

'Everyone says so,' he replied, 'but I am cool. I have just come to my Lisbon house from my house in a village on the other side of the moon.'

He was a distinguished man from a poor family who, he said, couldn't get far.

'For fifty years I worked in the same bank. I introduced American Express to Portugal. Then I travelled, New York, London.' He paused, 'Do you know that this is the lowest of Lisbon's seven hills?'

I didn't. He'd stopped filing his nails in deference to me but I noticed how immaculate his manicure was, how beautiful his hands.

'I'm making for Campo dos Mártires da Pátria,' I said, 'to see Dr Sousa Martins.'

'Ah yes, you should. It is still called Campo Santana, though its name was officially changed many years ago.'

Campo Santana I knew, a contracted form of Santa Ana after the convent I'd not yet seen. Also known as Campo do Curral, when a cattle pen was set up in the present Jardim dos Mártires for bull-fights and fairs.

'Your Marshal Beresford,' said the *senhor*, 'who fought under Wellington in the Peninsular War, he stayed on to govern Portugal when it was ruled theoretically from Brazil by our royal family. Twelve men led by the Grand Master of the Masonic Order – the *Maçonaria* that spread liberal ideas in Portugal – plotted the downfall of Beresford and the British for our self-respect.'

I nodded.

'The conspirators were tried,' he said, 'and executed by firing squad up there.'

The images coalesced: last rites for bulls in clerical black, crumpled men corralled within cloisters. What I found in the Campo Santana was Lisbon's imposing Faculty of Medicine building, set between the Bacteriological Institute in Santa Ana's old convent and the Institute of Forensic Medicine and Morgue. Its neo-classical façade looked out on a lake of birds backed by trees in the tranquil Martyrs' Garden across a busy road junction. In between, on a traffic island, yet another bronze statue stood on a stout column overlooking the eastern city. It seemed, now, just the place for a rational, calm approach to matters of life and death.

But no, the monument's circular base was spread with tributes: lighted candles, cut flowers in vases, lavish bouquets, photographs of supplicants, wax models of organs and limbs, and what at first sight looked like printed cards. These were stacked and propped around the column's pedestal, on which sat a modestly-draped woman. The white stone *senhora* held an open book on her knee and offered up a rapt, almost beatific face to the erect robed figure of Professor Dr José Thomaz de Sousa Martins (1843–97). He must have known how to treat women. The heaped cards were marble slabs, like hundreds of little gravestones, engraved with messages of thanks. Some said simply *Obrigado*. Others were florid tributes to 'Brother Sousa Martins for all the many mercies received . . .' finished off with the initials of the healed. A few were heart-shaped, embossed with photographs. Above them all the blackened doctor, in his frogged ankle-length gown with ruffled epaulettes, looked more magus than medical man.

A swarthy individual in black laboured over a galvanised furnace where candles and wax votive offerings burned *en masse*. A woman genuflected before the flames. Every day students and doctors came and went on the cool steps of the Faculty of Medicine. Did they look this way and laugh, or pause to consider healing virtue, power and immortality?

Beyond the traffic, stalls set on upended fruit crates offered flowers, candles, crucifixes, devotional postcards, lockets of the Virgin, pictures of Dr Sousa Martins, prayers to Dr Sousa Martins, statuettes of Dr Sousa Martins under glass domes or *en plein air*. I asked a woman for a leaflet. She may have been a gypsy but she looked like Sousa Martins's mother.

'Please, *senhor*,' said a devout minder who appeared from somewhere, 'that one is very cheap, good value for money at only five hundred escudos.'

I demurred.

'Four hundred.'

I moved swiftly to a stall at the end of the row where a large warm black woman sat with a doll-like young white woman.

'How much, *senhora*?' I asked.

'Here, naturally, it is much cheaper,' said the spiritually-minded pimp hard at my shoulder. Naturally.

'*Senhora?*' I insisted. Birds lifted, clattering, from the lake. Here among the colourful trash it felt like Brazil or Africa.

'Fifty.'

'Thank you,' I said.

'May God bless you,' said the man, with the slenderest of smiles, 'May God be always with you.'

'And with you, brother.' I could smile too.

I opened the leaflet. It afforded me 'Five minutes with Dr Sousa Martins', a prayer to the doctor's spirit: 'Send to my aid this spirit of Light which works so much for us sinners. Spirit of Dr Sousa Martins, in the name of God come to my aid. Brother Sousa Martins hear me. Brother Sousa Martins see me. Brother Sousa Martins heed me . . .'

This was the man whose death the king had described as an irreparable loss, a national loss. 'He went, putting out with him my kingdom's greatest light,' said Dom Carlos. 'He was the tender-hearted and dedicated friend of the poor and of poets,' wrote Guerra Junqueiro, foremost poet of the 1910 revolution. 'His hand guided. His heart forgave. His mouth taught. He dignified Portuguese medicine and all those who procured in him a cure for their ills.' The mourners' past tense has changed to the continuous present. The doctor has become a saint, a clinical Sebastião. The novelist José Cardoso Pires described him as 'the ever-popular and continuously effective Dr Sousa Martins, on whose pedestal guttered the candles of pious spiritualists . . . a surgeon dead but still in active practice'.

'The good doctor was a ladies' man,' said the *senhor* with the well-kept hands, 'but then, perhaps this too is a cure.' He'd walked up to the café in the Martyrs' Garden and waved me over to join him for a beer. He took off his dark glasses and the blotchy parchment of his skin creased in a big smile.

'I have had cataract and prostate operations in London. I am old. But old people, how they love to say what they suffer from and how, how much they have suffered. So much! Morbidity is a most serious disease.'

He assumed a most serious expression and pushed his snack plate towards the young waitress.

'This is not good,' he said sternly. 'This was badly prepared.'

She looked crestfallen.

'No, my dear, listen,' he urged, 'it is not your fault. Please tell the cook from me.'

He smiled again. She wiped an eye, nodded and carried the plate off like a doubtful trophy.

'She is not to blame,' he added. 'But this used to be a good café. These buildings by the Martyrs' Garden are embassies and suchlike. Diplomats and politicians like their food, you can at least trust them for that.'

I imagined that Campo Santana's gypsies, medical students and prostitutes enjoyed tasty snacks too. The *senhor* fixed me with his bright brown eyes.

'That one,' he confided, 'is now the German Embassy. In Salazar's time it was a government building and every week a government car brought Álvaro Cunhal up here from prison to study for his doctorate in law. He got it. He was the leader of the Communist Party for half a century. Now, nobody ever escaped from Elvas or Peniche. But he did. Dirty politicians!'

What wheels within wheels was he hinting at? People did escape. Cunhal and nine comrades did indeed break out of the impregnable fortress of Peniche in January 1960. Famously, seven more escapees screamed away from Caxias prison in an armoured Mercedes that Adolf Hitler had presented to Salazar.

'But I digress,' continued the *senhor*, 'from the case of Dr Sousa Martins.'

Patients hope to languish gracefully on sofas, or to be miraculously cured. Political prisoners hope to escape from gaol or be cast as martyrs. All kinds of pretenders hope to become, or to be plucked from morbidity by, a modest messiah. Hope may be more dangerous than death, but at least it seems to have a future.

'One day the doctor visited a lady in a very big house. He diagnosed her problem. He asked the maid in attendance to bring him a glass of water.' The *senhor* pursed lips and raised eyebrows. 'Now, it is a very big house and there is just time for him to complete the cure before the maid returns with the water. The patient asks, not unreasonably, When will you come again, doctor? He smiles a professional smile for the maid's sake and winks at the lady in bed, When I am thirsty, *senhora*.'

6

THE MAN IN BOOTS

Cacilhas and Montijo

THE WORLD IS divided between people who see no point in going anywhere and those for whom life in one place isn't worth living. Think of Lao Tzu: 'The further you travel the less you know.' Thoreau at Walden: 'True and sincere travelling is no pastime but it is as serious as the grave, or any part of the human journey, and it requires a long probation to be broken in to it.' Fernando Pessoa: 'To travel! To lose countries!' Ape, after too long in the concrete jungle: 'I gotta get away!' Stucley at Alcântara Mar with the niggling question, 'What the hell for?'

So, let's be cynical. Let's not pretend we can embark on an odyssey today. Pilgrimages are suspect deals. If there's anywhere exotic left it's somebody's home. It always was. Your great journey is my commuter route. Travel agents are toy shops. Drop in and pick up a package. Don't unwrap it till you're off the plane. The industry spends millions to convince us that *there* is more interesting than *here*, and more, that the most interesting thing about *there* is us there. *There* is interesting if we're interested. Mostly we don't look twice. That's why we resort to resorts. There are too many places in the world where we can play, ski, swim, drink, doze, dance and screw our way through boredom. 'At our expense, OK.' But in how many ways do we pay?

Why leave Lisbon at all if, as they say, it offers you four continents for the price of one? When at seventeen Fernando Pessoa returned, after nine years in South Africa, to Lisbon, 'city of my childhood, dreadfully lost', he almost never left it in the remaining thirty years of his life. He didn't risk loss of city or self again. Once, a friend

invited him to stay near Oliveira do Hospital on the edge of the
Serra da Estrela. He said no, as if his mythic image of 'Portugal'
might be smudged by reality; a reality that was my first taste of
deepest Portugal: nights camped beside a river loud with frogs, the
high village of São João, boys climbing trees to pick me fat cherries,
a local white wine of exquisite fragrance, and a small church with
a big bell and painted scenery lowered from the chancel's 'flies' to
change the altar's backdrop according to the spiritual season. Pessoa's excuse for not going anywhere near all that was that he had
'an insufficiently panoramic soul'. He was, he said, planted in
Lisbon's soil, if not like a root at least like a post.

The area around the Largo de São Carlos was his 'village within
the city'. His world of work, of commercial translation for various
firms, was the Baixa, the grid of streets between the hills of Alfama
and the Bairro Alto. *Baixa* means 'low'; it gives 'downtown' a new
meaning. Three main thoroughfares stuffed with shops and banks
and businesses – Rua do Ouro ('gold'), Rua Augusta and Rua da
Prata ('silver') – link the city centre and the river. The assistant
accounts clerk Bernardo Soares, whom Pessoa invented as 'a simple
mutilation of my own personality' to author *The Book of Disquiet*,
worked out his days in an office close by the lodgings where he
wrote at night. 'Yes, Art, living on the same street as Life but in
a different room . . . Yes, for me Rua dos Douradores embraces the
meaning of all things, the resolution of all mysteries, except the
existence of mysteries themselves which is something beyond resolution.'

A white marble plaque in Rua dos Douradores is inscribed 'Casa
Antiga Pessoa', and red neon announces the Restaurante Pessoa. *In
memoriam* the great poet, I first thought. Most people do. But in a
diary entry for 27 March 1913 Pessoa wrote, 'I had lunch in the
Restaurante Pessoa, with money borrowed from João Correia de
Oliveira.' Despite, or because of, a menu still too rich for clerks or
poets, I could sense him in the narrow streets – Douradores which
he gave to Soares, Assunção where he first met Ophélia, and Fan-
queiros where he posed for a photograph dedicated to her – but I
could hardly imagine him walking down today's pedestrianised Rua
Augusta. White hands ten feet high pointed skywards and wobbled
on springs. A pair of Ecuadorian pipe bands danced at sea-level but

played with a breathy high-altitude soulfulness that quite over-powered an old man with a scratchy violin who sat firm at his regular pitch and sawed away inaudibly as if the exotics who flanked him didn't exist. Another beggar stood stock-still near a bank's cash dispenser, his face entirely overtaken by growths, blebs and bulbs of flesh, livid and ruby, except for the dark glitter of a single eye which fixed and followed me.

At the end of Rua Augusta stands a mighty triumphal arch. What did that one eye, indeed any late-twentieth-century Portuguese eye, see in it? On it stand figures nobody now notices, if they ever saw them: Glory crowning Genius and Valour, the Douro and Tagus personified, the heroes Viriato, Nun'Álvares, Vasco da Gama and Pombal. Through it, the gleam of the river and the rump of Dom José I's horse. The mounted king dominates the Praça do Comércio, a square described even by one Frenchman – Valéry Larbaud – as the most beautiful in Europe. The English nicknamed it Black Horse Square. Natives still call it Terreiro do Paço, 'terrace of the palace'. Here was Dom Manuel the Fortunate's riverside residence. From here, on Tuesday 24 June 1578, the Feast of St John, Dom Sebastião's armada of galleys, galleons and ships' boats set sail for North Africa and disaster. Here, after the restoration, were estab-lished the royal chapel and music library of the Braganças. Here by the water religious spectaculars were staged by the Inquisition: *autos-da-fé* in which, after processions of victims in conical hoods, after awesome ceremony in the face of very hell, wild fire was set in neat stacks of faggots under the feet of Jews and other heretics.

Within the palace Bartolomeu Lourenço de Gusmão, a young Jesuit father, expounded his theories on 'navigating by the element of air' and first demonstrated his flying machine. By it people would be carried far and fast, over enemy territory if need be, goods could be transported overseas, polar regions discovered, the problem of latitudes resolved and infinite benefits achieved which time alone would show. On 5 August 1709 a paper globe with a small fire-boat suspended beneath it didn't get off the floor, but two days later a new balloon lifted fifteen feet towards the ceiling in the king's presence. On 3 October that year another 'instrument of flight', with wings and tail, was launched from the Casa da Índia's bridge and rose to a good height. Gusmão called it *Passarola*, 'big bird'.

63

The people acclaimed him *Voador*, 'flier', and tradition has him taking off from the castle of São Jorge and touching down in the Paço de Povo. With the benefit of magic realism, José Saramago takes him to still greater heights in his novel *Baltasar and Blimunda.* However spectacular Gusmão's flights, the king did not fund further research and development, though he honoured him with member-ship of the Royal Academy of History, a privilege which in theory granted immunity from the clerical thought police. Nevertheless Gusmão died upriver at Toledo in Spain, a disappointed man of thirty-eight, after suffering harassment by the Inquisition.

The waterfront palace was shivered by the 1755 earthquake and swept away by the following tidal waves. Dom José's horse prances high above a glittering sea of parked cars. In a blue haze of exhaust a man thrust a chunky ring and a gold watch under my nose. On the promenade above the Tagus's mud banks another hissed and whispered, 'Hashish! Good!' as he passed. Below me, a third pissed in a shining arc onto a rock. Floodlit by sun I walked down the expansive stone landing stage which descends by broad raked steps to the water. I stood with other dumb actors and watched water. At either side of us a pillar bore the weight of a stone ball, and an inscription that might have commemorated a royal embarkation or some exotic expedition's departure. But no, they noted lesser voy-ages: on the left, one of Salazar's, on the right, President Carmona's, going about the New State's grandiose business. Someone had pushed a *papier mâché* head onto the right-hand ball and turned the pillar into a stiff effigy of the current prime minister. Beside me a man warped his long fishing rod and reeled in weed.

At the bar beside the ferry terminal I entertained elemental but inconsequential thoughts about the lively and deadly powers of earth, air, fire and water. And firewater. At the next table a white girl was flanked by two black boys. One, in wire-framed glasses and pointed black-and-tan cowboy boots with soles like steaks, trod the paving like a man treading grapes. The second, slight one played with himself in his jeans. She, all tight tits and buttocks and eyes that would cut glass, patted him on the arse and thrust her tongue down the first one's throat. I swallowed a beer and leant on the parapet. Gouts of commuters flowed off and on orange ferry boats. Immediately beneath me a sewage outfall spewed its load. Pulsing fish fed voraciously at the murky fringe, flashed as they surfaced. It was a velvet fan edged with fluttering silver leaf.

'Often enough I've wanted to cross the river,' wrote Pessoa in the voice of Soares, 'those ten minutes from Praça do Comércio to Cacilhas. And always I've felt intimidated by so many people, by myself and by my intention. Twice I've made the trip, nervous the whole way, never feeling my feet on the ground until I'd returned. When one feels too much, the Tagus is an endless Atlantic and Cacilhas another continent, or even another universe.'

I've only once crossed to Cacilhas to see Cacilhas; usually I've been meeting someone or going on to Caparica and the long lazy beach. Cacilhas is a gateway to that southern continent. The great LisNave shipyard there spelled voyages. It put great hulls on the high seas. In the past tense. I watched tiny men in a cradle suspended from a crane blasting rust off a cliff of a cargo vessel with pressure hoses that filled the *cervejaria* where I sat drinking soup and wine with a mighty rushing that even vigorous shaking of the head couldn't shift from my ears. A siskin chirped like a mute in a dirty cage above my head. Well, I was slumming it. Cacilhas is famous for its smart fish restaurants, but I was poking around a funfair temporarily doing slender business directly opposite the shipyard. The rushing scoured everyone's skulls. No one bought tourist tat or basketwork from women squatting behind stalls. The dodgems were undergoing some sort of therapeutic deconstruction. A pair of young dogs were scrapping and yelping, how seriously they weren't quite sure, one of them with a German shepherd's body on the legs of a dachshund. It was one of those delicious no-hope places that poignantly promise good times. At the ice-cream stall I thought of asking for a *Morango Fizz*, a cheap strawberry lolly that was always sold out, but didn't bother. They existed only in glossy pictures on the sides of freezers. The rushing noise died and the men in the cradle struggled to steady themselves against the hull and damp their pendulum swing as the crane eased them sideways. Soon they'd be sold out. The yard would close for good. I climbed uphill and round the front of a utilitarian block of flats with sublime views across that ten minutes of water to the capital's glorious waterfront and the swell of its hills. Women for whom the view was just the view gossiped from balcony to balcony; I gazed at it through chain-link fencing. Above the city the Tagus was wide enough to be a sea, *o Mar da Palha*, the Sea of Straw. Below it, I fancied I could glimpse the ocean. I imagined standing here, the fence cutting into my hands, watching Lisbon shudder and burn, then hiss beneath the overwhelming waves. Here in Cacilhas there's a procession each All Saints' Day to celebrate, and thank God for, the town's narrow escape from the 1755 earthquake.

A holy miracle should be prized. The people of Lisbon were offered one sixty-odd years later. The government, the English-dominated Rossio regency that ruled following the Peninsular War, advertised an unholy miracle. Billboards promised that a man was going to walk from Alcântara to Almada, walk on water, walk across the Tagus in boots made of best Portuguese cork and step dry on to the far shore without help of wind or sail or hull. If *Cristo Rei* had been standing above Almada hill then, he would have stopped directing traffic and raised his hands in blessing or in horror. When the day came crowds flocked on foot and in every available boat to the place where the man in boots was billed to step on to the river.

The people of Lisbon got their 'Holy Miracle' during the Peninsular War, when a relic of that name, *Santo Milagre*, was evacuated to the capital from Santarém for safekeeping. The holy miracle's story may come later; it's enough to say now that the man in boots was enlisted because Lisbon had hung on to the relic, so prized for its virtue, long after the French had packed up and gone home. The people of Santarém demanded it back. Serious civil disturbance was on the cards. It ranked as a little local difficulty for ironic English rulers. But Protestant minds enjoyed setting miracle against miracle, credulity against credulity, and devised a rational, witty scheme to defuse the riots that lack or loss of the Holy Miracle would spark.

At the precise moment the man in boots was due to walk on water the *Santo Milagre* was solemnly carried aboard an upriver boat. The relic left unnoticed, but landed at Santarém to an ecstatic reception. The people of Lisbon waited most of the day for a sight of the man in boots. They debated the volume of cork required to give him buoyancy. They hoped that neither current nor tide nor wind nor breakfast brandy would upset him. It was rumoured he was so-and-so's son-in-law and his courage had failed him. By the time they sloped off for their dinners he had sunk, metaphorically, without trace.

The Transtejo ferry *Madre de Deus* trudged, metaphorically, for almost an hour across the Sea of Straw. It was the feast day of São Pedro, Peter the fisherman who walked on water until fear overtook faith and Jesus had to heave him out. A man led me from port to starboard and back, pointing things out with a hand that was two digits short of a fist. Two more were bandaged. If he was a sawyer or a butcher he was fast running out of fingers. Ten miles from Lisbon as the crow flies we disembarked at Montijo's quay. Though it hadn't seen a steam-boat for years and had just been reconstructed with European money as a new Estação Fluvial, 'river station', everyone still called it the *Cais dos Vapores*, 'quay of steamers'. Our swell juggled *barcos* with sharp sterns and bows lifted like the points of Turkish slippers.

We'd passed fishermen in a variety of small boats, traditional and modern, hoping on this saint's day for a great draught of fishes, but the crossing had been dominated by the sight of oil terminals and storage tanks, helicopters rising from the naval base on the point, and new pastel-coloured flats stacked along Montijo's expanding waterfront. Here though, after an ear-splitting mortar salvo to start the day, ancient rites took precedence. A skiff, densely rigged with bunting, left the Cais dos Vapores escorted by fishing boats which were bright even before they were decorated. Every line and detail of the shipwright's work was enhanced by contrasting colours and motifs common to travellers' caravans, canal boats and old-fashioned fairground gear. Their intricately-wrought names – such as *A Pombinha*, 'little dove', *Algatejo* and *Deolinda Maria* – were set within scrollwork or panels of painted flowers. Prows and rails and wheelhouses sprouted gladioli and carnations. Staffs, masts and shrouds seemed to fly every colour, ensign, pennant, streamer and burgee in the vocabulary of flags. The water was a sea of glass spangled with confetti.

At the Cais das Faluas, 'quay of sail-boats', São Pedro was ceremoniously disembarked. His fine doll's face was bearded and serene beneath a high crimson crown, his left hand held the papal cross, his right the keys to the Kingdom of Heaven. Four fellow-fishermen, the *pescadores*, took the arms of his palanquin, padded with crimson, on their shoulders. They wore black breeches, broad cummerbunds, thick check shirts and black tasselled stocking caps. One was weathered, wiry and well-cured, with eyes alert for the glance of any well-rounded woman. Two were stout, with well-basted faces more suited to the town's autumn pig festival – *Feira Nacional do Porco* – when fifty thousand people come here to savour suckling pig, spicy sausage and coriander-flavoured trotters. The fourth stared ahead, his face pale and gravely lined. He, I felt, had seen the waters close over his head and heard the cock crow thrice. His barefoot walk from the quay to the main square would be no day-trip. It was pilgrimage and penance. With due ceremony and celebration, flowers precise and lush, holy water and fire, the procession of fishermen and shoulder-borne saints set out, accompanied by *Cristo de la Buena Muerte*, a group of Spanish musicians from Ayamonte just over the border in the far south. St Peter is supposed to have achieved his 'good death' on a cross, like Christ's, but upside-down. Today, with solemn enjoyment, and hints of that matter-of-fact ecstasy which Anglo-Saxons find so difficult to carry off, São Pedro drew everyone away from the water along the palm-lined promenade on a holy trek towards Montijo's *Igreja Matriz*, or 'womb church'.

Montijo and Alcochete, and the peninsula between them, are hardly noted in the guide books. The place is devoted to the raising of bulls, to pigs and pork, to the making of guitars and *guitarras*, to cork oaks with flagrant orange trunks and dull gnarled limbs, and to the shimmering and crystalline acres of saltpans. There are wild areas, like the Tagus estuary nature reserve, with its autumn flocks of rose-pink flamingos, birds supposed to have drawn gypsies to Andalusia and on to Alentejo, home from their Nile valley home, giving them an emblem for their banners and poise for their *flamenco* dance. There are mysterious places, such as the circular hermitage of St Anthony of Ussa, bizarre and romantic, set down by a lake in an ancient *quinta*. There are the enticing beginnings of open spaces where Lusitanian horses are bred and *campinos* (herdsmen) ride with bulls so skilfully that sweat and cunning, muscle and terrifying momentum are transmuted into dance:

> On a hot August afternoon,
> Under a burning sun,
> They take a bull from the herd
> So lightly, so docilely,
> Like one who takes a flower
> On the point of a goad!

Alcochete has an August festival named for both the herdsmen's green stocking cap (*barrete verde*) and the saltpans (*salinas*). The town dates from soon after the Moorish conquest of Lisbon and its name comes from the Arabic for 'lime-kiln'. It was very hot and blindingly white. I found a light breeze at the end of its long pier. All down the *Praia dos Moinhos* (Beach of Mills) there were unmoving palm fronds instead of turning sails. Rainbow-coloured boats were anchored in shallow water, moored at the pier or grounded on the beach. On one stood a watchful, silent dog. Profound stillness might have been mistaken for serenity. But there were human touches too: boys rained rocks on burrowing crabs, seaweed-shrouded tubular-steel chairs sat in mud beneath the promenade waiting for the tide, and the dog's master squelched into sight around the hull of his boat with a pot of pitch in his hand.

Glaring cobbled streets were given depth by sharp shadows – of scalloped eaves, balconies, lamp brackets, satellite dishes – and populated by panting dogs, occasional women in black, and bronze statues: a man taking the bull by the horns, arms round its neck, feet in the air; the hunched bulk of Padre Cruz whose cult was celebrated on tiles set into many house walls; and, dignified with crown, sceptre and armillary sphere, King Manuel the Fortunate whose birthplace this was. Before the south bank became unfashionable the House of Avis used to relax and conceive heirs here. Now Alcochete, like Montijo, was waiting for the future to collide with it. Small-time playboys lounged under an awning between a new wine bar and an old sports car.

In the cavernous Barrete Verde restaurant, crammed with bull-fight emblems and all but empty of customers, one man stared at me unremittingly from behind his newspaper. Then, tiring of disguise, he put the paper down and I saw the odd light in his eyes. He turned in his chair to fully face me. I felt that some long-brewed resentment, some deep hatred of strangers was about to erupt. He simply gazed. The patron and his daughter disappeared into a distant domestic interior and the man rose, approached, loomed for a moment over my table, said 'Enjoy!' and loped out into the bleaching light.

Just before noon I squeezed into Montijo's *Igreja Matriz*. It was packed wall to blue-and-white-tiled wall. I leant at one of the stolid pillars that nevertheless soared to a nave roof panelled pink and green. It was a foothold in the human tide. In a thick haze of perfume and sickly aftershave I was pressed between best suits and dresses, crisp shirts and long-sleeved translucent blouses, oiled hair scraped back and pastel interior-sprung perms. However few the devout in the confessional and at the altar-rail on other days, on the feast of Peter the fisherman there was nowhere else to be but in the 'womb church'. Before a reredos, all gilt and spirals and piles of holy emblems, stood the altar and, before that, a replica fishing boat. *Pescadores* with black caps folded on their right shoulders aimed for it, pushing their way barefoot to the front. A woman fussed with São Pedro's crimson robe and pinned a banknote to it, one of many mothers spoiling him rotten. Other saints stood about on beds of flowers. There was a stiff descent from the cross with gore and gladioli. Children perched on stone steps that climbed around a pillar to a pulpit like a balustraded balcony. A girl in a red dress with white polka dots played and posed within it as if it were a playpen above the congregation's heads and she the only one of us with space to lie down or dance her way through mass, through the chanting and singing, the scout master's announcements, the lessons read by the admiral, the matron, the bank manager. Before all that, just as the priest launched the service into the swell of *Cristo de la Buena Muerte*'s hymn, bells in twin towers chimed with methodical gaiety and heavily struck twelve as the first of several salvos of firecrackers went up and for ten minutes filled the outer world.

Out there townsfolk, sober and raffish, tarty and prim, pressed up the church steps to the open doors and stood on tiptoe. Above them a huge picture of São Pedro was flanked by electric stars. A woman with sparse black hair and a pale pinched face sat on the steps to the right fanning herself with her hand. To the left a dark gypsy, with a silver-tinged beard and arms folded on his knees, watched his daughters, or granddaughters, wrestle. On the bottom step, at the townsfolk's feet, a gypsy woman cradled her sucking baby between uptilted thigh and downturned face; she was slender but folded into curves: bound hair, neat ears, fine jaw, turned wrist, bent back, shapely buttocks, one strong calf escaping a white wrap-around skirt and one hard heel lifted nakedly from a black clog.

There was nothing idyllic or poignant about this beauty, this mother and child, unless I added it. I couldn't help it. Indoors, where the fisherman with the keys to the Kingdom held sway over devout revellers, over the bourgeois and the compliant poor, a mother and child with gilded haloes had forgotten the flight into Egypt. These others were outside, apart and contained. They came of a race supposed to reproduce on the road, not like the Portuguese wedded to soil or sea, not like the Pessoas or da Gamas. They were travellers of another order. The baby was a girl, I felt sure. If her skin contained anything bigger than herself it was a goddess. This gloss of mine, this politically correct atavistic nostalgia, pleased me. And angered me, because the sight of her was not a vision and it was enough. She too was once-and-future clay.

Gypsies have good reason to remember Montijo with sour pride. The brave Jerónimos da Costa, a gypsy from Alentejo, took João IV's side against Castile and fought for three years with his own arms and horse and without payment or reward. He was killed at the battle of Montijo in 1646. The very next year the king issued an edict against gypsies in a comprehensive attempt to suppress their way of life.

This afternoon is set aside for official *saudades* in Montijo's cemetery, but not for gypsies. Tonight St Peter and his priests will pronounce benediction upon the boats and the river. Tomorrow is the Feast of São Marçal who protects against fire, a saint easily confused in the confusing folk memory with Mars the war god. It will be a macho day when the bulls are let go again, and not for the last time during these *festas populares de São Pedro*. The pagan and the Christian consort effortlessly here in popular dances, in nights of *fados* and in ritual. Five nights after St Peter was borne across the water, Montijo will placate the Tagus with a sacrifice.

71

After a torchlit march and a display of fireworks we'll witness the cremation of a skiff. Its ashes will be fed to the waters, fresh and salt, that mingle in the Sea of Straw, to sate their appetite for another year.

The past, like the poor, is always with us. The future collides with Montijo and Alcochete. Between them a new road from the south surges north-west and leaps the Tagus, to Sacavém and Lisbon's resurrected east side, on the new nine-mile-long Vasco da Gama Bridge. All at once it makes this place snug with the capital and closer to the Alentejo's heart. It brings the north and the south to this peninsula, or simply through it. People talk, as optimists and pessimists faced with change always talk, of development and devastation.

Instead of a return voyage on the *Madre de Deus*, I'll catch a bus back over the bridge, but not for a year or two. It's a vision that will soon be a site. The road, the bridge and the connecting bus, metro, rail and air links on the north side should be in place for Expo '98. While the bridge remains invisible, I'll need Bartolomeu Gusmão's big bird, with fire in its belly, to carry me back through the air, or a pair of buoyant boots for the ten-mile walk on water, with good reason to be 'nervous the whole way, never feeling my feet on the ground until I'd returned'.

7

WAITING FOR *TOURO*

Vila Franca de Xira

WHAT ARE WE waiting for? I'm waiting for lunch. At the next table a family in their Sunday best is already eating, but craning and twisting necks waiting for something. It's not Sunday, it's Saturday during *Colete Encarnado*, the Red Waistcoat festival at Vila Franca de Xira. I'm reading the programme while at the next table they're waiting for the bullfight. Some of us spend our lives waiting for things. For death. For love. For money. For messiah. For Sebastião's return. For the policeman's knock on the door. For God to strike me dead. Expectation is not hope, it is also dread.

They're waiting for the bullfight on TV. The tinny band is braying and oompahing *Viva Espanha*, appropriately for once, they tell me, because the fight is coming from Badajoz in Spain; but the matador they're waiting for is a young Portuguese whose initiation this is. They watch each nuance of ritual preparation in his dressing room. They're waiting for blood sacrifice, mopping their plates with bread and sucking down the last of the red wine. I swivel on my chair in time to see the god on the screen lifted and dropped into his suit of lights. He's shaken down like shopping into a small bag.

'Red waistcoat' is a weak translation of *colete encarnado*. 'Red' may be *vermelho* or *escarlate* (scarlet) or *carmesim* (crimson), but Vila Franca de Xira sports multitudinous waistcoats incarnadine in shop-window and balcony displays, on flagpoles and lamp-posts, printed on T-shirts and worn authentically, together with green stocking caps, black breeches and long white socks, by every *campino* in town. *Encarnado* is more than a colour, as any Macbeth knows; it's a fleshy word, stained with blood. The straightforward word *sangue*, 'blood', does not occur in the *Fado de Vila Franca*:

> . . . And if a catch is valiant
> No one hurries from the arena
> The people quiver elated
> In a bullfight at Vila Franca.

Sangue does not occur in the festival programme either. I'm more surprised by something that does: an article on the nineteenth-century writer Almeida Garrett. It's like finding a feature on William Hazlitt or Benjamin Disraeli in a football fanzine. Well, it is until I think about it. How shall I explain? For now let's just say, inadequately, that balls and bulls are both part of the culture, but that bull culture is more art than sport.

If I came to Portugal as a stowaway on novelist Henry Fielding's *Voyage to Lisbon*, then it was in the wake of Almeida Garrett's *Travels in my Country*, ninety years later, that I decided to steam upriver to Santarém. The quotation from it at the beginning of this book hints at his ironic view of travelling and writing. 'Garrett was not only a man of letters,' wrote Rebelo da Silva, 'but an entire literature in himself.' He revitalised the theatre of his time, wrote its finest lyric poetry and struggled all his life, 1799–1854, to liberalise the Portuguese psyche and society. Mix Laurence Sterne and Sir Walter Scott, combine a travel book with a romance, do it playfully and passionately and you'll get some idea of the texture of his work. It's said that the Inquisition and the earthquake delayed the birth of the novel here by the best part of a century. When Garrett took hold of it he dragged it into the world kicking and chuckling.

On a July morning in 1843 at Lisbon's Terreiro do Paço, Garrett embarked with his companions on a steamer and, as they made upriver, observed in leisurely fashion 'the majestic, picturesque amphitheatre formed by Lisbon's east end'. He thought this part of the city, set on the Tagus at its most expansive 'like a small Mediterranean sea', outdid the rest, except perhaps Belém, in beauty evocative of history.

On a July morning more than 150 years later I caught a slow

train out of Santa Apolónia station. Opposite me sat an elderly couple with goods in packages tied with string under their seat and on the rack; one cardboard box was pierced to let air in to a subdued canary, and intermittent snatches of song out. The woman, all in black with white hair and fleshy jowls, slept. Her husband wore a white vest, a black shirt, navy-blue pullover and a worn but beautifully-tailored jacket. Rheumy eyes in his rough-hewn face caught mine. Like an adolescent he withdrew his great hand from where it rested on her thigh. She stirred, grasped it and drew it back to its place.

There were moments of aged elegance, tired villas and colonial-style mansions about Braça de Prata, but mostly the way out of Lisbon conducted us down the declensions of decay: cracked tenements, busted warehouses, derelict sites. It's around Marvila and Chelas, a little to the north, that Lisbon's underside can be glimpsed. There, shanty towns are piled at the feet of hi-tech blocks of flats; tin-can and corrugated cities fill depressions where allotments and remnant olive groves fall away from solid housing. There, where the city's underclass spends its nights, pimps and drug barons tighten their grip.

Between Cabo Ruivo and Olivais we traversed a concrete desert spouting pipes: BP, GALP and Mobil's oil terminals. On sixty hectares of run-down industrial land the Expo '98 complex has sprung up. Its theme is 'The Oceans: A Heritage of the Future'. Its spectacular oceanarium will draw the crowds, and in the long term the area will swell to 330 hectares of residential, commercial and leisure development with integral fibre-optic communications, plumbed-in bars and a marina with five hundred moorings. It's a *fin-de-siècle* vision of what society aspires to be. It aims to reverse Lisbon's population drift, from the west and Cascais/Estoril and the coast, to the burgeoning east. At a stroke the ocean has been relocated north-east of Lisbon, in the direction of Brussels.

The new international East Station, by Spanish architect Santiago Calatrava, is described as a rail-metro-road mass-transit interchange with airport connections. Meanwhile we shudder past Moscavide's prefab slums, regimented tower blocks and Lever Brothers' plant at Sacavém, botched rehearsals for the Lisbon of the new millennium. The long bridge from Montijo will step off its stilts and come down to earth here. The world will change. On a misty morning in a bulletproof limousine flanked by raven-black outriders Dom Sebastião will drive north across the Tagus to the luminescent oceanarium; he'll cut a ribbon to open the mouth of Leviathan who will spew forth the prophet Jonah preaching repentance and the Empire of the Spirit to a new age.

I'm travelling to a picturesque Portugal, not squalid, not visionary, but full of pride and skill and sweat and the colour they call *encarnado*. But at Bobadela it's cork bark in stacks. At Santa Iria it's the Dan Cake factory. At Alverca it's a car plant, an aircraft factory and museum of the air. Alverca's full name is Alverca do Ribatejo, and we're entering the province called Ribatejo, 'Tagus riverbank'. In between towns and the industries that the line attracts the real country begins to show, the river meadowland, *lezíria*, the water's edge, *borda-da-água*. Here are rice paddies and fertile *quintas*, wastes, heaths and the open spaces where bulls and horses are bred.

Southwards the eye is led away to a long horizon. Northwards it meets hills of olive and eucalyptus or butts up against inland cliffs of sandstone. Garrett calls the town of Alhandra on the north bank 'breeder of bulls'. Its terracotta roofs and tiled façades are dulled, and its air polluted, by a cement factory. On a high hill above it the mighty statue of Hercules marks the end of the Lines of Torres Vedras, the Duke of Wellington's surefire last-ditch stand. One line runs from here through Torres Vedras to the coast, the other from Povoa da Santa Iria through Mafra to the sea. A plaque up there pays homage to Neves da Costa, the Portuguese engineer who designed them, and to J. Fletcher, the English officer who built them with forced labour. Imagine the surprise of the French, poised to drive the allies into the sea in 1810, at finding themselves drawn towards the mouths of 436 cannon in 180 forts they had no idea were there. Imagine too the locals' chagrin as the demoralised army scuttled back into Spain with all the Portuguese conscripts and horses they could take. Imagine the people's suffering as they tried to live off earth the British had scorched. In 1846, just a month after the last part of *Travels in my Country* was published in a Lisbon magazine, the liberal grandee General Saldanha defeated radical rebels up there along those old inglorious lines.

If you enjoy a mixture of melodrama, farce and *grand guignol* the

76

political history of nineteenth-century Portugal is entertaining, but its entrances, exits, false climaxes and codas need a long script to themselves. Steaming past Vila Franca, Almeida Garrett merely remarks on its changes of name, from de Xira to da Restauração, then back to de Xira. The royal pilgrimage of 1823, that had the town and absolute monarchy as its destination, was known as the Vilafrancada. A reaction to the 1820 revolution, it meant exile in England and France for Garrett, Saldanha and other liberals. But the very idea of restoration quickly 'fell into such loathing and execration that not even a wretched town wanted to be named after it'.

That particular passage is not quoted in the programme I'm reading. The young Portuguese matador on the TV screen at my back has the blood of a Spanish bull smeared on his face and its severed ears in his hand. At his *alternativa*, his initiation, he has been honoured with not just one but both. It is a triumph. The climax is over. There's a noisy clearing of tables.

The town is dressed. Windows and balconies are shrines tricked out with crossed goads, green caps, red waistcoats, brass-inlaid box stirrups, carnations and roses, framed photographs of mounted heroes and, here and there, the mounted heads and horns of bulls. The place is consecrated to the tauromachic cult. Rua Luis de Camões leads to a tiered graveyard, bright with flowers, whitewash and marble opposite the flag-flying bullring named *Palha Blanco*, 'White Straw'.

Beyond, I find myself walking alone into a wide yard dotted with straw bales and stabling under canvas, where *campinos* prepare themselves for the crowd. One with a fag in his mouth gallops, steadies, weaves, sidesteps, turns on an escudo and rears for sheer exuberance: the man's exuberance and authority, the horse's discipline and wildness. It's dressage with abandon. No one minds me wandering here. Four thick-set bow-legged herdsmen line up, adjust the red headbands of their green caps jauntily, drape black jackets over their forearms, puff out plain white shirts and red waistcoats to smile at my camera. They are comrades in a proud tradition. They are gnomes with goads instead of fishing rods.

The breeders and other gentry are duller but well-groomed, light

77

opera rather than pantomime. Their jackets are in dark ochres, greens or greys, their trousers and full skirts black, but each white shirt or blouse that swells above each tight waistband is ruffled and pleated and finished at the neck with four gold studs. A man with dark glasses above a black moustache twists a wide-brimmed black hat onto his head, slides into a short black jacket and flexes fingers in black leather gloves. He leads his black stallion towards me to show off its points. It shows me the whites of its eyes. With an imperious flashing of teeth the master says, 'Now we pay homage to the herdsman.'

I've seen *campinos* outpace a bull, the leading pair at a gallop beside it, each with a leg snug between flank of horse and flank of bull, goads crossed in front of nose and horns, judging pace and temper until it can be let go into the corral's mouth like a stone from a sling, or brought to a stand and hobbled, as yearling bulls are for branding and vaccination. Now the *campinos* trot two by two into the town square.

I stand above most of the crowd with my back against the Manueline whipping-post. The carved stone *pelourinho* is topped with a bronze armillary sphere. It is more than the world up there: its rings and orbits comprise the Portuguese universe, the nation's imaginative space. On a podium before the town hall the air force band strikes up. Beyond the bunting and the buildings, cliffs of raw rockface with houses on shelves rise to the seamless blue. Everything is possible. Here in April 1974, the crowds aimed for the *pelourinho*'s steps too, crammed the square with the banners and red carnations of revolution, and celebrated the release of political prisoners from Caxias and those other prisons and 'bullpens' whose bars had cast long shadows across the imagination of the nation. Men perched on balconies and straddled the gaps between them, backs pressed against white stucco. They, the banners and the loudspeaker lashed to the pillory, proclaimed the victory of the captains of April, and cried *Fim da Guerra! Viva a Democracia!*, and the Chilean slogan *O Povo Unido Jamais Sera Vencido!* – the people united will never be defeated.

Waiting for the ceremony to begin I'm an outsider, an observer amongst aficionados. Idly, I wonder how the secret police here, the agents of the PIDE, felt on that distant day. Did they mingle in this square? Did they drink in the cafés where they had habitually grazed gossip. Some clutched their cover yet more closely about them and hoped to sell themselves to the next bidder. But many were known, their professional arrogance curdling in terror, in fear for their health, yearning for the safety of a cell. The band gusts sweet and golden, syrup with a pulse. Shoed hooves cut through it, tap dancing and skittering on stone setts. Last to settle into their ranks are the gentry on magnificent mounts with permed manes and chequerboard rumps, wonderfully proud and aloof or benignly smiling at grooms and *campinos*. A young couple I saw cavorting and laughing in the yard by the bullring are almost unrecognisable now, with hats, jackets and solemn expressions in place and their spirited horses held in check.

The chief family sport pale grey hats and rich green jackets. He surveys the scene with the mien of one who owns most of it. She is a handsome star who loves admiration, upstaged only by her palomino mare with its white blaze and blonde mane. Their son needs no lessons in bearing; perhaps ten, he keeps a good seat in his brand-new brass-studded saddle. He looks about him with a finely-honed contempt, born of a talent for disdain that is inherited, never earned. Like his elders he carries no crop, but a long switch that might have been plucked from a hedge and trimmed this morning. Behind him, in the second rank, his green-eyed aunt in shapely green velvet is the only rider without a hat to contain her loose fiery hair. She earns a testy grimace from the boy as her fiery horse sidesteps and bucks and dances, unsettling his for a moment. She's easy, and her horse rears up to inject a little of her anarchy into the show. It points up the discipline in this hot-blooded, thoroughbred assembly. A little anarchy is not a revolution.

Other ranks are the gently jostling, comradely *campinos* with long goads in their right hands. Each, according to the *fado*, recalls a king on his charger who

> makes of his ox-goad a lance;
> has for breastplate his waistcoat.

With great courtliness Joaquim dos Santos, who merited the distinction last year, hands on the Goad of Honour and a bouquet like a

79

bride's, pink carnations in a mist of gypsophila, to his peer Pedro da Foz. The two men doff green caps and embrace on horseback. We pay homage to a man born the year Salazar became prime minister, who has worked all his life with *gado bravo*, 'wild wealth', on the ranch and in the ring. A well-known song, they say, expresses his beginnings perfectly: 'In the morning, only ten years old and already he goes to work; he learns the ABC of sweat, anguish and sorrow . . .' But sixty-two-year-old Pedro da Foz, a farm worker with the Palha family for the last twenty-eight years, remembers with *saudade* 'a past that despite having been full of pain, had its positive side'. He'll certainly never scorn the *campino*'s uniform, he says, 'for it represents the principle of my life'.

A woman is lifted up to ride sidesaddle behind him. She wears a hat like a squashed bowler tipped forward on her head with a poppy in its brim; her face is wrinkled but she's loaded with gold like a dowry-bearing bride: heavy earrings catch the sunlight, a dozen chains and sacred pendants swing from her neck, medallions are pinned to her shimmering deep turquoise blouse, gold bracelets chink on her wrists. Is she really Leontina, Pedro's wife of forty years, mother of his only son? Is she the goddess of the *campo* who gives life in exchange for the blood of bulls? Or is she queen of this feast, that she should ride with the king? Lance at his shoulder and the queen at his back, Pedro da Foz, *el-rei* for the day, carries her off at the head of his force of a hundred horse, brash green and *encarnado*, dark and sophisticated, clattering out of the square as firecrackers spill jagged noise in the sky and the air force band unrolls a fandango in three-eight time like a deep red carpet.

I am waiting for bulls. Meanwhile, there's plenty to think about. Since the homage ceremony, I've made a small pilgrimage down Rua Dr Miguel Bombarda, a road named after a republican psychiatrist who once specialised in persecution mania. His murder by a crazy patient on 3 October 1910 sparked the revolution which finished the monarchy. Towards the end of his street I found the sixteenth-century church of the holy martyr São Sebastião who lent his name to a crazy sixteenth-century king. Oh, the beatific pout, the pert arrows, the pretty blood. The oddness and the weight of history first stimulate, then bear down on me. In every place its

King Sebastião in his niche on the mock-Manueline façade of Lisbon's Rossio station. Hardly anyone seems to notice him standing just above their heads as they pass.

A glimpse of the dictator Salazar's New State: mighty *Cristo Rei* and the Monument to the Discoveries on either side of the River Tagus.

In the miraculous cloister of Jerónimos, the monastery built to celebrate Vasco da Gama's discovery of India.

Eça de Queirós: 'Upon the strong nakedness of truth the diaphanous cloak of fancy.'

Left: A small world within the paved compass or 'rose of the winds' at the foot of the Monument to the Discoveries.

Right: Chiado's stage-set. Resurrection after the Lisbon fire of August 1988.

The Tower of Belém. A serious fortress, an icon of *saudade*.

The steps of Montijo's packed womb
church during mass on the feast of São
Pedro. A mother and child who have
not forgotten the flight out of Egypt.

Fishing boats that escorted São Pedro
across the water.

layers are a palimpsest which, if we could decipher successive sig-
nificances rather than half-sensed fragments and scratches, would
start real tears and tough decisions instead of saccharine *saudade*. I
hurried out to refresh myself with coffee, to forget for a moment
everything but the present at number twenty-seven, the Amenésia
Café.

Now I am waiting for bulls. That's what this event, *Espera de
Touros*, means. *Espera* is 'expectation', which is not quite *esperança*,
'expectancy' or 'hope'. I have trudged up streets thick with sand,
past doorways protected by barricades that you can skip behind if
the bull comes too close. In the past I've seen men crushed against
such barriers and heard the ambulances scream. Today I am waiting,
not hoping. A man advised me to get a seat on a shaky stand
overlooking a sandy expanse between the bullring and the gate
through which the bulls will be funnelled into Rua 1° de Dezembro
and town. I'm glad to see he's taken his own advice. He and his
wife are natives of this town, now working in Europe. They've
travelled home for *Colete Encarnado* and brought the family with
them, including their son of eighteen who's never seen this spectacle.

It's a long wait, hardly relieved by the succession of men selling
beer and wine and fizzy drinks, sweets and ice-cream and cakes,
fans and hats and sunglasses, green caps, toy bulls and glittering
bandarilhas. Boys play football on the sand. Lads choose the best
perches on the railings and rehearse hand- and foot-holds that will
lift them out of trouble. They sit and stand on the far wall which
is papered with posters advertising a bullfight in Montijo today
and one here tomorrow. Suddenly, behind them, a rushing silver
train blots out the deep-blue Tagus. The bull-run was due to start
an hour ago. A woman comes to her deserted balcony, shades her
eyes, sees nothing, retires into the shady interior. In a rush *campinos*
come out of town, goads aloft, at a gallop, escorting brown-and-
white steers, brass bells round their necks clanging dully, a chiming
that sounds further off than they are. Head-down among the steers,
calmed by them, come the black bulls. This is what we've been
waiting for. The surge of energy, the rumble of hooves, the rush
of adrenaline, the hot momentum clears the corral and rocks the
crowd even after beasts and men have disappeared into the bullring.

We are waiting for bulls. At last, after the boys have resumed

81

their football game, one by one they emerge. The woman is on her balcony again, now with her own crowd. The first bull finds itself alone in a great space populated by young males, each ready to preen himself and measure his nerve against the next man's, as if courage was something that grew in his trousers. The young bull lunges at a few and runs away into town. The next tumbles out in a flurry of sand and stands quite still, bewildered. Men and boys tempt it, shout, '*Hé touro!*', run past him, the bravest touching a horn. He doesn't want to play.

We are waiting for bulls. After half an hour *campinos* and clanking steers round him up. The third paws at the sand, charges a few lads but gives up too soon. A man taunts him repeatedly but keeps his distance, a display of spirit that reaches a climax when he flings a wooden fruit crate which gashes the bull's rump. A boy goads him with a long stick. A handsome would-be *toureiro* with a cape attempts passes. A stylish young man, in golden trousers and magenta T-shirt, the colours of the cape, makes him turn and toss his head half-heartedly. The crowd hisses. We are waiting for bulls. The fourth charges a few times, sends men up the rails, up the wall, swinging from hoardings above his horns, but he ends up standing as close as he can to the door from which he emerged forty minutes earlier, saying, if I translate him correctly, 'Let me in!'

What has my friend been saying to his son all these years about glory days at Vila Franca? What stories there are of flair, courage and foolhardiness! What tales of exhilarating terror, of the man pinned to a door between horns, the boy tossed on to the railway line, the car *touro* wrote off. Where are the broken bones, the squealing ambulances I've heard before? What of the hefty bull that burst into a café, shattered the marble bar and chased the daughter of the house upstairs? Most of the stories are true, but what does my friend say to his boy who today is waiting for bulls, and for men?

'The bulls are small this year,' he says to me. 'They've imposed a weight limit, because every year people were killed.'

'Every year?'

'Yes, two or three killed every year. Ai! it is not what it was.'

Has an enlightened town council imposed this new regulation

on the mecca of the *esperas de touros?* Is it a law applied by Lisbon to all bull-running towns? Or is it an EU directive that Pamplona must also obey? I've had enough. As I make my way down the rickety stand the *campinos* ride in with a new batch of bulls. One breaks out between the steers and flanking horses. Separated from his peers he is *tresmalhado*, 'strayed', a 'dropped stitch'. A *campino* wheels to gather and knit him back in, but he charges, chases and gores the horse's hindquarters to hisses and boos from a crowd for whom the greatest sin in ring or run is to let a horse be touched. The horse bleeds badly, not with blood the crowd wants to see.

In the lush park beyond the tracks I walk by the Tagus waiting for a train out. I've decided not to stay for the Holy Martyr's grilled sardines; I'll give the *fados* a miss, the folk dancing and the all-night popular ball. A grain ship is moored beside silos on the quay, and traditional boats beside that, strenuous curves of many colours blending in the breeze-blown surface. Upriver the long bridge quakes. It's still hot. Dusk comes slowly down the broad river. An indefinable unease is coming with it. A sense of loss I can't locate. The day has been full of tradition still rooted here, but I sense also a creeping blight that sanitises, that begins to prise ceremony from the soil and transform it into 'entertainment', a word not meaningless but without significance. I surprise myself, finding that what I miss is catharsis. If bulls are too green, too light, what are we waiting for? What hope is there? What dread? If grey-suited men in the town hall, or in Lisbon or Brussels, turn ritual into a family show, how will the goddess be satisfied? If the king's a eunuch what will the bride-queen do?

The last I'd seen of the rites, as I climbed wooden barriers and crossed the sand-strewn road, was an athletic youth jinking, fending off a bull, his hand planted between black-tipped horns. He vaulted the railings, the bull stopped short, snorting. Two old women, black as the beast and tiny beside it, poked sticks through the barricade and beat at its head with a kind of impotent hunger.

8

SAFE GROUND

Salvaterra and Caneiras

WITHOUT CORK boots or a boat, the first place you could cross
the river and keep your feet dry, before the erection of Lisbon's first
bridge in 1966, was at Vila Franca de Xira thirty miles from the
ocean. There the inland sea formed by the Tagus estuary ends, or
begins, at the bridge completed in 1951 and christened the Marshal
Carmona Toll Bridge after the president of the republic. For centuries before that the first crossing place was another thirty miles
upriver at Santarém. It gave that town a strategic importance and
consequent dramatic history hard to match. For Almeida Garrett,
Santarém was the place where the nation was consecrated; it was
the cradle of Portuguese pride and the symbol of his disillusion.

Garrett's *Travels* of 1843 don't take us to India and back like
Camões's *Lusiads*. They don't transport us to China or Brazil with
the discoverers. They lead us all the way to Santarém. In the next
century Fernando Pessoa understood, temperamentally and intellec-
tually, that in a time when you can easily go almost anywhere travel
means loss. Garrett had been exiled in England and France; he'd
joined Dom Pedro's constitutionalist forces in the Açores before
laying siege to Porto, his birthplace; later he served as a diplomat
in Brussels. But when, after travelling in his bedroom, he resolved to
embark on a great odyssey, it was aboard a small steamer chugging a
few miles up the Tagus, backwards out of the big world.

At the prow, intent on a smoke, he found a *campino* smoking a
cigarette. But before he could ask for a light he was offered one by
a fisherman from the north, a figure in the wide Greek skirt and
braided Sicilian tunic favoured in coastal Ovar, a stark contrast to

84

the 'Mozarab from the Ribatejo' who was on his way home from grappling bulls in the ring at Sant'Ana in Lisbon where I met Dr Sousa Martins on his plinth. These two at the steamer's bow belonged to factions engaged in a debate, south versus north, countryman versus fisherman, land versus sea. The *campino*, says Garrett, 'has the stamp of African races; these others are of Pelasgian stock', by which a nineteenth-century anthropologist meant the pre-Indo-European 'aboriginal' Mediterranean race, or north Aegean 'sea-people'.

'It's to Almeirim we're going,' said the fisherman, speaking of a district across the river from Santarém, 'that only the other day was heath and is now a garden, God bless it! But it wasn't the *campinos* who made it, it was our people who hoed and planted and made it what it is, and made soil of the sandy waste.'

'It's strength we're talking about,' the *campino* retorted, to shift the question on to ground that suited him. 'It's strength we're talking about: one man of the *campo* flings himself on the withers of a bull that a whole company of boatmen couldn't seize, begging the gentlemen's pardon, by the arse!'

'Well now, what about strength, I'd like to know, and these gentlemen shall say, which is the stronger, is it a bull or is it the sea?'

'So that's it!'

'We'd like to know.'

'The sea is.'

'Well then, we who battle with the sea eight and ten days together in a storm from Aveiro to Lisbon, and this lot who fight one afternoon with a bull, which is the stronger?'

Garrett disembarked on 'the dismal wharf at Vila Nova da Rainha, the ugliest bit of alluvial soil on which I've ever set foot'. I'd like to have taken a steamer or a colourful *barco* up so far, or farther, all the way to Santarém, but for me the river journey would have to wait until there was no other way to travel. For now I could go by rail on the north bank and by road on either side of the river. For Garrett there were mules and donkeys on offer and he imagined himself, in wide trousers, green tailcoat, white hat, brilliant cravat, and with a rubber switch in his hand, mounting a poor little mule.

He despaired of the caravanserai and imagined that a bedouin village in the foothills of Morocco's Atlas Mountains must be cleaner and more comfortable. To his relief, he got a lift in a four-wheeled, curtained carriage as far as Azambuja, 'the first place to show that we're on the fertile banks of the Portuguese Nile'. He doesn't mention the fact that the town was given to Flemish Crusaders in 1200 as a reward for helping to dismantle Muslim civilisation hereabouts.

Towards the end of the century King Dinis, known as *o Lavrador*, the farmer, ordered a pine forest to be planted between Azambuja and Cartaxo. It was a glorious Christian forest that, over centuries of progress about which Garrett is so ironically eloquent, became a druids' wood of childhood nightmares, an ancient demon-ridden forest where we may set our worst dreams, our darkest secrets, everything that's hidden in the gloom that hedges about the civilisation where we think we live, but only half live. The forest is outside us, where our shadows glide. Wildwood surrounds house and garden, town and city. It and its denizens are uncultivated. The urban and the civic embody values, urbane and civilised, to set against the forest (meaning 'outside'), the rustic or pagan ('of the country'), the heathen ('heath-dwelling') and the savage ('of the woods'). The very language, English or Portuguese, is loaded against nature. Wilderness be*wild*ers the urbane because in it lurk the land's aboriginal inhabitants, of whom all conquerors, however long settled in cities, must beware. Forest is the outsider's native heath. Gypsies encamp there and are felt to prey on those within walls. Brigands and highwaymen fall upon those who dare to travel through. The royal forest thickens, deepens, grows subversive. Childhood dreams and stories, the scenes of our beloved fears, the forests grow up rife. Or are cut down, for cutting down is what grown-ups do best.

The Azambuja forest was notorious for footpads in the eighteenth and early nineteenth centuries; it was a haunted place with which mothers could threaten their daughters. Maybe Garrett's mother said he never should play with the gypsies in the wood, but when he got there he found 'a handful of measly, stunted pine trees through which the surrounding vineyards and olive groves are almost visible . . . It's the most complete and extreme disappointment I've had in all my life.' I saw what Garrett saw. I feel it. It drives me wild, by which I mean not crazy, but awfully sane. 'The pine forest of Azambuja has moved . . . it's been *consolidated*. And if you don't know what that means, read the budgets, glance at the lists of taxes . . .'

Meanwhile, on the opposite bank, just upriver from the tributary River Sorraia, lies a town with a magical name founded by Dom Dinis, developed by the Infante Luis, brother of Dom João III, and favoured by the kings of the Bragança dynasty. A palace, an opera house and a bullring were among the glories of royal Salvaterra de Magos. Was this 'safe ground of the Magi' so called because it was pronounced an auspicious site for a royal residence by wise wanderers from the east, or by one of the Jewish astrologers who served the crown? Was it a haven for the mentors of princes, a repository for the secret teaching of which Dom Duarte spoke? Was it a place where the monarchy could inspire, breathe in, its own spiritual destiny? Did the holy dove of the fifth empire hover here or, as an imperial eagle, stoop to the royal wrist with jesses trailing? The poet Robert Southey wrote of 'Salvatierra where the Prince annually hawks'. One of Salvaterra's surviving wonders is the royal falconry: three hundred-odd empty cages. Almost everything else save the palace chapel was razed by a mysterious fire.

So much for safe ground. Run to it, say 'Pax!', savour the taste of ashes. But long before the flames licked the place clean, weak King Fernando made peace here with Juan I of Castile on 2 April 1383. Sober memory should have lingered here to temper the triumphalism of young Dom Sebastião, the longed-for but ill-fated king who spent time each year at his palace of Salvaterra. If you live on safe ground you grow to think yourself invulnerable. Nobles nerved themselves for war by taking on brave bulls before a battle; tradition has it that Sebastião entered the ring to fight on horseback before embarking for Morocco. We know he hawked and hunted with a passion, and rode until he dropped or fell into fits, 'whereby it seemed that some furious destinie lead him headlong to his end'. I imagine the fanatic king testing himself against bulls here, unknowing all the while he faced disaster.

The Count of Arcos fought a bull from horseback here in the presence of the eighteenth-century King Dom José. A dart hanging from the bull's neck caught at his clothes. He was dragged from the saddle, gored and disembowelled. His father, the seventy-year-old Marquis of Marialva, descended to the ring with a drawn sword. The king ordered him to stop, but the Marquis took two more steps down towards the blood-soaked sand. A courtier took the old man's arm.

'Does Your Excellency disobey the king's command?'

'The king gives orders to the living,' said the Marquis, 'and I am going to die.'

He drove his sword up to the hilt in the bull's neck.

The story, as told by Rebelo da Silva, is called 'Last Bullfight in Salvaterra'. Well, it happened, that's for sure, but it wasn't the last. There's a brash bullring here once more, filled on summer nights with braying music and the thud of hooves. Outside, it may seem secretive and safe, this ground, but it's undermined by an abiding apocalyptic undertow. Down by the water's edge at Escaroupim the *barcos* of fishermen nestle beneath weeping trees and their houses stand on stilts. The land is consolidated by planting but they live always half-waiting for it to be carried away to the sea.

Some way into Azambuja's non-forest Garrett had to alight from the smart carriage in which he'd enjoyed a lift and mount a mule. In Cartaxo his mule was refreshed and made good time on to the heathy plain. Cartaxo's good wine, that had sustained both Wellington and Junot during the Peninsular War and Saldanha during the Wars of Succession, roused Garrett to a diatribe against French mouthwash and an impassioned appeal to the English to remember that they are nothing without the Portuguese, that without Portuguese alcohol they would revert to aboriginal Saxon uncouthness: 'What is an Englishman without Port or Madeira, without Carcavelos or Cartaxo?'

It was not Cartaxo wine but the heath beyond that went to his head. 'I have only to sit at sunset on a rock in wild deserted moorland . . . and it tells me things about heaven and earth like no other sight in nature.' He fell into a state of distraction, but came to himself with the realisation that here was the place where Dom Pedro had reviewed the liberal army for the last time in 1834, just after the bloody battle of Almoster. From poetic musing on the heath he was propelled into bitter memories of the losses his generation had suffered in the War of the Two Brothers. 'Civil war is always dreadful.' The jagged wounds are poisoned. Each side lays claim to the nation's myth, as much as to territory or crown jewels. Dom Miguel had recruited the shade of Dom Sebastião and won the loyalty of a people who longed for an absolute ruler. But 'the usurper' could not prevail against the quadruple alliance of France, Spain, England and the forces of Pedro 'the liberator' who succeeded in imposing constitutional monarchy and enlightened reforms upon a populace that didn't want them. Miguel returned to exile in Austria. Pedro died three months after his victory; his body was sent back to Brazil, his heart he bequeathed to Oporto, where it remains in a silver urn in a mahogany box behind a locked grille in the chancel of the church of Nossa Senhora de Lapa. Periodically inspected, it stays perfectly preserved through chaos and dictatorship, revolution and reaction. I thought of troops from Santarém who so recently crossed this precious heath, full of apprehension and optimism, on their way to Lisbon in April 1974. In sadness Garrett and I reached the bridge over the Asseca river where, in a Peninsular skirmish, Marshal Junot was wounded in the face.

At the time one French official had commented, 'He'll be a handsome boy no more.'

'He was wrong,' Garrett remarked.

'Wounds heal,' I added, 'but superficially.'

Over the bridge we found ourselves in a delicious place, the Vale of Santarém, home of yew and bay and honeysuckle. Not Paris, nor France, nor any Western country but Portugal has anything this beautiful, Garrett gloated, 'and it makes up for the many things we do not have'. It also makes a setting for the romantic novel that is interleaved with his *Travels*.

Joaninha, green-eyed lady of the nightingales, lives here with her blind grandmother who spins thread. Their cottage becomes Dom Miguel's last outpost, while Joaninha's lover, Carlos, advances from Lisbon with Dom Pedro's forces. Friar Dinis visits from Santarém each Friday, possessed by terrible secrets. Garrett makes this idyll a microcosm of the Portuguese imagination, caught between bitter factions. In Camões the *barões*, barons, are heroes. In Garrett they are opportunists who gain from the revolution

89

without having fought for its ideals. Ten years after the liberal victory, of which Garrett was a part, Joaninha's grandmother continues to wind yarn, insentient, a dead woman awaiting burial. Now, after April 1974's coup, and ten years after joining the EU, it's not a bad time to go travelling with Garrett in the barons' Portugal.

I came across a puzzle about three miles short of Santarém, some way from the main road near the riverbank settlement of Caneiras. There were fields of sunflowers there, and maize too. No puzzle about that: there were EU grants for their cultivation, and a flourishing scam for reaping more loot than you ploughed in. Rising above weed-ridden ground, a multitude of sunflowers nodded indolently but looked me straight in the eye with an expression of incorrigible innocence. There's honest dirt and there's invisible dirt packed under the fingernails of the soft hands of accountants. The fields had been fenced with barbed wire stapled to posts that were nothing more than stout sticks, each one glittering with snails, hundreds of them, bumper to bumper, more like coral than timber. At this time of year every other bar displayed a slate chalked *Há caracois!*, but I'd never seen so many snails gathered together in the wild.

'Look at this, Helder,' I said. 'Have snails!'

'Snails?' he said and he looked. 'I've never seen that before.'

Helder had brought me to Caneiras. He was a teacher who had studied this place. He was passionate about the people here, but didn't show it. He guided me round with suppressed excitement, but didn't know the answer to this puzzle. Why, when there were so many weeds and such well-subsidised crops, did snails yearn to slide *en masse* to the top of a bare branch? There had to be something in it for them. Perhaps they'd have said, 'Because it's there.' Or were they particularly Portuguese, exhilarated by the prospect of distant horizons? I liked the idea of an exhilarated snail. I'd heard about the one who took a ride on a tortoise and said, 'Wheeee!'

The people here at Caneiras migrated this way for a reason. They were fishermen who tired of the battle with the sea and moved inland a century and a half ago, backwards out of the big world. They came from Praia de Vieira, 'scallop beach', about halfway between Nazaré and Figueira da Foz, and from an Atlantic Ocean which had grown increasingly cruel.

'Damned life!' wrote the novelist Alves Redol. 'Whole winters saw the sea rise up to sweep all before it and not leave a crust of bread for the mouth of a little one.'

To begin with they came seasonally, three days' journey by foot or wagon, resting at night, starting at daybreak, a caravan with awnings for shelter and dogs for company. They became known as nomads of the river, who lived on boats, fishing the tasty and abundant *sável* (shad) from January to June for the local boat-owners. Later they brought their families with them; they built their own boats and worked for themselves.

'The two main families, the Mendeses and the Pelarigos, first set themselves up across the river on the Almeirim side,' said Helder. 'They had to cross the river daily to take fish to Santarém market. They've ended up here on the right bank, paying rent to the river authority, a low one though, and always for an area less than they occupy.'

After fifty years of seasonal migration they had settled for good in small family groups on the bank of the Tagus. The cursed life at Praia da Vieira was finally behind them, but almost a century on they are still *os Avieiros*. At first, sparse catches and the need to move to and fro along the river meant that they habitually lived aboard their boats, stretching awnings over bent willow wands, or else set up temporary shelters on land. Then they constructed more permanent thatched shelters made of reed: Caneiras takes its name from the reed beds which gave them houses and still restrain the flood waters. Later still they built wooden shanties, but to those who feared and despised them they remained *ciganos do Tejo*, gypsies of the Tagus.

Helder and I walked through old Caneiras: a street of wooden shacks on stilts. In times of flood they would stand above the waters. Mostly they had tiled roofs, and steps of wood or concrete leading directly up to low doorways or on to verandas overstuffed with geraniums. Kitchens were set apart from living quarters, along with ovens, cellars and chicken-coops. Between buildings on the riverside there were gaps where we could scramble down the bank to the *barcos*. A woman rowed strongly past, blue oars flashing, though the pointed stern was pierced for a hefty outboard motor.

'She is a widow,' said Helder, 'for she fishes alone. Married couples go for nights on the river, lamping for fish from sandbars and making children in the bottom of the boat. She used to fish with her husband, and now she might go with a brother or son, but with no other man. It is very strong here. Nothing must look bad. She'd rather walk into town than accept a lift with a man.'

Like other older women she wore sober colours, black blouse and skirt, woollen footless stockings, a grey apron and a grey kerchief knotted on her head. The boat was a brightly painted, flat-bottomed one with pointed prow and stern, built with techniques brought from the coast and influenced by the *moliceiros*, or Mesopotamian-style seaweed-dredging boats of the Aveiro lagoon.

'The woman rows, the man puts out nets fast and gathers them in. The fish are kept alive beneath the willows, fresh for market in Santarém.' Helder frowned, 'The *sável* are finished though; dams and hydroelectric schemes prevent migration from the estuary upriver to spawn and agricultural pollution has made the lower river inhospitable. Now the Avieiros harvest eels and barbels, plentiful *fataça*, a kind of mullet traditionally grilled on a tile, and *saboga*, prized for its roe.'

A man, Senhor Mendes, ducked out of a kitchen door. He was strongly-made with short legs, a big smiling moustache and flamboyant ears. He was not dressed in skirt and tunic like the fishermen from the Aveiro region that Garrett met on the steamer, but he wore the uniform of today's older generation: cap, check flannel shirt, rough navy-blue trousers secured with a belt and rolled up at the bottom, and bare feet.

'Do you never wear shoes?' Helder asked.

Senhor Mendes's eyes were creased against the sun but I saw a flash of atavistic pride in their depths. He took us inside. It was a place for cooking, sure enough, but also for receiving visitors and watching TV.

'Inside and outside, I never wear shoes. On land and in boats, I never wear shoes. When I go to town I don't wear shoes, even when I visit the bank.'

Senhor Mendes was not the cobbler's friend. His sturdy feet had in-turned big toes with prominent whitened joints. It was as if he wore fresh air one size too small. But I believed what he said when he gazed down at his feet and spoke quietly.

'For me to put shoes on is to put my heart in a vice.'

A few doors down a middle-aged couple made fishing nets. She wore a floral apron and sat on an upturned beer crate, stretching nylon twine between left hand and right big toe, plying the shuttle with her right hand.

In the bar there was music, beer and ice-cream, but no *Morango Fizz* even here. Adolescent natives sat around with glasses in their hands and shoes on their feet. Mostly they came from concrete-and-brick houses set among fields away from the water, and tasteless mansions built during the tomato-boomtime. No pillars or stilts under those. It was safe ground. Ground was safer than river, just as river was safer than sea. Here was a people in retreat, rapidly joining the rest of us.

In the shady courtyard of one concrete house young adults played serious cards while their elders worked the fields. They were a different species from their parents, on a different planet from their grandparents. The fishermen Garrett met had transformed waste into fertile soil, 'like sowing seeds in butter', but it wasn't until the mid-1940s that need drove these people to work as poorly-paid labourers. They hated working for any master and went on fishing to keep pride alive under the weeping willows, even if it was unmarketable. In the fifties they rented land for themselves and cultivated melons, watermelons and tomatoes. Exploited by both landowners and canners, they nevertheless bought land in the seventies, rented more and were able to employ their own sweated labour, women and children, to harvest tomatoes in 40°C heat.

Until the factories were glutted the Avieiros made a lot of money. The nineties brought a crisis of overproduction, as well as EU grants for other crops. Young Avieiros leave to find jobs in businesses or factories. Those who stay want progress on a plate, shoes more than pride. And wheels. Fast cars, that is, not tractors. A mighty red-and-white-and-chrome motorbike glittered in a reed shelter beside the card-players.

'This was a gift,' said Helder. 'Parents get themselves into bad debt to give their children things. They want everything money buys, and some things it doesn't, well, not here, not yet.'

He surveyed the beaming sunflowers in fields that stretched away to the road where the real world used to begin. The subsidies stretched still further.

'An Avieiro with a hundred hectares had a daughter who could not pass exams,' Helder continued. 'He offered me a thousand *contos* to get her into medical school.'

That's a million escudos, or £4000 for the chance of having a doctor in the family. The gypsies of the Tagus have come a long way. God save us, we're all Europeans now. Despite that the river flowed westwards as we contemplated it once more, this time from the balcony of a log house, and not one belonging to a native, nor one sold to weekenders by Avieiros who had lifted their feet from the floodwaters and set them in concrete. This was a Swiss chalet on stilts built by a town hall official on land he'd bought for a song. I wanted to hear the lyrics, but the shutters were tight.

Below his balcony the most beautiful *barco* was moored, kept for leisure, not fish. A bee-eater made brilliant forays amongst vegetation at the water's edge. A frog croaked profoundly. Soon flocks of white egrets would be back. If you look you can still find an idyll, an Eden in the Ribatejo. When despised river nomads moved to the fields it was a good opportunity to buy up a bit of chic ethnicity cheap.

It hasn't all gone that way. In the shadow of a concrete house, and beside a humble kitchen, men were tiling a brand-new wooden house on stilts.

'Now you must meet the star of Caneiras,' said Helder. 'She's the oldest woman here.'

And there she was, in black, with grizzled grey hair, gold earrings and memories that went back to when? She scratched her head, mumbled and smiled at me over a glossy hydrangea bush. Then a phone hanging on the outside wall of the concrete house rang and she was called away.

When a dumb *campino* arrived at heaven's gate, the story goes, São Pedro asked for details to enter on the registration form. The man said nothing. São Pedro repeated the question. But even a saint's patience runs out and he turned the man away. Just then a bull strolled by. The dumb man threw his arms in the air and grunted, '*Hé! Touro!*'

'Ah, so you're from the Ribatejo,' said São Pedro. 'Come on in.'

Avieiros of the old school had an understanding with Pedro the fisherman; they simply winked and crept in on bare feet. Now they roar up on big hairy bikes and drop the saint on the gate a few *contos* for a deckchair beside the glassy sea.

Even from this distance I can see the pearly city shimmering on its hill above golden fields. I'm making for it too.

9

A SAINT WITH WET FEET

Santarém

FAR BELOW ME thick vapour rises off a dull molten stream. As if a lens focused sunlight, a patch on the river brightens and glows golden. The early-morning mist burns off above a sandbar and then, like drapes billowing in a slow-motion breeze, it parts to show early traffic, sparse and barely audible, scurrying across the centre of the bridge down there. Until the mid-twentieth century this was the first crossing of the Tagus. A farm lorry and two cars dive back into milky clouds. I am walking the walls of the pearly city, the gothic capital of Portugal. The sea of mist laps around Santarém's scarps. It is a tide that ebbs, downwards and upwards at once, unfurling steep slopes, a skyline of churches and, at the feet of promontories that project above the Tagus, the ancient riverside settlements of Alfange and Ribeira de Santarém. Across the river, before heat haze blurs the middle distance, the rich flat Lezíria runs away past the old royal residence of Almeirim to the horizon and the Alentejo.

This high garden inside castellated walls is the sun's gateway, *Portas do Sol*. The broad riverbed of gold and azure and buff sand materialises, bends and unrolls south-westwards. In time of flood it haemorrhages, panics inhabitants below who find streets turned to water and, just downriver, rushes beneath the floors of calm Avieiros at home on stilts. Today the river is low. Between the town's spurs a man leads his donkeys down to grazing. Close by, bells clonk erratically, an audible illusion. It's not until I lean out over sheer walls that I can see white and fawn and chestnut goats stepping fastidiously along a ledge, curling lips around wisps of

grass rooted in the masonry. They stare up with predatory wistful-
ness as if I may satisfy some unspecified goatish appetite. I reprove
them for tempting me with the pathetic fallacy.

Palm trees and planes cast shadows like furrows across the promenade. Sprayed light fills a high cage. A man in faded blue is hosing
down a dovecote built as a pagoda around the lower trunk of a tree
whose gnarled branches writhe under the claws of game birds and
pigeons. Guinea fowl scream. A deserted hole in the ground, roughly
ribboned off like the scene of a crime, is an archaeological dig into
the foundations of a Phoenician dye-works. Under the heroic eye
of a bronze war-memorial soldier an abstract marble couple on a
veined block sit apart, back to back, in blank sorrow.

Almeida Garrett found the Portas do Sol a melancholy viewpoint.
It had been a place of execution. The view was majestic but sad.
The bluff that plunged to the river was tufted with sagebrush
introduced by the Moors to bind the soil. So the story went. Garrett
thought the country's African temper and geology were sufficient
reasons for this vegetation; no need to invoke Moors. But Portas
do Sol's garden grows on the site of a Moorish stronghold that
should have been the guarantor of Muslim civilisation in the Ribatejo. It fell, however, to Afonso Henriques. Depending on your
point of view, big bearded Afonso Henriques was either a northern
bandit warlord or a noble Christian warrior. His men acclaimed
him king after his victory over the Moors near Ourique on 25 July,
the day of Santiago (St James), in 1139. Before battle he'd been
granted a vision of Christ and a glimpse of Portuguese destiny, the
universal empire of the Holy Spirit. By 1143 his territory extended
from the northern province of Portucale to the Tagus, though
Santarém and Lisbon were still in Moorish hands.

Afonso Henriques took this town, the guardian of the Tagus
valley, by surprise on 15 March 1147. *En route* for Santarém he was
overtaken by guilt and doubt. So the story goes. Guilt, planted in
his heart by his confessor, that his troops should be fighting Muslims
here rather than in Palestine; doubt planted in his mind by
Santarém's famed impregnability. Tradition permits him to ease
both heart and mind with a promise to St Bernard that he'd build
an abbey to the Virgin at Alcobaça if he won. He entered and took
Santarém through the Atamarma Gate, one of seven the town once

possessed, that Garrett calls 'Afonso Henrique's triumphal arch, Portugal's noblest monument!'

Garrett tells us that the civic authorities had more than once been high-minded and big-hearted enough to consider knocking it down. 'The idea is worthy of the age.' Luckily, there was insufficient money for demolition. I went to find it. I found a little pillar inside a flimsy painted fence of spears and battle-axes upon a meanly-constructed plinth. The Atamarma Gateway surmounted by a shrine to Our Lady of the Victory, dedicated – so the story went – by Afonso Henriques himself, had indeed been torn down in 1865. A stone marked the spot until 1917 when the first attempt to raise the present meagre monument was made. This one bore all the symbols of Portuguese nationhood, but in a reduced form. It was like finding the Arc de Triomphe on a crazy-golf course. If Garrett was saddened by the neglected gate he saw, what dirge would he sing now. As it was, his diatribe echoed Christ's lament for Jerusalem:

Oh, Santarém, Santarém . . . raise yourself up, giant skeleton of our greatness, and look at yourself in the mirror of the Tagus . . . Raise yourself up, Santarém, and tell thankless Portugal at least to leave you in peace, among your ruins, to bleach your glorious bones . . . Tell her not to allow your temples' bricks to be sold, not to let them turn your churches into barns and stables, not to order soldiers to play football with the skulls of your kings and billiards with the shinbones of your saints . . .

From the skeleton of Portugal's greatness I tried to creep downhill to see Santarém's saint, the saint with wet feet. She was supposed to stand beside the Tagus in Ribeira de Santarém, but I wondered if she'd still be there. Immediately below the castellations I found rife rubbish, glittering crimson poppies and rampant convolvulus of a purplish blue so vibrant, so veined with gold, that it made me gasp. Below the palm trees, bamboo thickets and thorns closed on me. I pushed between them but the path grew very steep and took me round the wrong way, to beehives propped above makeshift houses and the stertorous growling of dogs. They sounded big and hungry. The houses of Ribeira were out of sight now; there was only the Tagus and a hazy horizon. Of Santarém, with its elegant shops and echoing ruins, all I could see were the old castle walls falling towards me as clouds fled north. The close invisible dogs had started sweat on my palms and, far above, I could see what impregnability looked like. It was easy to imagine the fear of blades, bludgeons and fire that must have gripped the guts of anyone trying to scale the heights unseen, sneak through the Atamarma gate and take the stronghold of Santarém by surprise.

I climbed back towards the Cabaças Tower, that has arched windows like look-outs' eyes near the top, and a slim door at the bottom. Probably part of the medieval walls, later modified, it was surmounted by a great bell hung in an iron frame below eight earthenware cups – called *cabaças* or 'calabashes' – which were supposed to amplify the chimes. It sounded no alarm or tocsin as I got to it. It clanged eight, resonantly. Across the road the church of São João de Alporão was shut tight like a battered stone coffer. It is an archaeological museum full of bits of Santarém: Roman Scallabis, the Moorish fortress, the gothic capital. It was locked every day I was in town. Built in the thirteenth century on the site of the Al Koran mosque, one of its own glories was Dom Duarte de Menezes's hyperbolic gothic sepulchre, erected by his widow to contain a tooth, all that was recovered after he was hacked to pieces by Moors in North Africa in 1464. I couldn't get in to see it. Perhaps I'd never prove that OTT was an acronym for One Tooth Tomb.

I regained my breath in Snack-Bar Tico-Tico in the main square. The day's pastries and desserts were being delivered: precision-made components for civilised life. I needed coffee and rolls. The saint in Ribeira would have to wait while I broke my fast. Across the square more saints suffered torment or *ennui* in pillared niches on the baroque front of the seminary church of the Royal College of Our Lady of the Conception built in the seventeenth century on palace ruins given to the Society of Jesus by João IV. Since then Pombal had expelled the Jesuits from Portugal, the whole place had been turned into a town hall and a hospital following the liberals' 1834 victory, and the year after the Carnation Revolution it had become cathedral for the newly-created diocese of Santarém. I'd been inside. There was a glorious painted ceiling and an atmosphere of devotion and dark suspicion. The chapels were all encrustation and sculptural elaboration, gold leaf and inlay, jasper and marble, relics and definitively dead statuary. Now, in front of the church's heavily-carved closed doors, a man brushed the broad terrace that topped a plinth of steps.

Tico-Tico's coffee was strong, eye-popping. I could see why men took a glass of firewater with it first thing in the morning, as a sedative, to prevent the day gaining an unstoppable momentum. The man with the broom worked steadily and to a system he may have employed every day but which looked made up as he went along. I saw him as an archaeologist, delicately brushing off the latest layer of excavation to expose frail finds. The whole town needed that, to be disinterred chronologically so that inhabitants and visitors could make sense of it.

If he swept the cathedral away, he'd have to clear up earthquake debris and then the old royal palace. While he was at it he could flush blood off the square where two of Inês de Castro's murderers were executed. Afonso IV had not been able to bring himself to kill his son Pedro's Galician lover, but three of his advisers carried out his wishes thoroughly. When his father died Pedro signed a treaty with Castile to extradite the hitmen. One, Diogo Lopes Pacheco, hid out in the mountainous Beira or got away to Italy. Pachecos still gather in June to celebrate his escape. The other two were brought here; their hearts were publicly torn out, from Alvaro Gonçalves's chest and from the back of Pedro Coelho. It's not a children's story, but the latter's name means Peter Rabbit. King Pedro had Inês exhumed and set beside him at his coronation, so that the court could kiss her hand. She was crowned too, so the story goes, though that would have been difficult since she'd been beheaded. Pedro and Inês are buried in sumptuous tombs, so that they will rise face to face at the resurrection, in the glorious abbey Afonso Henriques built at Alcobaça to celebrate the conquest of Santarém. If the man with a grey cap and a springy broom before that mannerist church façade brushed long enough he might sweep away the whole hill of terrible history and get down to primeval water-level at last.

I went down there as fast as I could, not diverted by snarling dogs or more breakfast, or history like layer-cake diced in trifle. I was making for Rua Luis de Camões which twists and turns down into the Calçada da Atamarma, but before I got to it I passed a chic new café. It opened only yesterday with due ceremony marked by a man in white make-up and top-hat and tail-suit who stood on a chair in the square outside opposite the Bank of the Holy Spirit for a long time without moving in the face of taunts and temptations of all kinds and the puzzled admiration of those who sunk the first drinks the new place served. This kind of busking, requiring not a voice nor dance skills but silence and stillness, is familiar enough; here it's reminiscent of the 'statue' who sometimes stood on a barrel in the bullring, safe as you like until his slightest movement caught the bull's eye. Even whimsical diversions turn serious. But this is not a real-time diversion. I kept walking, it's a digression in my account of my walk downhill, a digression such as one finds at every corner in Santarém.

The plunging *calçada* crossed the main road and became long steep steps beside a curving wall which two women were painting with long brooms dipped in limewash. They giggled and let me by unspotted. With their brushes they added yet another thin layer to the story of place. Past washing and a faded carpet hung beside a house of flaking gold, I climbed steps to the derelict churchyard of Santa Cruz. Weeds and rubbish were post-thirteenth-century additions. Inside, the church was a delight, a broad-flagged floor, simple arcades, and flanking walls tiled with seventeenth-century Moorish-style *azulejos* that gave back a submarine light. The Renaissance pulpit was delicate-rugged. The apse was a glowing cave. The government department responsible for restoration specialised in interiors only. The official at the desk took no money but happily answered questions. I was a rare migrant to his habitat.

'Whose tomb is this?' I pointed at a huge sarcophagus borne by lions on the north side of the nave.

'It is the tomb of a king.'

'Which king?'

'One of our kings, that's all I know.'

Ribeira de Santarém was on a different latitude to the city on the hill; still north of the river, but on another continent. It was hot and humid down there. Under a tempestuous sea of pantiles were washes every shade of white or of faded gold, rose, ox-blood, aqua-marine. Stucco peeled. Pye-dogs slumped in the shade of scrawny public trees. Children played in doorways. Up narrow alleys there were deep shadows, glimpses of bright paint, yellow and red, terra-cotta pots of flowers. I came upon a charmingly naive, scrubbed baroque church. In a niche above the door stood a saint in a nun's habit with a sword in her hand.

'Is that Santa Iria?'

'Yes it is, that's Santa Iria all right.'

The man took off his pork-pie hat and ran a thick middle-finger nail through the silver hair above his ear. He seemed as pleased as I was that I'd found her. A woman joined us.

'Santa Iria, Santa Iria,' she said, 'Ah, Santa Iria.'

It was going to become a litany. She grinned and tapped my arm repeatedly for emphasis as she began the story. The man put his hat back on and butted in now and then with what he saw as essential details. It added up to a mixture of unforgiving folk ballad and the perverse monks' tale.

Iria was a noble maiden born in seventh-century Nabantia, now Tomar. One day her father turned an unknown knight away from their door. Of her charity Iria persuaded him to relent and offer shelter. The knight kidnapped her from bed, carried her off, attempted to rape her on the heath and, when she resisted, killed her. Years later, finding a shrine to St Iria on the fatal spot, he begged forgiveness but received her curse.

In the monks' version of the story she's a nun who stopped a noble's advances by casting out the devil in him. But the devil entered her spiritual director and filled him with lust. She rejected him. In revenge he dosed her with a tincture that swelled her. This phantom pregnancy revived the noble's passion, and added to it foul jealousy. His servant crept up on her in the secret cave by the river Nabão where she meditated, stabbed her to death and tipped her corpse into the river, which carried it to the Zêzere and so into the Tagus, which laid her to rest in golden sands beneath ancient Scallabis that would take her name and become Santarém.

Iria's abbot saw it in a vision, carried a cross the length of the fields of Golegã and reached Ribeira where the waters parted to reveal a sepulchre of alabaster carved by the hands of angels. After he'd removed relics the river closed over the saint. But six centuries later it opened to the gaze of the queen St Isabel, wife of Dom Dinis, who led the whole court dryshod between walls of water to the tomb but could not open it. Tools broke. The king had a lofty brick column built to mark the place after the waters rushed over it again. In 1664 it was rebuilt in ashlar, and Iria's statue was later perched on top.

I found her, beyond the railway line, on reclaimed land in a shabby little park beside tennis courts not far from today's river-bank. Her plinth said 1775. She was overshadowed by a canopy like an umbrella fringed with wrought-iron curlicues and topped with weathervane and cross. Despite her sword and holy book she looked more puppet than saint. Set above parched grass instead of rushing river, she had moved effortlessly inland from the sublime to the ridiculous.

Her pillar cuts the water like a prow each time there's a good flood here. If the river wets her feet, it will be the Deluge. The big one. Come back Noah. In the floods of December 1876 the river's volume approached sixty thousand cubic metres per second, a record for a European river. In lesser floods Ribeira's streets and squares become canals, a squalid Venice. The photographs are pretty: a watery town sitting on its reflections below Santarém's old walls. But without benefit of the river-gypsies' stilts, people must carry all their goods upstairs. It happened recently, in 1985, 1988, 1992 and New Year 1996. Ribeira, with its merchants' homes and ware-houses, was once the main port for the Ribatejo. Now progress and the river have left it behind, but not high and dry. In November 1967, after heavy rains, the Tagus submerged 275 miles of roads and bridges and made more than two thousand families homeless on Lisbon's outskirts. It was the worst natural disaster in Portugal since the tidal waves of 1755. If the Tagus wets St Iria's feet, so the story goes, Lisbon itself will be washed out to sea.

The poet Miguel Torga describes how the Tagus, seen from Portas do Sol, swells and outlines contours never before revealed by nature. It's comfortable watching from up there. Up there I'd met Célia Ferreira who had filmed the floods.

'Doesn't the river ever rise up to touch Santa Iria's feet?' I'd asked innocently.

She looked at me as if I was some sort of superstitious freak.
'Oh yes.'

Down here, I crossed a filthy channel on a narrow beam, all that
was left of a broken footbridge. I wandered beside the sluggish
river, lagoons between sandbars dotted with scrub and a tent or
two. On a wooded spit I walked into a small gypsy camp. Here,
almost in the shadow of the road bridge, was the place to dare the
river. There were shelters of plastic sheet, heaps of wood, fragrant
fires, black eyes in Romany faces. There was a polluted river, rubbish, poverty and beauty. Children played fights and a willowy girl
approached me just to look. She wore nothing but pants and had
a winning spark in her eye that might be fanned to joy or fury.
Beauty excused nothing, improved nothing in this scene. But when
one of the small boys ran squealing to his mother she looked squarely
at his pain and did that absurd, gratuitous, efficacious thing mothers
do. Roughly, she kissed it better. She kissed it better. He could
spend his life looking for that kiss again.

Down here, João II wallowed in the limpid river on a hot June
day in 1491. Known as the Perfect Prince and lord of all secrets,
he yearned for the lands of Prester John. He'd summoned his only
son Afonso to swim with him, but Afonso had just married a Spanish
princess, daughter of Ferdinand and Isabella, and was reluctant to
leave the bedchamber. With a wink in his voice he shouted that
he had matters to attend to in Spain. Maybe Spain closed its borders,
for Afonso grabbed a robe and a horse and galloped downhill. The
horse hit a pothole and threw the prince. Unknowing, the king
swam on. Fishermen gathered Afonso up in nets but by the time
they'd carried him uphill to his mother he was dead. She couldn't
kiss him better. Her brother, Manuel the Fortunate, was the one
who'd succeed and realise João's marvellous dreams.

It comes down to nets and plastic sheet, food and fire, blood and
dreams. But up there, as tourist guides proudly quote, 'Santarém
is a book of stone in which the most interesting and poetical part
of our chronicles is inscribed.' The guides don't continue Garrett's
purple passage. 'It was,' he slips into the past tense, 'the most
beautiful, most precious book in Portugal.' It should have lasted
for ever, until the Creator erased it; but this Pompeii was not

overwhelmed by catastrophe. Its people exist, but they fell into childish ways. 'They were given the book to play with and they ripped it, mutilated it, plucked out its pages one by one and made kites and dolls and paper hats with them.'

Santarém amused me. Like Garrett, I dutifully visited all the monuments and crept down all the alleys. I'd come at the church of Graça from the rear and seen its bulk. At night I'd looked at its deep, richly-carved portico, like one of Batalha Abbey's. I'd ignored a glittering prostitute in the shadows and wondered at the subtlety of its great rose window carved with flamboyant assurance from one stone. But when I went through the doors in daylight I saw what a gothic masterpiece I'd entered. Pillars thrust an arcade towards airy vaults and, more wonderful still, a flight of steps fell steeply from the threshold to a gleaming floor. Whether those who laid its first stone in 1380 and topped it off in 1420 realised it or not, they created a church for the Augustinian friars that seems built in four dimensions. Pedro Álvares Cabral, who took Portugal to Brazil in 1500, could hardly have discovered a more sublime resting place.

Everything else in Santarém seemed slightly smaller than life. The church of the Holy Miracle was dark, over-restored and self-obsessed. After early-morning mass worshippers glowered at me. Perhaps they feared I'd come to steal the *Santo Milagre* back to Lisbon in the knowledge that the man in boots wouldn't fool anyone a second time. The miracle occurred in 1266. A woman – a Jewess, Garrett says – tried to win back her husband's love by indulging in a little magic. Her neighbour, who was not shy of occult arts, urged her to steal a consecrated wafer during mass. The woman managed the sleight of hand and hid the host in a chest at home. It held the power to focus spells by which her husband would be drawn back to her bed. The account in the church porch stressed the woman's admission of theft, not her man's adultery. Surprise, surprise. His heart melted. The crumb of wafer began to bleed. It was preserved among crystals in a gold monstrance locked inside a sacrarium up stairs behind a side door in the high altar. Pilgrims from all over the world still come to the relic to be blessed.

Swifts screamed and housemartins relaunched themselves from eaves like swimmers making racing turns at a pool's end. Black redstarts too. And dogs, slumped in shafts of sunlight from *travessas*, licked their balls and shampooed vermin. On one side of the Travessa dos Capuchos dwarf terraced houses were full of half-glimpsed signs of life; on the other stood the long blank wall of police barracks. Wide-eyed, a tousled-haired woman with an infant on her arm launched herself at me from a side alley and harangued me in whispers. A crone in rusty brown squatted in an entry and extended a bony hand.

Flowers were emptied from a small van into one florist's, then another. Scents smothered the smell of baking bread. They should have told me something. The morning enlarged into the Largo dos Capuchos, wide sky, river, Alentejo and, on a spur that echoed the Portas do Sol, a cemetery like a disappointed bridge to the next world, jammed with stationary marble traffic.

The Largo was a plateau above the earth with only the dead and yesterday's wilting flowers between me and the horizon. I sensed a watchful eye. An old man gazed at me from the first-floor window of the barred and shuttered Café Cervejaria Flôr do Pereiro. Later, when it opened, I entered the 'Pearmain Apple Blossom Café' and encountered reserve for the first time in secular Santarém. *Pereiro* also means 'ox-goad', and the flower of the goad is a bull. I felt like a bull in an undertaker's. The middle-aged couple behind the counter were all in black. His thinning greasy hair sprang from a nut-brown ball of a skull. He relaxed when I spoke Portuguese. Her hard fine face softened when I sympathised with her heat. A silver-haired customer in a soft red shirt escorted me and my beer to a table outside and put my plate down there. A bent woman crossed the plateau with a syphilitic walk; matchstick legs in purple tights flexed exaggeratedly. As she tipped a basin of waste water into a ditch round the bole of a tree, she raised to its branches a young face in an aura of golden hair. A man in worn brown corduroy zig-zagged across to the café clutching what looked like a bible. He left without it. At my back, in a cramped yard full of gas cylinders, two tables of raucous mourners guzzled snails.

Among the fresh-dug plots, the flower-strewn numbered stones and the ostentatious mansions of the dead, an obelisk stood on a tall plinth whose sides were divided into oblongs labelled like drawers of a filing cabinet: many names and many *ossados não reconhecidas*, unrecognised piles of bones, victims of the 1896 catastrophe at Clube Artistico. Nobody I asked in town could tell me anything about it. I imagined an anarchist's bomb. A marble angel pointed steadily upwards; the sharp obelisk raised by public subscription pricked the perfect blue.

Would I be any the wiser by the time I left town? Do we travel for wisdom, did Garrett on his mule? The proverb says:

> *Quem burro vae a Santarém*
> *Burro vae e burro vem.*

'The ass who goes to Santarém, ass he goes and ass returns.' Perhaps we go just to look. Between Cine-Teatro's billboard and a bullfight poster I saw a beggar in a wrinkled fedora with a bundle and a stick and a withered leg displayed like meat. In a new burger bar I saw a mural depicting a cow being winched from a helicopter into a mincer; it would have been vegetarian propaganda anywhere else. In a glazed niche at the doors of the fire station I saw an effigy of St Marçal, patron saint of *bombeiros*, fire-fighters. I smelt flowers before I knew they meant death. In Rafael's restaurant I drank the best wine ever from Alpiarça, and ate the best fish; in cavernous Solbar I could barely swallow the greasiest fattiest bloodiest *Cozido à Portuguesa* I've ever met. I heard swifts, I touched hands.

It adds up. I travel to sense the world, and to make some sense of it. Before I left Santarém I went to the old royal convent of St Francis, the last place Garrett visited.

'I'm definitely going away, I can't stay here, I don't want to see this,' he wrote. 'I am not so much shocked as sickened, disgusted, furiously angry.'

Some say it's Santarém's greatest architectural treasure, but it's not even mentioned in the guide the tourist office gave me. It was founded in the early twelfth century and rebuilt by King Fernando in the next. Garrett was nauseated by its desecration, for it had been turned into a military depot and vandalised unmercifully. Soldiers had hacked into the tomb of King Fernando hoping for treasure and finding – what else? – bones and dust. Now the gothic church has been re-roofed with concrete beams and raw tiles to preserve the ruins, the soaring or bellying arches, the moments of architectonic genius. Loose stones lie around. Fragments of exquisite carving are propped around the cloister. In it there's a stack of masonry. Devastation, once tidied, is less than romantic, but in roofless chambers saplings drape young foliage about useless pillars and flatter them with elegiac dappled light. 'In vain I question it stone by stone, block by block,' says Garrett. 'It answers that it knows nothing, has forgotten everything.'

But the soldiers are still here. Beyond the ruined parts the monastery is restored and run with military precision. This is the School of Cavalry where Captain Salgueiro Maia trained in the sixties and which he and his men took on the eve of the Carnation Revolution. Prearranged signals were broadcast loud and clear: Portugal's Eurovision Song Contest entry at 10.55 p.m. on 24 April 1974 by one radio station, and José Afonso's *Grândola, vila morena* by another at 12.30 a.m. on the twenty-fifth. Grândola is a town in the Alentejo celebrated for resisting the Salazar regime; the song became the revolution's anthem:

> Grândola, dark-skinned town
> Land of brotherhood
> The people are in charge
> Within you, O city!

But it was from Santarém, elegant and ruinous, historic and smaller-than-life, that Salgueiro Maia launched his peaceful assault on Lisbon. By 7.30 a.m., with two hundred men and a few Patton tanks, he'd reached the Terreiro do Paço and, reinforced by other units, began occupying the ministries ranged around the square. Then he asked the way to the old convent of Carmo, the barracks of the National Republican Guard. There, the day grew exquisitely tense. But at 5.45 p.m. General Spínola arrived to receive Prime Minister Caetano's surrender. There was rapture, days of it. Red carnations ran out and more were rushed in from the Netherlands. Monarchists wore white ones. Dom Sebastião had stepped out from the repressive fog.

From the Portas do Sol I watched late sun burnish the Tagus. A mother lifted a little girl in a straw hat horizontally, like levitation, her mouth open over the drinking fountain. Lads tormented caged birds. Men cruised the battlements for men. Kids looked up from stone tables in the picnic area where they lay on top of one another, gave me a loud '*Boa noite*' and giggled hard. I've rarely been told to bugger off so politely.

At the far side of town I walked through a Santarém without smart shops and bijou bars, a high-rise, make-do, get-by, real-world Santarém. I climbed to a pleasant apartment where I'd been invited by one of Salgueiro Maia's friends, Luísa Mesquita. She sat me down at a burnished table with a glass of Alcanhoes, an old strong sweet white wine, and told me how she met him.

'I got married and went to Guiné Bissau where my husband was posted. Don't go, stay, my friends said. But I must go. In a bookshop there I bought a volume by Maxim Gorky. At once the PIDE called on me. Don't be seen on the streets with that, they said. Why not? I said. Because there are many planes for Lisbon. So there I was, in Guiné with Fernando Salgueiro Maia and many other soldiers who would become Captains of April.'

They had a long view of suffocating Lisbon and a close-up of superannuated colonialism. They discovered doubt, and like-minded comrades with whom to foment the forbidden idea of change. They forged a language that at home was unspeakable. Their nostalgia was for a Portugal that lived in their dreams. Salgueira Maia returned to Santarém in October 1973, more ready than he knew. Luísa spoke movingly of the way the twenty-nine-year-old captain cajoled his fellow-officers here, and in Lisbon on 25 April. He took on superior GNR forces with words and, not least, neutralised a mortar position near Rossio station that was aimed at the Largo do Carmo.

Neither he nor his fellow Captains of April could have foreseen the political surrealism that would follow, the fantasy millenarians who would tug at the reins of power, the fake idealists who would capitalise on the courage and faith of the few. Without fail, those self-dramatising dream merchants lost power to self-interested prag-matists. Garrett said it all: today's barons are not Camões's heroes, they are greedy opportunists who vandalise the very notion of nationhood.

Just before he died Salgueiro Maia told a friend, '*Ganhou, o gajo, ganhou*': 'He's won, the guy' – meaning the cancer – 'he's won.' He was less than fifty. But who has won?

'Before and after his death,' Luísa said, 'he was accorded many honours, decorated by the president of the republic. But he left a widow and two children. She applied for a pension and was refused. At the same moment PIDE dependants applied successfully!' She grimaced. 'There's a complex of feelings here, of anger and disillusion; betrayal is felt on both sides, the Captains and subsequent governments. Salgueiro Maia's widow gets no pension, secret police families do.'

At midnight I walked in the Garden of the Republic by the convent ruins and the Cavalry School. I'd grown to like the town, the way you get to like an old scoundrel. Of course, I could never be as angry with it as Garrett was. The park seemed almost deserted. Water piddled into a moat around a bare bandstand floodlit by moonlight. A carp splashed.

'Got a cigarette?'

'Sorry, no.'

The young man asked me where I was from. He'd come to mainland Portugal from the Açores to make a bit of money.

'I've no work now though.'

He felt around, produced a cigarette from somewhere on his person and lit up.

'So why do you stay in Santarém?'

'My girlfriend is from here. She's great, I'm sticking with her.'

He took a long hollow-cheeked drag and slumped on to a park bench, lost in an exhaled mist.

'I've come to look for her,' he went on. 'We plan to go to the Açores when we've got the money, and then Canada. I hope she's doing good business, this really is my last cigarette.'

He waved in the direction of the convent. At that end of the park cars paused now and then, stop lights glowing.

'She works from here, it's her regular pitch.'

'Well, I'm for bed,' I said. 'I'm leaving in the morning. *Boa sorte!*' What else could I say?

'Good luck,' he said in English.

10

CASTLES IN NOT-SPAIN

Castelo Branco, Castelo de Vide and Marvão

A STONE IS NOT AN EGG. A stone is not bread. But stones can sustain and contain. Soups and castles. In Almeirim they are proud of their stone soup, *sopa da pedra*. It's fairy-tale stuff. If you have nothing but hunger, try the recipe: take one stone. Add water and boil. It's that simple. If you happen to have a handful of beans, throw them in too. Scratch around for some vegetables. Scraps of meat, seasoning, anything goes. Soon you sit down to a nourishing broth made from almost nothing, not quite *ex nihilo*, you're not God, but from water and a stone.

Waiting for the bus to Almeirim I watched a big man like Captain Pugwash, in a broad-striped blue-and-white T-shirt and espadrilles, briskly cleaning a small man's shoes. Lovingly he cracked his cloth over mirror-black toe-caps. His customer sat upright, gripping a white-handled stick between spread knees; he wore a stained grey suit, a watch chain, an enigmatic smile and pebble glasses under a grey fedora. Only later I realised why I stared at him. He was an aged Fernando Pessoa, not the poet who died aged forty-seven, but the one who lives on.

A woman with red carnations done up in cellophane and ribbon asked me if I was going to Fátima. She may have wanted help with a bundle tied up in a blue gingham tablecloth, but she spoke so fast and laughed so much that I don't know. No, *senhora*, my pilgrimage is a shorter one, to the town where stones are made bread. But I imagined her stepping off the bus into that dusty waste, tumultuous on festival days, spread before the temple in which she'd proffer flowers to Our Lady of Fátima. Poked down the barrel of a gun, red carnations are the symbol of a revolution that might never have happened. Given to your love, they mean passion. For this woman they stood for the Passion. She called them *cravos encarnados*. *Cravos* means 'carnations', but it also means 'nails'. Blood-red nails.

The bus-driver restrained himself. We ground over the bridge from Santarém behind a three-wheeled moped with an empty trailer; it whined at jogging pace the breadth of the Tagus. The south bank was devoted to tomatoes, melons, vines, sunflowers and maize. We gave a wide berth to a black trap drawn by a white horse. Then we were in Almeirim, favourite residence of the House of Avis, hunting ground of Dom Sebastião who did for the dynasty. After his defeat at Alcaçer-Quibir and the death of Cardinal-King Henriques in 1580, Antonio was acclaimed king here, but not for long. Antonio, the Prior of Crato, a bastard nephew of João III, fled into exile when Philip of Castile moved in. For an historical instant Almeirim was the moral frontier between Portugal and Spain. It fell. The royal palace is extinct. The place is famous for wine and stone soup.

Under purple bougainvillea in the square, the park-keeper sprayed his elderly buddies with his hose. On top of new four-storey apartment blocks, strawberry and cream and pistachio with tall vanilla chimneys, a builder on flimsy scaffolding threw orange tiles one by one to his mate on the roof. Young women in pastel house-coats filled a street with strings of flags cut from fashion magazines and dressed skeletal stalls arranged round a circular shelter shrouded with green boughs. It was the set for tonight's *festa* in aid of the playschool where they worked.

'Where have you come from?' one asked.

'Santarém,' I confessed.

Tossed heads and pitying looks were enough to tell me that Almeirim might not have monuments, but it had the life. They told me anyway. One, called Sandra, in transatlantic English.

'Yeah, I grew up in Canada,' she said. 'Come meet my folks at Fazendas de Almeirim, Vito's Bar. Just ask for the Italian.'

I went the next Sunday. The bus-driver was unrestrained; I clung on with the farmers and their wives until he dropped me, after I saw Vito's Bar sail past, somewhere between Almeirim and the place still called Palace of the Negroes. I walked back. This was wide, flat country. *Fazenda* means 'ranch' or 'plantation', and the bar was part of a plush ranch-house compound behind tall blue railings. A man in a vest unlocked the gates: Vito, Sandra's dad. He opened the bar and got me a beer and some nuts. When his well-tailored wife, Maria Odete, appeared he went to smarten up.

They had met in West Park Hospital, Epsom, when he was a nurse and she was a cleaner; a wonderful country, England, but for the 1968 smog and the twelve pounds she put on in a month drinking tea with sugar, the people so polite and educated, not like here, and warm not cold like the Canadians, so after Canada it was tough for Sandra to adjust back here at home, Maria's home, where they opened a bar in Almeirim first but kids did drugs there, brought in by blacks of course after the revolution, and several OD'd, died, so they opened up out here, though the youth have cars anyway, they want it all, people want too much, it's never enough, and parents give them everything, house, furniture, effects even if they can't afford it, even if the kids don't get married, not like the older generation who worked like Vito and Maria worked for this place, their apartment in town, their house by the coast, and you have to be careful because people get funny and only two days ago the big German shepherd that should have barked at me but didn't was killed when someone pushed poisoned meat through the railings.

Vito was back, in a crisp shirt and an aura of aftershave. Sandra Rafaella had emerged cool and smart and confident, and all three talked at once. Framed posters showed the Colosseum and Marcus Aurelius on his horse. A local man with a big belly, baggy shorts and legs that seemed to start very far apart, danced in and demanded an orange juice. He banged a cassette of Italian pop music down on the bar. When in Rome.

'He's a very funny man!' said Sandra. 'It's six years since he touched cigarettes and alcohol. He used to be an alcoholic. He is a funny man.'

'You're the image of Benfica's trainer,' the funny man squinted at me, then Sandra. 'Isn't he? Benfica's trainer without a doubt!'

I hate football but I thanked him. What greater credibility could

I ask for in Portugal? I'd really feel at home when I left Rome, the Italian's bar that was his castle.

Questions of identity recur. Portuguese nationhood, consecrated at Santarém, was tested and retested within the country's frontiers, against Moors, Castilians, the French and against its overbearing ally, the British. If Portugueseness started in Guimarães, Afonso Henriques's birthplace, and was consolidated here in the Ribatejo, where does it stop? At the borders? Certainly not at the seaboard. The frontiers of Portugal have been almost the same since 1249; they're as clear on the map as waist size 24-inch in Marks & Spencer or Eurosize 16. But the frontiers of nationhood are like knicker elastic. Peoples, like people, have wildly neurotic notions of how they look, of how gross or slender they are. One Englishman's England, for instance, may be greater than another English person's Great Britain. After 1434, when the Portuguese pressed beyond Cape Bojador down the Saharan coast, a century's voyages expanded imagination's frontiers across a 'world' whose very meaning grew and grew, each caravel's wake like weak elastic, overstretched by the vastness of the globe and the appetite for it: 1487, Cape of Good Hope; 1499, India; 1500, Brazil; 1513, China; 1520, Fernão de Magalhães's circumnavigation of the globe; 1522, Australia; 1543, Japan . . .

Salazar even redefined 'colonies' as 'overseas provinces', a piece of consummate self-deception made easy by his failure to visit them. Then everyone knew what the propaganda ministry's posters told them, that Portugal's 'real size' was that of its provinces from the Açores to Angola, from Macau to Moçambique. Now the people who say, wistfully or with relief, 'Once we were so great, now we are so small,' can gaze at their slender reflection in a long mirror. Even if Portugueseness does not stop at the Atlantic coastline, Portugal does. It has always stopped at the only other border it's got, the border with Spain.

Bread rises. The Portuguese cockerel pecks its way out of an egg. A stone is a stone. One upon another is a wall. Wrapped around us it's a castle. Castelo Branco is the white castle, in not-Spain. The town is the capital of the province of Beira Baixa that has been trampled by invading armies on the way in from Spain and on the way out again. It had been the Romans' *Albi Castrum*. Moors took it from Goths in the eighth century and Afonso Henriques took it in the twelfth. History on a chessboard: black knight takes white castle, white king takes black castle. It was given to the Knights Templar who rebuilt the town and gained it a charter in 1213. So much for the big pieces who figure in black-and-white 'history', the grey-and-grey ache of what really happened in the Castilian usurpation, the War of the Succession, the Peninsular War, the War of the Two Brothers, the Liberal Revolution, the squabbles, the sackings, the costly liberations. We can only imagine the stories of the pawns who suffered and made love and populated its streets.

At the *bombeiros*' building – a firemen's headquarters of solid whimsy, rounded angles and peaked dormer windows at the base of the castle hill – I left the spacious modern town behind. The old town walls had been breached by Spanish forces, after four days' resistance, in May 1704 and further broken down when it was retaken two months later. As I climbed I penetrated a world grown increasingly narrow, dense, medieval. I came upon the Praça de Palha, Square of Straw, sounding soft and incendiary within a nest of stone. Beyond it, houses grew smaller in streets named for pottery workers, furriers, horsemen, small birds and one, Rua dos Cabeças, for heads. Heads? At the head of the hill steps ascended out of the steep maze to the castle, hollow granite teeth holding within them a sugary morsel of church. A tiny woman, bones in a black cardigan and thin white hair under a blue scarf, greeted me with a gaping grin.

Her head was a skull and her hands were chill. She showed me the summit, the red-and-white television masts and satellite dishes, the battlements and towers. The church of Santa Maria do Castelo had been burnt by the Spaniards. The Virgin was a victim, and townspeople were so enraged at St Anthony for allowing their town to be plundered, contrary to the terms of the contract they had with him, that they broke his statues to bits. They knocked the head off one especially venerated and stuck the head of St Francis on its shoulders.

The old woman urged me down, down to the Miradouro São Gens. Down to a viewpoint? I wanted to walk the castle walls. She skated through the dust in carpet slippers and wrinkled crepe stockings. Below us, eighteenth- and nineteenth-century Castelo

Branco spread from the base of the hill, with accretions of recent apartment blocks and factory units, all set in an undulating plain of tawny and green surrounded by blue hills and mountains like low cloud-masses. The cadaverous crone's insistence pushed me down steep steps on the north side to a viewpoint of paving, rectangular ponds, walled beds and blue-and-white tubs and pergolas all a couple of sizes too small and built, it seemed, by a DIY freak with small-minded notions of grandeur. Below it, a blue pumping-station and more steps that led through a yew tunnel to sunlight, folk music and cobbles.

There were delights and relics, mouldings and carved coats of arms. In Praça de Camões a stairway mounted beneath emblems of state to the old town hall. Where the old quarter ran out, a medieval tower wore four heavy-browed clocks on a spire pierced for bells. Nearby, men waited beside a picture-window hearse, all tassels and drapes, outside dwarf doors set into studded gates in a high wall adorned with a fading picture of workers under the red flag and a demand for 'the voice of revolution in the legislature'. The clock-tower chimed eleven with charming vigour and the cortège moved off.

Last night there'd been estates, mud-caked jeeps and glistening all-terrain vehicles in the streets. They contained not coffins but cages for hunting dogs. Their passengers carried guns. A party of them in the next room had woken me up early.

'Ooo, these hunters!' a woman said. 'I hate it, the first day of the season. The killers are here. I hope they miss.'

I thought of the noble sight of well-born men with bows and spears striking sparks off setts as they rode down from the white castle and out into the forest, that 'outside' where aristocrats, *arrivistes* and their pawns still go to do the one thing they do best, kill, kill rabbits, hares, partridge, woodcock and work up an appetite for the other things: eating, drinking and copulating.

Perhaps we should credit them with the buildings and works of art they commissioned out of vanity or pious fear, but I prefer to credit the artists and craftsmen whose vision was bought with their gold. I ignored both the sacred and secular buildings in downtown Castelo Branco and made for what the place is famous for: a folly built for, not by, a bishop. In 1725 Dom João de Mendonça, Bishop of Guarda, commissioned a garden to be created beside his winter palace, a bower of orange trees and bougainvillea that should embrace the Portuguese universe.

I passed beneath the town's old north gate, a bridge of steps climbing to the palace garden, flanked by balustrades of empty pedestals. The statues that used to stand on them were knocked off by vandals, a word justly or unjustly spelt *franceses* here, the French. General Junot made it his HQ in November 1807, *en route* for Lisbon, and his troops stand accused of bearing off the bishop's best statuary, even though stone is not bread. The poet Robert Southey enjoys telling the tale of their sojourn which, in his version, is briefer than in reality but at least as destructive:

> The night which the French passed in Castelo Branco is described by the inhabitants as an image of hell. The men pillaged as they went, and the very officers robbed the houses in which they were quartered; and, as if they had been desirous of provoking the Portuguese to some act of violence which might serve as a pretext for carrying into effect the threat which Junot had denounced, they burnt or mutilated the images in the churches and threw the Host to be trodden under foot.

The bishop's garden was to have been an image of heaven, an iconic tableau of the spiritual universe, a platonic parade of the powers stopped in their tracks so that, paradoxically, they should move endlessly through time before the eyes of all generations. Once I'd bought a ticket from a man loitering at the gate I faced two stairways, each manned by a pair of archangels, celestial bouncers. The bishop himself, on a panel of *azulejos*, looked at me sideways out of leafy shade. How seriously or playfully I wasn't sure. Like an understudy for Joseph's dream I ascended the steps, running Miguel and Rafael's gauntlet, and entered a chequerboard of sculpted box: pillars and hedges of the vegetable baroque lining paths and dividing beds of scarlet salvias and golden marigolds. It was a maze where you couldn't get lost, each turn punctuated by personifications of the seasons, the 'continents' of Asia, Africa, Europe and India, the cardinal and theological virtues, the four elements, the signs of the zodiac and, at the four corners, the Angel of Judgement, Hell,

Paradise and Death. This last was a shrouded skeleton; some wag had wedged a half-smoked roll-up between the jaws of his skull.

A great dance was in progress according to a preordained pattern, frozen in this meagre moment, but ever stepping and turning in the next dimension. On a higher level a rectangular pond was set with three fountains, each one of four entwined dolphins bearing a crown and cross on their tail fins. By the raised pond ran a promenade with stairways climbing to a fourth level at either end. Reflected figures shimmered in the water. To the west, two lines of saints, apostles and evangelists stepped down to earth from an imposing walled pool. To the east, facing the saints, the kings of Portugal flanked the descent. At the landing where the stair turned down towards the mazy dance, three kings and the queen-saint Isabel of Aragon waited like flunkeys at a banquet. Beside them stood diminutive statues of Cardinal-King Henriques and the Castilian Felipes, I, II and III. These dwarfs put the Spanish usurpation, between Dom Sebastião's defeat and the restoration, into clear perspective. Young granite Sebastião stood apart, surveying the still dance between box hedges and vivid beds. Perhaps he waits for a climactic unreeling of the inaudible music, an unravelling of dance steps, a moment when history, the saints, the continents and all the heavens cohere in the Fifth Empire and, here, in a new Eden where the one-so-longed-for will reappear in innocent flesh with a fig-leaf for his armour.

The blue-and-white-tile bishop looked enigmatic as I left his little garden. Was it a serious entertainment, a sort of four-dimensional chess, he'd had laid out in the shadow of the Templars' castle? Was it an arrogant emblem of transcendent nationalism? Was it a measure of glorious hope? A van juddered to a stop outside the cathedral church. The rear door sprang open and a gypsy woman ejected herself and her baggage from it, shouting with a deep, full-throated, aggrieved voice that filled the space before the stern façade. She was about thirty, haggard but handsome. When words ran out she strode across the road, brown skirts swinging, and dumped a grey plastic sack at the bus-stop. The church forecourt and the triangular park facing it were ominously silent. She crossed back to the taxi-rank, but stopped almost in mid-stride, stared at her people in the van with a look so stony it might have petrified them, and smashed herself hard across the face with an open hand, a slap that stunned the air. Then she was haggling with a taxi-driver, taking coins from an old woman who came to her side, being driven off at high revs, the van full of her tribe creeping in her wake, men in the front grinning bravely.

A solitary man in a wide *sombreiro* waved a national flag and criss-crossed Avenida General Humberto Delgado shouting 'Por-tu-gal! Por-tu-gal!', a lung-busting mantra. He was off to catch a coach to a football match. General Delgado had been a patriot too. Sent into the streets by his father with a green-and-red paper flag at the age of four he'd cheered the fall of Dom Manuel II. Later he was at Salazar's side and had links with the ultra-right-wing Portuguese Legion. Then, in 1952, he went to Washington to head the Portuguese military mission. 'He was an old-time right-winger,' wrote Mário Soares, the Lisbon lawyer briefed to investigate Delgado's death, later President of Portugal. 'But everything changed after he went to America.' The blimpish general turned on Salazar and pursued his new duty with all the conviction of a messiah. French OAS men were offered £225,000 to assassinate him. After flamboyant failed coups he emerged from exile in Brazil in 1965, crossed from Morocco into Spain and made for a conspirators' conference, or a trap, at Badajoz. He'd have played Sebastião, but the PIDE, secret police, killed him and his secretary and hid them in shallow graves near the town of Olivenza. Poignantly, for Olivenza had been Portuguese Olivença until 1801. The people there speak a language closer to Portuguese than to Spanish. Elsewhere, apart from Tras-os-Montes where the dialect is a kind of Galician Portuguese, the linguistic boundary is dramatically distinct. The Olivença district is a hernia in the ancient frontier, a vestigial pocket of the Alentejo that stirs hearts more than any number of lost colonies. General Delgado the patriot was buried in not-quite-Portugal. The patriotic fan beneath the white castle in not-Spain raised his flag, screamed 'Por-tu-gal!' and lurched past graffiti on the wall: *Nova PIDE Não!* New PIDE No! *Soares/Pinto.* The socialist ticket. Already, men with caged dogs in their vehicles were returning with more small corpses than they could possibly eat for dinner.

*

Less than fifty miles south of Castelo Branco as the raven flies is the Alentejan town of Castelo de Vide. If you look at a map you'll see that a sliver of Spain thrusts west between them, like a tongue-tip feeling its way down the Tagus. Driving south, I tasted a landscape of mighty boulders, hulks, torsos. In it, Nisa with its castle, its exquisite sheep's cheese, its brimming amphorae and its Renaissance fountain. Granite and water. Granite and cheese. Bread and wine in a smoky bar.

At Alpalhão I relished the rural Portugal of all our *saudades*, mule-carts, wiry men in fleeces, pinched women in black hats and scarves; a harsh place whose nostalgic charm depends upon partial amnesia. I stopped at a granite rock with a slender cross on top and an oval niche carved in it. The saint that once stood there had been liberated. The soft bells I could hear hung round the necks of sheep. They chimed in erratic concert between the olive trees. Belled red Alentejan cattle with jaunty horns backed off, clonking, into the shadow of a granite ridge. Megalithic cut stones, *pedras talhas*, stood in scrubby wastes and fields. Ridges became mountains, the range of São Mamede and its northern spur, the Serra de São Paulo with at 1,500 feet a massive dun castle squatting on a foothill at the top of the white and terracotta town of Castelo de Vide.

A mediocre new development on the old threshing-floor and pastel-coloured boxes stacked up the ramparts were poor preludes to a spa town of astonishing prettiness. The expansive lower town was punctuated by fountains, wrought-iron railings, balconies and window-grilles. Praça D. Pedro V, corralled by small baroque palaces, was a wide space where the wind eddied around the grandiose bulk of Santa Maria's parish church and sieved through the town hall's mighty iron gates. Men sat on ledges with planted walking-sticks or pliant whittled twigs.

Castelo de Vide means 'vine-twig castle', founded in the best romance tradition by young lovers: the Spanish beauty whose father forbade her marriage to the Portuguese gallant. They eloped to this upland where a vine grew and healing waters gushed from springs, this border post where the Romans built a fortress on the trans-Iberian highway. It was sacked by Vandals, settled by Moors, conquered by Portuguese and contested by Prince Afonso and his brother King Dinis who, when it was his, prepared for marriage to Isabel of Aragon here and rebuilt the castle. Later it fell all too often to French and Spanish forces, Spanish and French. Disputed borders embody new allegiances and changed identities. Wars and marriages. They say, *Nem bons ventos nem bons casamentos de Espanha vêm.* 'Neither good winds nor good marriages come from Spain.' Still, a lovers' paradise is more ballad-friendly than a trampled stronghold.

Stone and water. Not far from the spa bath-house, in a square that's hardly square, a trapezium of cobbled levels that tilt every which way but level, the first and oldest spring trickled from four spouts beneath a bud-like phallic urn in the shelter of a pyramidal roof supported by six marble columns. All over Portugal goddesses of sacred rocks and springs have been superseded by Our Lady of this and that, but the *Fonte de Vila* was still a water temple which soothed and brought its surroundings into harmonious proportion. A bent man with a cap balanced on the back of his bald skull assured me that its outpourings – rich with potassium, chlorates, bicarbonates and nitrates – were good for the skin, for gut problems, high blood pressure, gall-bladder troubles and diabetes. Oddly, he didn't mention either fertility or *o fígado*, the liver, that national hypochondriacal obsession. I sipped the waters. They tasted fine, so he must have been wrong about their virtue.

The town climbs two ways: to the eighteenth-century fortress of São Roque and to the ancient castle. As it climbs it draws itself tighter. Narrow streets, steep glimpses, worn steps, pots gaudy with flowers, low houses, Manueline windows, gothic doorways and, in the thirteenth-century *Judiaria* or Jewish quarter, a pointed arch into the small synagogue. It's said to be the oldest in the country. I stood within its fragrant dusk and remembered the importance of Portugal's Jewry. King Dinis made the chief rabbi head of the treasury. Jews were astrologers to the royal family, physicians, crafts-men, tax-collectors, merchants, bankers. They were Portugal's first printers and the best map-makers in the world. The astronomer Abraham Zacuto's perpetual almanac allowed Vasco da Gama's fleet to calculate latitude by declination of the sun.

Jews like him had been expelled from Spain, or fled from Inquisi-tor General Torquemada's reign of terror, and found brief sanctuary

in Portugal. Then Manuel 'the fortunate' was given the Spanish
princess Isabel as wife on condition that he empty his kingdom of
Jews. But, he said, only unbaptised Jews had to go. Baptised ones
could stay for twenty years. Many, like Abraham Zacuto, refused
to convert. Many became New Christians, though in practice that
hardly reduced the scope for more than two centuries of *autos-da-fé*.
Burning at the stake as public entertainment was the cautionary
beacon at the pinnacle of a tall, dark tower of imprisonment, torture
and slow death. The Portuguese Inquisition lasted from 1536 to
1820.

Fernando Martinho, poet and critic, had told me about this
synagogue over a glass of his excellent port.

'New Christians took family names from plants or birds or animals,' he said, 'such as Pereira, meaning "pear tree", Perdigão,
"partridge" or Coelho, "rabbit".'

They came to be called Marranos, meaning 'excommunicates' or
'unclean'. Hidden Jews were baptised, married and buried according
to Christian rites, but privately they celebrated the Jewish feasts.
They still do. Salazar refused to admit refugee Jews to Portugal in
the Second World War because it was contrary to the teaching
of Fátima. The Portuguese consul in Bordeaux nonetheless issued
thousands of visas over three days and nights. He was recalled,
dismissed, disgraced.

'That consul, Sousa Mendes, was posthumously reinstated in
1988,' said Fernando. 'Soon afterwards President Soares at last apologised to the Jews for the Portuguese Inquisition. And recently I
came to the opening, or reopening, of this synagogue. It was very
moving. After four and a half centuries. Jews from Lisbon and local
peasants, all looking simply Portuguese, took their hats off to show
their skullcaps. Very moving.'

By the castle gateway I found a new monument built against
the ancient wall. White marble sculpted in triangular forms was
grafted onto rough rock with bronze lettering, 'In memory of Salgueiro Maia Captain of April,' crossed sabres and the date, 'April
1994'. Castelo de Vide was the birthplace of the young officer who
had led his unit from Santarém to Lisbon twenty years before. Just
inside the archway to the castle quarter that Afonso IV fortified a
man was selling wooden pecking birds. A small motorbike was

parked beside him with rusty handlebars and a doll's head for a horn bulb. Emblazoned granite lintels, narrow stairways and chamfered arches took my eye in the medieval village wrapped within walls. The church of Our Lady of Joy had a sullen façade, but a climb onto the western ramparts gave me a sudden sight of Portugal's breadth; but for haze, I felt I should have seen as far as walled Obidos, Peniche fortress and the ocean. I dropped back into tight alleys and found myself off the sightseeing track, hard by the north wall in a cobbled lane between what looked like battlements on decayed brick walls. They were oblong chimneys sprouting regularly from weed-infested roof-tiles. The houses they served were mostly bricked up, but a handful were unblocked. Cement *lavadouros*, washtubs, stood at doors overhung by fig and vine. An old woman and two younger men waited to use the communal latrine at the end of their 'street'. In one home I could make out a jumble of goods, pots and rumpled clothes on iron bedsteads. A shrunken woman came at me out of darkness, shrieking, beseeching, like a bat with a walking-stick and an outstretched hand. I climbed to the castle and a long chill hall with a glowing barrel-vaulted roof of brick rising from stone. Above, a well of echoes and deep reflections within the keep and twin stairways up to dwarf doors and the sky. Five round towers and walls like a lasso. A tight town within and a town spilling without. Facing, to the south-west, the mount of the Lady of the Rock with the white chapel on its summit where I saw the lamp lit last night as darkness fell. Mountains to the east and the rough pelt of hills, cover for deer, hare, fox, wild boar. White storks. Egyptian vultures. Eagles. The hilltop fastness of Marvão. Spain.

Water on rock. It rained hard as I drove between poplars and wet fields past the site of the Roman city of Medóbriga. High in the watery sky upon a steep bare scarp stood the battlements, buttresses and watchtowers of Marvão. The road wound up the far side to a monastery founded in 1445 on a great rock outside the walls, a site revealed by shooting star. A shepherd had followed it and found the burial place of *Nossa Senhora da Estrêla*, an image of Our Lady of the Star. She is said to have been hidden here before the Visigoths abandoned Marvão to the Moors in about 715. She stands in her monastery and repels invaders. I entered the town through medieval arches. The rain had stopped but only a handful of people moved. I wanted to be alone here, at three thousand feet, high and out of the world.

The place was a dream. A proud and beautiful village surrounded by intricate defences and capped by a grave and elegant castle. It's a fine example of Vaubanesque fortification, a system translated into the Portuguese vernacular from the seventeenth-century French of military engineer Sébastien Le Prestre de Vauban. Sebastião preserve us! Mostly he and Our Lady of the Star did just that. One massive Spanish assault had been repelled in 1641, and more in the next twenty years, as they tried to regain the Portuguese throne. French and Spanish were seen off in the War of the Spanish Succession, and again in the Seven Years' War. The French were sent packing in the Peninsular War. They say Marvão was only really taken once, during the internecine squabbles of the 1830s, and then by a secret back door.

So, it was not always a dream. Often it was nightmare. Long ago it became a military anachronism, a trinket on a hilltop. Its people were driven out; they fled from unemployment. An international tourism concern made a bid for the town as a job lot. The place was a ready-made theme park, real enough but ripe for transmutation into virtual reality. People who cared for it bought it house by house, saved it, restored it and made it live. By the church of Espirito Santo I fingered the rough grace of a baroque granite fountain. Beneath the castle, water played in a sunken garden like paradise on a barren peak. Within the castle court there was a cavernous vaulted cistern. Water and stone, pagan goddesses, blessed virgins, sustenance.

Every stone, each tower and bastion above the precipice, was sharply focused against blue distances. From the keep's high tower I looked at Spain. The Rio Sever flowed east and turned north to become the frontier as far as the Tagus. The frontier that's stayed firm, almost undented for so long. The linguistic boundary that's so distinct. A couple climbed the battlements chattering in 'the language of the navigators'. That's Jaime Cortesão's phrase. He compares Spanish, five clear vowels like castanets and the 'agitation of the *jota*', with Portuguese, that's softened by a multitude of diphthongs and 'vibrates dully like the voices from the bridge amid the fog and tumult of the sea'.

Far inland, on the brink of Spain and high up under a bruised sky, I could hear that ocean-going speech and stare across this frontier. Portuguese is bigger than Portugal. In the carnival atmosphere following 25 April, the monocled, kid-gloved General Spinola was cast as the new Sebastião. He announced that his government's first aim was 'to guarantee the survival of the nation in its pluricontinental entirety'. Some hope. The entirety that survives worldwide is linguistic. Fernando Pessoa, whose Sebastianic vision was of cultural universalism, says, 'My country is the Portuguese language.' It's a country of 150 million inhabitants. It ends in sight of Marvão, that's for sure.

The coast of Portugal is nothing like so clear a frontier. 'It is in the very fabric of our own language,' says Isabel Allegro de Magalhães, 'that we look for what is (or was, or was supposed to be) beyond.' That word 'beyond', além, again. That 'beyond', she says, 'reveals itself in the very stuff of our language, and in our ability to make something new with that same old stuff. A new poetic, perhaps, rather than a new patriotism.'

It was a dream, this most spectacular spot in all the Alentejo, poised above Iberia, beneath massy clouds. A blue-tailed kestrel sailed below the battlements. It was a short walk to Spain. I wanted to cross the border not by road, but by river. Ill winds blackened the sky. Sun pierced through and flashed on a maze of walls. Rain fell on rock, darkening it instantly. Forked lightning licked at wilderness. Thunder spoke.

11

THE TEARFUL TRAIN-DRIVER

Vila Velha de Ródão

THE RAILWAY line upriver from Lisbon via Santarém sticks close to the Tagus. Roads desert the river soon after Abrantes but the train presses along the north bank on a single track gouged out of hillsides. Both banks are steep, rocky and regularly tufted with olive trees, the texture of candlewick, soft green clouds hovering above deep shadows. Where small streams bleed new colours into the flow the train runs hollowly over tiny viaducts. Only when it reaches the town of Vila Velha de Ródão does it veer north-east, leave the river behind and make for Castelo Branco, Guarda and Salamanca in Spain. The rhyme says:

> *Na estacão da Vila Velha*
> *O maquinista chorava,*
> *Acabou se lhe o carvão*
> *O comboio não andava.*

'In the station of Vila Velha the engine-driver was weeping, he'd run out of coal and the train wouldn't go.' I believe he was crying because he had to say goodbye to the river. I'd resolved to stick with it. It used to be commercially navigable as far as Santarém and, before dams and hydroelectric schemes, by small craft as far as Vila Velha de Ródão. When Spanish kings ruled Portugal they had plans for vessels to ascend all the way to Toledo. The Tagus valley drew me, against the current, through terrain with no road or rail. I'd read in a recent guide book that a Roman road along the north bank linked Ródão with Alcántara in Spain. It was extra-

126

ordinary for the Romans to build along a riverbank, especially one interrupted by tributaries. But my information was that their road was paved with local slate set on edge and, except where dams raised the river level, was still to be seen winding in and out of gullies and desolate gorges. This Roman road I had to see. One way or another the Tagus would lead me to the Spanish border.

The first time I got off the train at Ródão I saw river and rail diverge. I saw geraniums on the platform, green tiles on the station, the town above it and a horizon of mountains. The train-driver had not run out of diesel and I can't swear that he was tearful. But there was a taint in my nostrils and, when the train slid out of sight, I saw a factory ahead with a red-and-white chimney pumping something more than steam at the sky.

Two women had alighted with me. The grey-haired one was a countrywoman in blouse and skirt. Her friend, about the same age, was blonde with black trousers and a designer jacket. She had a boutique carrier-bag and a confident air.

'What nationality are you?' she said.

'British.'

'Why come here? There is nothing here.'

I explained: river, rail, old road. She understood me but I could tell by her pitying look that I was at least three parts mad.

'I want to see that Roman road. Do you know where it is?' I asked hopefully.

'No, I don't know why you come here. But welcome.'

Her friend shook her head gravely, then nodded.

In Lisbon, a man cleaning the bacon-slicer in a favourite café had asked me where I was off to. I said Vila Velha de Ródão. His was daredevil hygiene. With a wet cloth in his red hand he mopped the spinning blade.

'You don't want to go there,' he said. 'You are welcome to stay in my house at Caparica.'

Ródão was not the long beach by the rolling ocean, but I'd received a welcome of a sort. People stared. It was very hot. Up by the church I rested under orange trees. A fountain played beside a monument faced with marble and *azulejos*, topped by a freestone bust of Manuel Cargaleiro. One of the country's most important living artists, he helped to rejuvenate the tile-painting tradition in the late 1940s. Ródão's famous son was born nearby in 1927, but moved to Monte de Caparica at the age of one. This I learned later, and remembered the bacon-slicer. Cargaleiro and his work had moved from Caparica to Lisbon, Brazil, Angola, Moçambique, Paris, the world. Under this sun I saw his playful patterns, his submarine metropolis. A girl on a tricycle, and her grandfather on his feet, moved unsteadily round them without noticing. It was only art. In front of low houses red, black and white washing hung between poles at the brink of a slope of poppies and yellow ragwort, raw orange roofs and the Tagus curving away among hills.

In a dim *cervejaria* the proprietor was hugely pleased to see me. A TV blurted Brazilian soap. The beer was chill.

'Roman road? I don't know about that.'

A gaggle of schoolkids, aged twelve or fourteen, poured in. The girls clustered at one table around a big bottle of Coke and many glasses. They ritually shared it, gulped, stared when they thought I wasn't looking. Their leader wore a CND badge and had no time for boys who circled in a blundering orbit among the café chairs, drinking beer and smoking expertly. A slight boy with glasses and a quiff like Tin-Tin's sat on a table, apart. He was asking to be asked, but I spared him confirmation of his swot-status. He was probably the only person in Ródão who knew where the Roman road ran.

From the town's high cemetery the view was large. The Tagus's elbow. The river sliced hills in two. The sexton said they were the Serra das Talhadas, 'range of slices'. He pointed to the highest peak, with its TV mast at 1,800 feet.

'That one is *Penedo Gordo*,' he said. Fat Rock. The plain below town was dominated by Big Belcher.

'What's the factory?'

'It is Portucel,' the sexton winced apologetically. 'For paper.'

Here's where the eucalyptus trees went, from plantations that threaten Portugal's native flora and lower its water table. Mottled trunks stacked at one end of the infernal city were sucked into it and pulped. Later I read the official town leaflet. It admitted that Portucel was the 'source of work and bread for its half a thousand workers (for the most part resident outside the municipality)' but confessed that, with nearby hydroelectric schemes, it produced grave environmental problems, not offset by benefits, with serious repercussions for the Tagus fishery and tourist development.

'Not good,' said the sexton.

'No,' I said. 'And another thing. Do you know the Roman road?'

'Roman road?' he shrugged.

The old quarter on the hill and the quarter down by the river were linked by a steep street of small suburban villas. In one neat driveway a cart heavy with hay stood in an olive tree's shade. A rick ladder hung on the wall beneath a marble stairway. Boxes of vegetables and fruit were propped outside another house, by a doorway curtained with plastic strips. A deep voice invited me in. There was no one behind the counter. On the floor was a man, or what seemed like part of a man. He lay on a low carpeted platform between piles of goods. His trunk was big, his neck thick, his face ruddy and weathered, his arms and hands rudimentary. One leg like oiled teak stuck a clenched, reduced foot out sideways. I had the awesome sensation that I was meeting a middle-aged foetus.

'That's right,' he said, 'come in. They're inside.'

I wondered if the boys ran in and mocked or kicked him for his blasphemous being. For their fear. Not Tin-Tin, of course.

'Thank you,' I said. 'Are the peaches good?'

'Yes, they're good.'

The tuna was good too. The tin said so: *Atum Bom*. I wanted to share the childish joke, but quietly chose peaches, bread, local cheese and tuna. The man's mother took the money but kept talking to her friend out the back.

'Many thanks. Goodbye.'

'Good day,' he said, 'till next time.'

I cooled off again at the bottom of town in Julio's bar. The lad behind the counter was bright and pleasing. He pulled beer, poured wine and expressed coffee with smiling precision. In between customers he went blank, drummed fingers on stainless steel and flicked pellets of till-roll or sugar-cube wrapping with alarming force. He clashed empty glasses and cups together and dashed them into the sink as if he'd practised hard to achieve maximum noise with minimum casualties.

'Have you a vacant room?'

'Not at the moment. We are under new management.'

I could see how that might make sense.

'Is there someone with a boat who would take me upriver?'

He shrugged hopelessly, but asked another customer.

'Maybe,' said the grey-faced man, sweating and thoughtfully sucking at his red wine, 'but I don't know.'

A young couple across the bar shared a plate of prawns. Both were slender with cropped hair. Urban, I thought, but utterly at home. She was pale and beautiful. Her eyes missed nothing while her long fingers teased firm pink flesh out of each snapped carapace and slipped it between her lips. I could hardly watch her enjoyment, it was so tenderly pornographic. In Portuguese, *gozo* means pleasure, a giggle, an orgasm.

'Can I help you?' she said in English, coming to my side. 'Try *O Motorista* for room, up the road to Portucel. You know? But a boat, I'm not so sure.'

'Thanks. Tell me, do you know the remains of the Roman road that runs along the north bank into Spain?'

'Roman road . . .' she mused. Her boyfriend chewed prawns. He shook his head very slowly. 'No,' she said, 'I do not know Roman road.'

I was an alien dropped out of the sky who could do nothing but ask wrong questions. But I liked the place. I crossed the road and walked down Rua do Porto do Tejo, which soon became a lane between wildflowers, stone walls and olive trees. The ancient port at the angle of the Tagus's elbow was now a small jetty floating on oildrums, a few sharp-prowed *barcos* in need of paint and a deflatable rubber dinghy, floating just beneath the surface. One boat moored under a bamboo clump was heaped with nets and plastic bottles for floats; oars were locked ready in rowlocks and a shiny outboard motor was cocked at the stern. It was waiting to take me to Spain. Women in scarves and hats scythed grass and young bamboo among the trees. They smiled. Two middle-aged bohemians, urban gypsies not in the least urbane, danced mischievously on the jetty and showed me their catch of small fish in a soup can.

'Do you know . . . ?' I began, muttering about a road and a boat.

'We're not from round here,' she laughed.

'Good luck!' he added, making for their 2CV and the road home to Lisbon.

I took their place on the floating boards. The smallest breeze came off the breadth of water, enough to emphasise the heat and carry the ripe scent of sewage. Hoopoes and sandmartins used the air space in their different ways. A just-perceptible swell rocked me, the river's pulse. Downstream, south-west, the road bridge's lacework of girders spanned stanchions standing tall against the spine of the *serra*. Upstream, south-east, shimmering light, water like shot silk, a lone luminous *barco* beneath silhouetted hills and a plume of bleached cloud. The oars flashed for some time before disappearing into a hidden inlet. The Roman road should take me to it.

Thinking about an old road, fifty miles of it along a riverbank, is one thing. You can't miss it. Until you set out to find it. I took a track parallel to the water. It was parched, on old hardcore that might somewhere turn into the edge-on slate I was expecting. A man was cutting a ditch with a mattock to irrigate a line of orange trees, with moats around mature ones and newly-planted saplings. I was envious of the shade in which he worked. After exchanging greetings I asked my question.

'What road's that?' he replied.

'Roman,' I repeated.

'Roman?' he said.

My road passed through the Garden of the Olive Groves. The trees either side of the track were gnarled, ancient. On a rise between track and river stood the small white chapel of *Nossa Senhora da Alagada*, to which devout folklorists made a *romaria*, a processional pilgrimage, each year. I made my own and found shade between a walled fishpond and the chapel court whose paving annually rang with the feet and skirling beat of Ródão's dancers and musicians. Now it was still and empty. Oranges like suns glowed in the dark foliage above my head.

It was crazy looking for a Roman road along a river whose baked banks fell steeply to the water in heat only relieved by polkadot puddles of shadow beneath groves of trees. I walked on anyway. Amongst the cultivated desolation, I heard the tinny sound of pop music. It came from the open door of a car parked with a motorbike by concrete tables and benches set like gravestones – one inscribed J.F. 1991 – under more orange trees. Tucked into the bank below the picnic site I found two fishermen with heavy-duty rods. Out where they were casting, big fish jumped and submerged beneath endless gilded haloes.

'*Olá!*' one of the fishermen called, shattering anything left of the silence.

'*Olá*,' I said and knew my question was going to sound silly if I couldn't ask it quietly. 'Do you know about a Roman road here, along the bank?'

'Not here, my friend.'

'Thanks. *Boa sorte!*'

The track stopped there. I pushed through foliage and found myself staring at another river. The *Ribeira do Açafal* ran in from the north. A few miles upstream a graceful medieval bridge crossed it to nowhere. Not that any guidebook I'd read mentioned that. One, though, had waxed lyrical about a Roman road. I wanted to interrogate its authors. I wanted thumb-screws on them. I was mad to come looking for it and the heat made me crazier. This was no time to hike upriver. I'd come back in the autumn and find a fisherman to take me to Spain.

Wamba seized power in Iberia at a bad time. It was 672 and the great edifice of the Christian Visigothic state was cracking up, split between the Roman party and Gothic nationalists. Gauls and Basques rebelled. Of necessity King Wamba drafted slaves and serfs into his army, contrary to the Germanic ordinance that only free men should bear arms. In perilous times few wished for freedom; it was a luxury only the strongest nobles could afford. The king conscripted clergy too, in defiance of canon law. His end was bizarre. He was shorn by a favourite. A cropped head was the sign of a slave, so a council of priests and nobles dethroned and banished him. Social tensions grew, demanded scapegoats. Wamba's successor, together with the Metropolitan of Toledo, a converted Jew, promulgated anti-Semitic measures. The same old story is always older than you think. Demoralisation and decline invited African invaders in. Musa ibn Musair's assault on Morocco in 710 had decisively claimed the Christian Berber state for Islam. The very next year, the first of his Muslim armies invaded Iberia and it was not long before they had seized almost the whole peninsula. Not unnaturally, Jews hailed the Moors as liberators.

At dawn in mid-October I walked through town to the Tagus Bridge. Set into the bank, the Restaurante Rei Wamba was tightly shuttered. From the middle of the 1889 bridge I watched martins and mist, a long shroud muffling the majestic jagged cleft in the hills where the dull green river funnelled downstream, the Gates or *Portas de Ródão*. A man with a big belly and a helmet like a white pimple rode a small motorbike across the bridge. Even his weight made it bounce. Back on the north side I climbed a minor road up *Barroca da Senhora*, Lady's Gully. From the depths below to brightening heights above it was thick with pine trees. Early sun fanned an ochre figure to fiery life, the flayed trunk and lower branches of a singular cork oak. Fingers of mist loosed their clammy grip on the summit and felt their way down between trees: a special effect for which directors of gothick horror would have given all the dry ice in the world, at once a veiling and an unveiling, the lowering of a diaphanous shawl from head to breast to lap. Its tatters lay a little in Lady's Gully before evaporating. Naked colour. At one thousand feet, a thing I must describe as a bright shadow loomed, turned honey-coloured and was revealed as Ródão's castle, a battered keep ripe for the reappearance of Gothic Wamba, to whom tradition but not history assigns it, or for the epiphany of some gothick Sebastião stepping down and down the craggy spine of rock from the castle to the sunlit pinnacle that stands up between the railway's single track and *Portas de Ródão*: gates ever open to a river's deepening blue, the Atlantic Ocean and the world.

I'd tried fruitlessly in Lisbon for further news of the Roman road running east, but hadn't completely given it up for lost. I repeated my riverbank walk in cooler conditions. Beyond the white chapel's stations of the cross and olive trees' agonised trunks and roots, I cut up to a raw road with a paving of white setts. It ran back to a brand-new Cultural, Sports and Tourist Centre co-financed by the European Fund for Regional Development. Could the effects of the pulp factory be complemented by a pappy notion of institutionalised culture on the raw edge of town? An abstract sculpture of *Portas* stood at the entrance. Ródão's promised new life was

133

confined within. I hoped the gates would open and let it out.

Thinking about rural depopulation I plodded down another track running east, between younger olive trees in fresh-ploughed soil, and downhill towards the Açafal stream's sweeping curve around a lush almost-island. This was no through route to Spain. There was a ruined *quinta* on the opposite bank and a farm of shacks on this. An alert dog barked and came for me snarling. It limped, but enough? I retreated and met a woman with a bucket and a suspicious eye. What was I doing coming out of the dawn with a howling dog at my heels and hens crowing in the holding below?

The *Rua do Cabeça do Salvador* took me to the town's temple. The turnstile was open and I climbed into the stand. I watched a ghostly match in which a glorious header, nodded from the goal-mouth in the direction of the new Cultural Centre, saved the town's honour. The Road of the Saviour's Head led me past plots for sale and then the rough and ragged air-brick-and-cement skeletons of new houses. Builders and labourers greeted me as they arrived for work. It was 8 a.m., Monday.

I'd woken up discouraged. Nothing had been easy. In the summer I'd checked out *O Motorista* and met the prawn girl in its dingy bar. Later in its big bright new restaurant I'd watched a gross man consume his meal and most of his wife's too before dismissing sugar and demanding sweeteners in his coffee from a tearful waitress. I'd seen her husband abuse her. She said I'd get a room in October. I arrived on the one day in the week when *O Motorista* was closed. I found a clean room above a nameless bar next door. A stern woman ran it and made rugs by the window when she wasn't otherwise wearing herself out. Her husband snapped his fingers at her, kept hunting dogs tied in the yard, cursed their yapping in the early hours and switched TV channels at night when she and I were particularly enjoying a show. I'd been there too long without finding a road. Or a boat. Except for a thirty-foot white-and-orange hull parked across the road among pink roses beside a garage on whose roof the proprietor's fat prim wife hung endless washing and from which her dull shapely daughter gazed down longingly at the taut bronze backs of young mechanics. The garage proprietor's boat might have yearned for water as fruitlessly.

On Saturday I met Lucindo, a charming trucker just back from

Cologne, who said he'd consider my problems. He did, and waved me over later that day to say hello to his daughter.

'No one knows this road,' he said, 'but go up to the old town, to the *Centro Municipal de Cultura*. They have a boat.'

'Are they open today?' I said incredulously.

'No,' he said, 'you must wait until Monday.'

I'd waited impatiently, and woken up feeling bleak. I couldn't believe that the small museum, which had been shut when I tried it, had a boat which would take me to Spain. I'd walked myself into a state of pleasurable resignation. From my room I could see enormous emissions of steam from Portucel. The clouds rose and spread. A white-coated man and his minion took readings at monitoring stations in slatted huts along the pipeline that ran all the way to the heat-exchanger, an obese concrete mushroom squatting in the river. The town above was blotted out. The goods train that hadn't moved from the station since yesterday was hidden. I'm sure the driver was weeping.

After breakfast in the café I felt suddenly tired. Then I showered and the sun broke through to dry my hair. Down the road, at the end of a long terrace of simple houses in every degree of repair and dereliction, it lit on a detached house. There was nothing special about it: single-storey with an ochre-tiled roof, a weatherbeaten wooden door and a deep-set window at one end of an otherwise blank expanse of limewashed wall. Its proportions were crude, its rendering was cracked and it sat beneath a shaggy palm tree in a plot of rock and rife grass with no elegance at all. But the door, the window and the edges of its walls – corners, ground, eaves – were framed in blue. The sun lit on that blue. Wherever I find it, around the Mediterranean, in Africa, the East or here, I ache. It seems a simple colour, a common one, but it acts on the optic nerve like a drug. It has depths. It weathers to illusory translucence. It is ether, azure, *azul* in Portuguese. It is water at its clearest and most opaque, that concentrates sky-blue by refraction, a hint of the vacancy of space caught between ocean's skin and earth's crust. Then the light changes a tad and it's summer air heavy with roses, or deep sea tainted with blood.

I had woken up feeling blue. Now I looked at that house and wanted to live in it. A sentimental desire of the kind I don't like to admit, but must because it and I are human. Its blueness met mine. All at once I knew for certain that this blue is the colour of *saudade*. It is not melancholy, it is a pigment compounded of regret and hope. Nostalgia is retrospective optimism, hopeless by definition. This azure was more than that, it was hopeful. Then the light changed again and it was heavenly. As the Portuguese say when everything's rosy, *Tudo azul!*

Despite azure-coloured spectacles I was pessimistic about the boat as I climbed to the pillory in the old town. I was sweating when I reached it. The *Centro Municipal de Cultura* was a small building full, today, of activity and well-displayed exhibits.

'Can I help you?' asked a young woman.

'I'm not sure. Do you know a man, a lorry-driver called Lucindo?'

'No, I don't.'

'Well, he told me to come here because you might be able to take me upriver by boat.'

'Why do you want to go?'

I explained myself.

'Yes,' she said, 'I will take you and show you the prehistoric rock carvings.'

'Wonderful!' I couldn't believe it. 'Talking of archaeology, is there a Roman road from here to Alcántara?'

Graça Batista consulted the in-house archaeologist.

'No, there is no Roman road along the river,' she smiled, 'so we must go by boat.'

I could smile broadly now. 'As I thought. When can we go?'

'This afternoon, two o'clock, does that suit you?'

> The sun is born in Castile,
> D'you want us to go there, my love?
> I don't like the sun to be
> In Castilian hands.

I bought fresh bread from the back of a van on my way down the hill and had a triumphant lunch as I packed my gear. At two o'clock a car and driver took Graça and me to Vila Velha de Ródão's old port where more than once I'd stood and hoped. In the museum she'd pointed out a photograph of the quay in 1900, showing lateen-rigged boats laden with cork bark moored in the foreground and the bridge, then only eleven years old, spanning the river behind. Now, beside the *barcos* and the sunken inflatable, Joaquim Duarte was waiting for us in a fibreglass dinghy with an outboard motor.

After a few pulls and breathless rewindings, Joaquim got us started. Soon we passed under the bridge, going downriver. On the base of its northernmost pillar someone had painted RED RUM in orange paint. Then I saw the Portas de Ródão in a new light. From town, from the heights, from the bridge the slice through the hills had looked impressive. From a small boat on the Tagus it looked mighty. Here in May 1811 Wellington brought forces across the river to join Beresford against the French in one of his feared pincer movements. The slice was a jagged tear through towering rock masses. Freshly-weathered chunks were all the ochres from clotted blood to old gold. Above, the rock loomed greenish yellow. On the south side, as our tiny craft slid between jaws, we peered into a great cleft.

'Downriver, between here and the Ocresa tributary, there's a collection of rock art from Neolithic times to the Bronze Age,' said Graça. 'It's considered to be one of the most important of its type in the world.'

In the museum I'd seen photographs and casts of petroglyphs: noble deer, schematic creatures, pin men, abstracts of dots and nets and spirals. I was ready to see the real thing.

'The waters behind the Fratel dam submerged the carvings almost completely,' she said apologetically, then added, 'but only after they'd been properly documented. We're going upriver.'

Joaquim spun us around and new bow waves criss-crossed the old as we sped back through the Gates of Ródão. The carvings occur in groups on the riverbank over a distance of forty kilometres between the Ocresa tributary and the Sever, which is also the border with Spain. A month after I made this trip the discovery of hundreds of similar carvings, in the valley of the Côa river at its confluence with the Douro, was made public. Scientists had been aware of them since 1992, and locals have been familiar with the pictures of deer, horses, bison and bears for generations. A dam project at Foz Côa threatened to swallow them up and archaeologists accused the national electricity company, EDP, and a colleague employed by EDP to survey the site, of conspiring to keep the rock art under wraps until building work on the Côa hydroelectric scheme had begun. UNESCO requested Portugal to suspend work on the dam. A pressure group, *Movimento para a Salvaguarda da Arte Rupestre do Vale do Côa*, was formed. A wine was christened *Rupestre*. Portugal's Institute of Architectural and Archaeological Patrimony was accused of gross negligence and complicity with EDP.

Even if I'd known all this then I wouldn't have been thinking about it. I was watching flocks of heron lift heavily from the river, the studwork of olive groves on the banks giving way to scrubland and lush bankside vegetation, a rare house of rush and grass on stilts, the occasional hill track down to a moored *barco*, small dark inlets like thresholds on mystery, vertical strata making jagged landings and rising by fractured stages to the sky or retreating downwards in water, drowned clouds and sharp-focus horizons in the clear mirror of the river. Its course was sinuous, its exit from the visible sheet uncertain and always advancing ahead, to left or right, far or near. If it hadn't been a watercourse with obligations to the science of hydraulics it might have been a maze. Steep banks swapped foreground and background as we ravelled up the current's thread. Small- and large-scale vegetation slid one against another. Arid islands and shaggy rocks marked subtle intervals in the melodic line. More herons strode from dishevelled water into the pure azure air.

Ahead, a man in a white shirt and a cream cap rowed his *barco* one-handed in a circle and drew in nets. Before we reached him Joaquim grunted in recognition and made for the rocky bank. As he stepped ashore we hit it hard. Joaquim ruefully bit his bearded lip and assessed the damage. A fracture, not a break, above the waterline. We slipped on slimy boulders and skipped over the dry ones while Graça cursed her unsuitable shoes and stayed by the boat. Joaquim seemed not to know where to look but every few steps he pointed to dots gouged in rock, lines engraved in softer seams, a crude bison, something like a shrimp, a bat or a bird, the rays of a prehistoric sun.

The ethnologist who found himself gazing at these carvings for the first time on 13 October 1971 described it as a most beautiful day whose sky was diaphanous in places, 'a wonderful autumn morning in readiness for a fine St Martin's summer . . . All was calm. And then it afforded this amazing fact by which we enter into the past.' It was, he said, one of the most marvellous days of his life. He saw engravings on the rocks. They were dated at between five and ten thousand years old.

The French archaeologist Jean Clottes has dated the Foz Côa collection at 20,000–18,000 BC. With Professor João Cardoso of Lisbon he came to far-reaching conclusions about the hunters who made the marks. The signature of a co-operative society. If they're not cut from the face and carted off like booty, the Foz Côa carvings may be drowned like those near Fratel. In any case, international 'experts' have been wheeled in by EDP to say that the carvings are really quite new. Some scientists have persuaded themselves that, given the hardness of the rock, water will best preserve them for future generations. Please explain that last sentence. Please. Without evolving gills and webbed feet Joaquim and I stared at each drawing until we ran out of them. It was only art. It's a whimsical question, but how many engravings would the hunters have given for power, a few lightbulbs, washing-machines, freezers, computers?

We joined Graça in the dinghy and drove onwards, a tiny arrow of wake, towards Spain. Around a bend in the river it came suddenly, a wall of concrete between high banks, a wall perforated by sluices and crowned with pylons, two walls in one holding back both the Tagus and the Sever at their confluence, the one flowing from the east, the other from the south, both marking the frontier. The wall was only a dam, the boundary just an invisible line made visible on dusty papers, treaties. How real was it? For getting me here, and for demonstrating that the Roman road the guide book had promised was even less real than a line on a map, I was grateful to Graça and Joaquim. I told them so. I was going over the top.

12

COLUMBUS DAY

Alcántara

I STRAPPED ON my cork boots and strode ashore beneath the dam. It is called the Cedillo dam, after the nearest village. Spanish Cedillo, that is, whose Portuguese name is Casalim. I climbed aboard the frail cockpit of Father Bartolomeu Gusmão's 'big bird' and, fired with a spirit of adventure, was wafted over the wall and high over the orderly tangle of electrical installations.

I landed on a waste tip in Spain: a plateau of shale and spoil bulldozed to the edge of a dead brown slope that fell first to a belt of coniferous woodland, and then to the river Tagus. The Portuguese 'Tejo' and the Spanish 'Tajo' look alike to Anglo-Saxon eyes, but you only have to hear them to sense the solidity of the linguistic boundary. *Tejo* has a limpid sound, 'Tay-zhoo', with a soft 'j' as in French, while *Tajo*, in which the 'j' or *jota* is guttural like the German 'ch', is a turbid 'Ta-ghho!'

Hydroelectric power is on the tip of this Spanish tongue between the rivers Tagus and Sever. From concrete massifs by the road that ran down to the power station I peered through eucalyptus foliage at two green reservoirs, right and left, behind white walls and their buttresses. A van moaned downhill to the generating plant. A man in overalls walked between railings on the dam's crescent. Otherwise, all was profoundly still. Apart from an unnatural step in both rivers and some disturbed earth, the illusion of wilderness was complete.

For some thirty miles now the Tagus was the frontier. Within sight, the Ponsul tributary ran in from Monsanto and Idanha-a-Velha in the north, a gash in the Portuguese bank. The Sever, fed by the river São João, brought its stream from Castelo de Vide and Marvão in the south. I got into my car, a hired Renault Clio with more realism than magic about it, and drove up the winding road away from the watery junction. Soon I came to a small bridge over nothing parallel to the tarmac, a dry stream-bed and the ruins of a house where a self-possessed woman in faded blue raised her crook and urged her sheep off the highway. The deep folds uncreased and became a rumpled plain leading to thin blue hills. Cedillo's pasture was parched and parted by dry-stone walls, its citrus and olive trees thickened with shadow, its roofs bland orange, its walls white. The church's steps and lower courses were of chunky freestone but the bulk of the building was dark sandstone with quoins, buttresses, arches and strings of red brick. The bells in the tower hung frozen in mid-swing beneath a lacy wrought-iron cross and a stork's nest.

Below, men were digging one of several ragged holes in the road. 'Trouble with water,' they said. Lack of water may have explained why Bar Gloria was so full and so loud, drowning my attempts to get my *b*s and *v*s sorted out, to extricate phrase-book Spanish from Portuguese. The talk around me was percussive, abrupt but unstoppable, the gestures aggressively flamboyant, the change slapped down on the bar. Yes, the linguistic, gestural boundary was distinct. I was in not-Portugal.

This was Extremadura, a shifting label applied to those lands bordering on Moorish territory, moving parts now settled and comprising the provinces of Cáceres and Badajoz. The name is popularly derived from the Latin, *terra extrema et dura*, 'extreme and hard land'. A pelt of white gold shimmered between solid shadows cast by holm oaks. Black horned cattle chewed cud and contemplated me from beneath long lashes. Bulls ambled away to the safety of a holm oak tree when I spoke to them. Sure, there was a fence between us and, at long intervals, limewashed gateways and long tracks leading to sprawling white ranch-houses. The *latifundistas*, owners of large estates, practise a culture characteristic of Extremadura, an oak/crop/pasture system called *dehesa* in which wheat, acorns, cork, cattle and pigs are harvested in season under the predatory eye of vulture and wolf.

Wilderness is highly cultured, even if not all its demons have yet been exorcised. Herrera de Alcántara was a village in the medieval outback. In a greasy fedora and cowled scarf, a weary couple with a donkey ascended a steep alley towards the squat churchtower and its pinnacle. Men were loading more donkeys into a lorry. The black of their clothes, of their hair, of the creases in their faces seemed blacker than Portuguese black. One donkey didn't want to go; it reared away from the ramp and, while the men regrouped around it, sawed the air with complaints. Between Herrera and the Tagus the road grew narrow, tortuous and steep. Hairpin bends, a crumbling surface and sheer drops were augmented by little rusty enamelled notices advertising every kind of *¡peligro!*. Danger. But at the bottom it was worth it. The swollen river that backed up from the Cedillo dam was a gorgeous lake, with late light enriching upriver colours, throwing levitating clouds into relief, showing downriver hills and half-submerged skeletons of trees in silhouette. Two dinghies were almost hidden in rushes by a boathouse, or was it the top storey of a flooded home? The glossy river was combed by breezes and pocked as if by buckshot: a multitude of jumping fish. I squatted on a rock, shut my eyes and listened for a long time. The unscored rhythm of water lapping and the erratic plashing of fish. The rich soundtrack of equilibrium and chaos which, at bottom, are the same thing.

At Membrio people made their evening promenade out of town and back, the young in bunches, the old and the timid in groups, girls and women together. The river Salor, in a gully between rugged hills, purled towards the Tagus. Tawny lands flanking Los Perales were marvellous before dusk: kindly last light gilded aromatic cistus, brooms, heathers and lichens on rocks; it domesticated the inhospitable, a landscape without walls, fences or trees, just a road and one long low ranch-house like an island set beneath a raft of cloud in a world bounded only by the raw ripple of mountains, layers of them on the horizon, an oscilloscope's screen making visible the flat earth's pulse. What long tradition of husbandry had nurtured this 'wild' place? Plover rose in a throng with throbbing wings.

Still looking for Roman remains, I arrived at Alcántara late. On the way into town I'd passed the Hotel Puente Romano but it had looked too smart, too new or refurbished for my taste. To eschew this Roman Bridge Hotel might have been a bad mistake. The modest square called Plaza Portugal boasted a restaurant and a couple of bars. I parked there and entered the old town on foot through a deep archway, the Arco de la Concepción of 1611, sole survivor of four gates in the town's second defensive wall. Almost at once I found a *pensión*. I roused a fat boy from deep slumber in front of the TV.

'We have no vacant rooms.'

'Where can I find one?'

'This is the only *hostal* in town.' Reluctantly he added, 'There is the hotel.'

I wrinkled my nose.

'In the season many private houses offer rooms, but now . . .' He didn't finish, he was going back to sleep.

Back in outer darkness a firecracker almost made me slough my skin. Kids in a side alley cackled and screamed. A small man stepped out of the pharmacy opposite and buttonholed me.

'You want a room?'

Before I could say much he marched me back to the *hostal* I'd just left. He shouted and the fat boy brought him a key.

'I have a room,' he said, 'with, if you don't mind, a small bed.'

The room was narrow, the bed too. And short. But very cheap. I thought there must surely be other places in town, but it was late.

'Half-price,' he said. I nodded. A firecracker shuddered the glass in the window frame. Then another. I shrugged. Not-Portugal was not unlike Portugal after all. I paid in advance.

Outside, a little girl pranced while a boy held a fizzing match to blue touch-paper. I retired immediately to the old town's heart. There were no other *pensións* I could see. None, I was told next day. What I saw in the deep dusk or in the sickly glow of street-lamps on brackets was a quaint village of chimneys on hilly roofs, doorways like proscenium arches, palaces, coats of arms and wrought-iron balconies, some adorned with brittle fronds left over from Palm Sunday, some glassed in like aquaria.

The convent of San Benito was the priory of the Knights of the Order of Alcántara. Grand Masters were entombed within its church of the Inmaculada Concepción. The gothic cloister looked inwards of course, at the still heart; but outwards too from three Renaissance storeys, pillared ambulatories hung like scenery between conical towers emblazoned with royal shields and topped with storks' nests. Spectral knights might have promenaded there and gazed down at the rising tiers of an amphitheatre made dramatic by moonlight. Their church was heavy, fortified, with clenched towers and high windows blinded by cataracts of something like mother-of-pearl. Translucent marble, I discovered in daylight. Now convent, church and amphitheatre seemed of different densities, disarticulated, in different dimensions. They made apparently illusory but real connections, like an Escher drawing in reverse. They were all sixteenth-century, but the order had begun in the twelfth as the Military Order of San Julian of Pereiro. In 1218 it had moved here from Pereiro in Portugal's Côa valley. The knights were a modern phenomenon compared with the rock carvings there.

Alcántara is founded on a rock above the left bank of the Tagus. I crept down a promising dark alley to see if I could get my first glimpse of the Roman bridge which gave the town its Arabic name. *Al-kantara*. All I saw was a ghostly curtain drawn across the valley. I guessed it must be the dam shown on the map. An absurd notion on a night set so many centuries back. Almost no cars moved. One mule. It was a town whose cobbles and setts demanded the percussion of shod hooves. On a narrow and deserted street named Solitude stood the eleventh-century Synagogue of Loneliness. In truth, both synagogue and street are called *Soledad* because Spanish, like Portuguese, doesn't distinguish between kinds of aloneness. It was in 1492, a year that began with the reconquest of Granada from the Moors and ended with Columbus's pilgrimage to America, that Ferdinand and Isabella were inspired by the dread inquisitor-general Tomás de Torquemada (with Jewish blood in his veins) to bring the century's anti-Semitism to a head and purge their dominions of all Jews who had not embraced Christianity. More than 160,000 fled Aragón and Castile. Present-day Ladino, the language of Spanish Jews in the Balkans, North Africa, Israel and the Americas, is firmly rooted in fifteenth-century Spanish.

Intermittently illuminated, a woman's shape moved, or rather quick-marched with unnerving concentration, to and fro, to and fro along the length of Plaza de España. The next night too. Was she driven by mania or doctor's orders? Close by I found a dark

Campinos on the day of the *Colete Encarnado* (red waistcoat) festival at Vila Franca de Xira.

Bull-running in the streets, that begins to prise ceremony from the soil and transform it into 'entertainment', a word not meaningless but without significance.

Above: Tending the first-floor garden, Santarém.

Left: At dawn, the Tagus bridge below Santarém.

Right: A barefoot *avieiro*, one of a tribe of fishermen from the coast who migrated inland to become 'river gypsies', in a street of houses on stilts at Caneiras.

Left: A beggar at the heart of Santarém.

Below: Riders and Lusitano mounts at the National Agricultural Fair.

Above: The hilltop fastness of Marvão, supervising Spain.

Left: Fonte de Vila, the oldest medicinal spring in Castelo de Vide.

Below: Kings in the bishop's garden, Castelo Branco.

street, Calle de Duende. It's a dark word, *duende*, but only made so by Christian abhorrence of earthly powers. It means 'hobgoblin' or 'sprite', 'daemon' not 'demon', and by extension 'magic'. You can have *duende* as profoundly or trivially as you can have *carisma*, the Holy Spirit's gift to public relations. For Federico García Lorca, death's poet, *duende* was a prerequisite of the qualities he prized, the vagabond spirit he adopted, the tragic dream of heroism, the heartbeat of the bullfighter, the *canto hondo* or 'deep song' of the gypsies of Andalusia.

From Duende I emerged into the halo of thin light around Santa Maria de Almócovar, a thirteenth-century Romanesque church on massive footings. It was built over the site of a mosque soon after Alcántara was won from the Moors. But, facing steps up to its great door and flickering in firelight, a monkish figure caught my eye. His fine head and sinewy neck protruded from a cowl like a carapace, his outstretched arms offered himself or nothing, he strained upwards from a bower of roses. In a corner below the terrace where he stood kids guiltily stoked a little fire of leaves. The monk was their saint, San Pedro de Alcántara. Behind him a humbler seventeenth-century church marked his birthplace. It looked in need of repair, but its south door was spilling light and music. Inside it was grand enough, culminating in a baroque reredos. Three guitarists accompanied a group of singers, including one tremulous heart-rending soprano who trod the vocal high wire above a crowd with their feet on the ground. Then someone hit a bum note and San Pedro's great acoustic ricocheted with laughter.

'Now, in October,' explained one of the guitarists, 'we have services in honour of San Pedro here in his home town.'

The conductor smartly clapped her hands.

'And tomorrow,' he added hurriedly, 'we will sing a special mass for *Día de la Hispanidad.*'

The conductor clapped, smiling broadly at me.

'Also known,' hissed the guitarist, 'as Columbus Day.'

The musicians soared once more. Outside, the fire had gone out and the kids had gone home. San Pedro gazed darkly up at Santa Maria's rose window. In a bar with a gory bullfight at blood-curdling volume on TV I ate an oily meal. The patron's daughter roused herself to cook it, leaving her infant slumped in a high chair.

He didn't stir. Near the *hostal* they'd run out of firecrackers. I curled up in my tiny bed and slept like a baby.

Tomorrow it would be *Día de la Hispanidad*, literally, day of Spanishness, as though there were such a thing and, assuming there were, that you'd need just a day to explain it. Except for Portugal, all the regions of Iberia not in Moorish hands had fallen under the hegemony of Castile by the middle of the twelfth century. Castile and Hispania became synonymous, though the title of successive Spanish monarchs was *Rex Hispaniorium*, that is 'king of the Spains', plural. However restless they were, and are, however fluently they cursed Castile in their own languages, the Catalans, Basques and Galicians have had to live in their own Spains. Only Portugal was not-Spain, almost never a Spain. In the fourteenth century it had to fight Spain off, although its borders had been recognised by Castile in 1297. If it so desires it can lay claim to a transcendent sense of itself. At least on paper, and except for sixty years following Dom Sebastião's defeat in Morocco, Portugal has preserved a remarkable independence.

Why? Crudely: it expelled the Moors three centuries before Spain did and it nurtured a sense of unity, and of pride, out of all proportion to its size, during the great century of discovery. Prestige and wealth came from the east. Unity and pride gave it the moral muscle to repel Spain. It stuck to its shelf of land between the Iberian tableland and the Atlantic seaboard. It should be added that at times of conflict, with Moors or Castilians and with the French in the Peninsular War, the English often seemed to turn up in the shape of motley crusaders, classy longbowmen, or an Iron Duke. Not that English influence was ever altruistic or always benign. We were after more than a glass of port and a round of golf. For centuries Spain was England's dire foe and Portuguese independence remained a strategic necessity to us. Alliance with and dependence on England kept Portugal afloat but encouraged long periods of misgovernment and decadence.

If Castile couldn't rape Portugal, it hoped to woo it. But from Spain come neither good winds nor good marriages. Brilliant dynastic alliances were contracted and annulled. Appalling acts were performed to stop children of Spanish mothers coming to the Portuguese throne. Remember Inês de Castro. Then, with Spain's ruin in the Napoleonic wars and loss of American colonies, the threat evaporated. Indeed, while repudiating dynastic union, nineteenth-century Portuguese liberals looked to Iberian solidarity – *iberismo* – as a way out of stagnation. The poet and philosopher Antero de Quental, who was to dismay and puzzle his brilliant friends by blowing his brains out, wrote of Portugal's 'unnecessary amputation . . . from the great body of the Iberian peninsula'. His comrade Teófilo Braga, future first President of the Republic, envisaged a republican Spain divided into fourteen autonomous states with which Portugal would, he wrote in 1892, 'be able to join without hesitation and with dignity in the constitution of the Federal Pact of the Peninsular or Iberian Free States'. That way Portugal escaped the British alliance and still kept her colonies. Such a pact was never sealed. The military junta that overthrew Portugal's republic and unrolled the long red carpet for Salazar received support and arms from Spain. In return, Franco's plot was in large part fomented in Portugal. The two dictators and their treaty of mutual assistance made a mockery of the notion of Iberian Free States and a dirty word of *iberismo*.

Now, despite a world of rife nationalisms, federalism is a Europe-wide concept and Portugal and Spain have, it seems, been members of the European Union for ever. A decade is an eternity in politics. A 1995 opinion poll showed that 58 per cent of Portuguese wanted to stay in the Union, though 72 per cent thought EU funding had been badly managed (so politely put). I've heard many express the fear that Spain will in effect buy up Portugal while 'exporting' Spanish unemployment, roughly four times worse, across the border. But in this poll 46 per cent perceived Spain as 'a friend and ally' while 42 per cent saw it as 'a rival and an enemy'. *Iberismo* has utterly changed its terms of reference.

On 7 June 1994, five hundred years to the day since Spain and Portugal signed the Treaty of Tordesillas, the Portuguese paper *Público* and the Spanish *El País* published a discussion between José Saramago and the Galician novelist Gonzalo Torrente Ballester. The latter was clear: 'I feel I am a man of the north. I feel European. The south interests me, but I feel northern.' Amid talk of northern, Mediterranean and Atlantic cultures, all of which Iberia shares,

Saramago felt subject to another pull. 'I invented for myself something I called *trans-iberismo*,' he said. 'An idea based on the following presupposition: that in the Iberian Peninsula there is a call of the south.' In his novel *The Stone Raft*, published the year Spain and Portugal signed the Treaty of Rome, he imagines that the Pyrenees split and set Iberia adrift to float first west and then south, ending up between Angola and Brazil, 'on the line which in those glorious days had divided the world into two parts, one to you, one to me, one to you'.

Once I stopped to buy bread, cheese and fruit in Tordesillas on my way from Vallodolid to Salamanca without realising its importance. It's a town with a fortress high on the right bank of the Duero, the Portuguese Douro. In 1493 the pope had drawn a line from pole to pole a hundred leagues west of the Cape Verde Islands. God gave Spain all the world to the west and Portugal all the world to the east in return for converting the heathen. This should have settled arguments arising from Columbus's voyage of 1492, but the line didn't allow enough sea room for Portuguese navigators. The treaty signed at Tordesillas on 7 June 1494 shifted it another 270 leagues west. So when Pedro Álvares Cabral on his way to India bumped into Brazil, on 22 April 1500, he could claim it for Portugal although (whisper this) Vicente Yáñez Pinzón, a Spanish navigator, had got there first, earlier in the year. A little Castilian town stands for the vast arrogance of a Europe that could divide the world in two to build the empire of one god above all others.

Tomorrow would be Columbus Day in Alcántara and all Spain. But was Cristóbal Colón Spanish? Was he a Genoese-born Spanish Jew? Was he really an Italian, like Cabral's pilot Amerigo Vespucci who gave his name to the Americas? Or was Cristóvão Colombo Portuguese? The Florentine cosmographer who urged him to go west believed he was. Columbus fought with Portugal against Genoa in a battle off Cape St Vincent. Recently, Dr Mascarenhas Barreto has claimed he was a spy for Dom João II, born illegitimate, but a great-nephew of Henry the Navigator, in the Alentejan town of Cuba. Maybe. Whatever Columbus's birthright, the Portuguese laughed at his arithmetic. They knew the Orient couldn't be as close as he thought, going west, although if he'd calculated in

Arabic miles rather than Italian ones he'd have been almost spot on. Still, Fernando and Isabella recruited him and his presumption for Spain and, while out looking for Japan, he found a few Caribbean islands.

12 October. Whoever Columbus was, I woke to his day, and Spain's. I stretched the deep creases out of my body at the open window. High above town an eagle cruised. Down in the street a boy emptied a fat water-pistol through a grille in the wall of a shuttered shop. At the back of San Pedro's church stood bags of rubble and a wheelbarrow. Beside it an ancient house was being patched with red brick, tiles and cement balustrading. A large woman in black tugged at a white poodle on a lead. A man in a pale blue cap saluted her from his mule.

The town ended abruptly at the ruined convent of the nuns of the Military Order of Alcántara. A man led a donkey laden with ripe oats into his yard. It stumbled beneath its wild blond thatch. But for the farmer's boilersuit the scene was medieval. Small tan pigs nuzzled the soil. A cockerel crowed and strutted before compliant hens. Cows with long bells at their necks chimed along their regular route to pasture between walls and terraces of Moorish fortifications that stepped, crumbling, down the hill. I scrambled along to one of several shepherds' huts. It was a rock igloo with a wispy toupee of parched grasses and corroded moss. Inside a low doorway dry-stone darkness was cool and rank. The corbelled roof effortlessly held off the sky.

A stone track, with angled setts like fishbones joining a central spine, dropped from town towards the Tagus. The Roman road I'd searched for along the far bank should have looked like that. Down below, the Roman bridge was no myth. It fitted snugly between steep slopes: six circular arches on five granite piers, two growing from the banks and three rising from slate-blue water to support a road and a triumphal arch 170 feet above the river. Such elegance was almost too perfect to be real. If its pillars had been strings and the Tagus a flow of air, it would have sung like an aeolian harp.

Below a hairpin bend in the track a stream seeped through a plot of cabbages and beans on poles, lemon and fig trees. Beyond

that, at bridge level, a man with a German shepherd dog opened
up a plastic bag. His grey trousers with a blue stripe down each
leg had once been part of a uniform.

'Food for the cats,' he said.

The dog sat. Stray cats in magnificent condition jumped up from
the vegetable garden and tumbled from fruit trees. The cats ate
warily, greedily. The dog sat. The man mewed.

'If I'm alone, they come close. They sit on my lap.'

I left him alone and they did. The bridge that had looked like
a neat scale-model wedged into the valley was a mighty monument
now. Sandmartins perched, appliquéd like heraldic birds, against
the masonry. Each arch, about a hundred feet wide, was constructed
of eight-ton voussoir stones. A temporary timber arch must have
been built off the springings, the stone segments winched up perhaps by treadmill-powered pulley-blocks and fitted together like a
puzzle. They'd been cut with such accuracy that the joints needed
no mortar. The architect Caius Julius Lacer had here in AD 105–
6 brought Roman bridge-building to its apogee. At its south end
he raised a small temple sacred to the Emperor Trajan and the gods.
Four-way skulls perched on its rear gable. How many died to bridge
the river in such style? Through an iron gate at the temple's pillared
portico I could see altars under a solid granite beam and information
framed behind glass. The glass was smashed, the writing illegible.
Two cars purred over the bridge's heavy-duty paving in the direction
of Portugal.

At that north end the sixteenth-century Torre del Oro, Tower
of Gold, reared up from the hillside, last remnant of many defences
that have adorned the bridge. It was built for Carlos V, one of
many restorers of the Roman work in a long history of war-damage
and vandalism. As it now stands the bridge's triumphal arch bears
inscriptions to Queen Isabel II and to him, who after repairing
depredations of war and age in 1543 wasn't shy of claiming a share
of the builder's glory: CAROLVS. V. IMP. CÆSAR. AVGVSTVS.
HISPANIORVMQUE. REX . . . 'Carlos V, Emperor, Caesar Augus-
tus and King of the Spains . . .'

Two contemporary guardians of the bridge continually patrolled
its two-hundred-yard length. One of them, a small round man with
fathomless eyes, made it his business to accost pedestrians. At most

there were four of us. I had to take my turn. He informed me that I stood on a Roman bridge and plucked me a sprig of dill. His companion paced to and fro. Mercifully, three cyclists waved me over. They were the serious sort – with grey hair, garish muscle-and-rib-defining shirts, black lycra buttock-shrinking shorts – but they grinned wildly.

'Will you take our photo please?'

They were Spaniards offering minute automated cameras. I took shots while they posed, jubilant at making it to *al-kantara* on Columbus Day. They wanted themselves, and bikes like pollen-heavy insects, framed by the triumphal arch. Or close-up with authentic sweat and a hand on the glinting granite parapet above the dwindling Tagus gorge. But not the view upstream, no, not the river sluicing out of a tall chill concrete dam.

On the far bank a track ran downstream between cacti, olive trees, figs and beehives like a terrace of tenements in a gully where a man repairing an old wall raised his trowel to me. Over the river Moorish walls and bastions made a maze of shadow on the hill. An eagle hung above it. A heron sat on a rock above a milky waterfall that I discovered later was the town's effluent. It looked picturesque. Hoopoes flashed and kingfishers quartered the stream. At my feet autumn crocuses spurted from parched soil like gas-jets. Broom or tamarisk dangled pale yellow bean pods. Cyprus trees mingled with eucalyptus. Crickets with banded legs kept up their inane electronic banter. Clouded yellow butterflies sunned themselves. And swallowtails.

An open gate and a cattle-grid led into a hunting preserve. The idea of a Roman road on this side had become so fixed in my mind, thanks to the description in the guide book, that I still wanted to see it although I knew better. I ignored the notice. I told myself that cow-pats were *cow*-pats not bull-dung. Here it was, shaly setts and all. I followed it until I could see that it ended, or climbed uphill out of sight. I knew it would. Hopes, false ones anyway, are a cause of lost energy, hours, lives. A dirty man in khaki with shotgun, cartridge belt and scraggy crème-caramel-coloured bitch drew closer and closer along the track. He passed me without a word. A sudden wind funnelled up the gorge, rippling the river like fear stroking skin. Back at the bridge, where stone paving gave way to tarmac, the pods on acacia trees rattled with the sound of shook foil.

That night bells called a stream, then a persistent trickle of people to San Pedro's mass. I went to the renovated hotel that had been *Hotel Puente Romano* but was now *Kantara Al-Saif*, 'bridge of the sword'. Moors gave the town that name. They smashed the bridge but lost the battle to the knights in 1214. Both sides knew the legend of the golden sword embedded within Roman masonry. A woman at the bar abused the barman for hanging on the phone. She smiled and stared at me. In the restaurant there were plenty of tables where I could think my own thoughts. A man in cycling gear joined me.

'My name is Augustín,' he said. 'I am Basque.'

He was pedalling through the Spains.

'When I have finished this tour I will have done all its provinces,' he said, adding, 'and Portugal's.'

Augustín, it turned out, was *trans-iberismo* on wheels.

'Today is bad,' he said. I anticipated a few Basque doubts about *Hispanidad*, but he explained, 'I have had four punctures and a camera malfunction.'

He had taken years of holidays to complete his route. He brought out a creased newspaper cutting with a photo of him studying maps. I thought of plans and dreams. Soon they would be finished. A hand comes up and draws Excalibur down into the lake. The golden sword lies deep within the bridge. The crock of gold sits at the rainbow's end.

'Still,' Augustín was saying, 'it's something to write back to my girlfriend. I write my diary and send it to her. I was married before but . . . Are you staying in this hotel?'

'No,' I laughed, 'I have a very small bed in town.'

'I have a tent. I'll pitch it out of town. The only real trouble I had was in Portugal, in Évora, where four boys beat me up. They broke my finger, but the bike was OK.'

We ate for some time in silence. A palely-loitering blank-faced waiter stood and watched us, playing with the small change in his tight white trousers.

'Crime in towns is increasing, but I like the countryside,' Augustín continued. 'I'm amazed to see working donkeys here, and seed still broadcast by hand. That's very rare now in Spain.'

More like 1492, I thought, when the urban crime rate was increasing, when blackamoors were driven out of Granada, when Jews were expelled from Aragon and Castile, when, in order to purge Hispania and convert the heathen, Columbus set sail westwards on a mission to misplaced China. By that time the knights of the Military Order and the nuns of the Holy Spirit had fought and prayed against the infidel for almost three centuries from their base in Alcántara. This lovely landscape was Extremadura, extremist and hard-nosed, from which so many *conquistadors* set out. Tomorrow Augustín would push on to complete his task. Before crossing the bridge to the old frontier I planned my own pilgrimage, a short one to the Hermitage of Nuestra Señora de los Hilos. *Hilos* means 'threads'. I planned to gather up loose ones there.

Next afternoon, I missed my way and blundered through farms above the Alcántara reservoir. When I found it near dusk, the hermitage comprised a sturdy church and quarters designed for a fat priest or caretaker, not an ascetic saint. Three men and a dog sat in the porch. It all dated back to the *Reconquista* from the Moors, but had been rebuilt in 1768 when a new image was installed. The light within was rare, the virgin backlit by a lustrous golden reredos. Always in Iberia the shock of contrast, disconnection, contradiction between outside and inside, *fora/dentro*. Our Lady was a numinous nymph. Outside, a sign read '*de los Hitos*'. The name on my Michelin map was a figment of the cartographer's imagination. The men laughed.

'Not *hilos*,' one thwacked his thigh with a switch, 'but *hitos*.'

No loose threads at all, but a line drawn taut for *Nuestra Señora de los Hitos*, Our Lady of the Boundary Stones.

13

HOW PORTUGUESE!

Idanha-a-Velha and Monsanto

A HUMBLE ROMAN bridge of four arches spans the piddling Rio Ponsul at Idanha-a-Velha. By the causeway leading to it a stout woman in a rusty-black fedora and wellington boots tilled a plot with a mattock beside her cabbage patch. Her peppers were festive lights. Pumpkins glowed like fire balloons. Her gingham apron with its bulging pocket was back-to-front like a bustle.

'This is rich soil,' she said, 'but our village is very poor.'

The alluvium here had once been rich indeed. A nearby altar was dedicated to Jupiter in gratitude for a find of fourteen hundred ounces of gold. Celtic Idanha had been developed by the Romans into one of the biggest, richest cities of Lusitania. It was called Igaeditania. An inscription of 16 BC tells us that Quintus Iallius of Mérida 'gave a sun clock to the Igaeditanans, out of good will'. It contributed gold to the building of Alcántara's strategic and prestigious bridge and heads the list of donor municipalities carved on the triumphal arch there.

It hadn't taken long to get here from Alcántara. I'd driven over the bridge, taken a last look at it, at the grey dam and the blue magpies flying between, then climbed into the rugged granite moorland around Piedras Albas, 'white stones'. Just before Segura on its hill I'd crossed the Rio Erjas (Spanish) or Erges (Portuguese). It flows into the Tagus at a point just seven miles downriver from Alcántara and is the frontier from there northwards to its source. By the bridge that crossed it I'd noticed the police checkpoint too late. It didn't matter; *trans-iberismo*, or rather *trans-EUismo*, had seen to that.

The road had at once become rough, potholed, with a swell on it at corners where the tarmac had ridden up in hot weather. How Portuguese! This useful phrase had been taught me by Lisbon friends. As a foreigner I could hardly employ it for fear of insulting someone, but they used it whenever they were faced with something second-rate or third-world. They'd toss the head, turn up the nose, make a disdainful *muxôxo* or 'tck!' with the tongue and say, 'How Portuguese!' It's subtle, because only a superior people can express an inferiority complex that way.

Every so often workmen were desultorily sifting gravel from shovels onto bald spots. There were miles of this apparently useless patching and, where tar had occasionally been poured, the tar-gravel mix had risen in boils and carbuncles. On one stretch Romany women with rough scarves knotted round their heads were crouched with buckets at the roadside, cleaning and buffing up the red-and-white kilometre markers. Our Ladies of the Milestones. At the Aravil stream a derelict bus was shored up by lean-to shacks and surrounded by motley cattle. A yapping dog launched itself from the verge and flew at the car. While I swerved the dog, tied to a long string, was brought up short with a curtailed bark. His gypsy master stood back by his immobile home and I hardly had time to register his sour smirk.

Soon I dropped down a slow hill with a sight of the holy mountain, Monsanto, in the distance and Idanha-a-Velha in the middle-ground. An instant of pure Umbria. This once-wealthy place was a small village, but boasted the buildings of an ancient town. The gold had run out. The sun clock's shadow might as well have turned widdershins. On a raised floor of massive flat stones two men and four women with flails threshed grain in a mist of husk. A patient hound sat up like a sentry. At intervals the men shovelled golden grain into tall sacks and poured fresh ears onto the threshing floor. All morning sacks moved across the floor, emptied, folded, filled. It was no idyll. The labourers were old and the work hard. In Portuguese, *debulhar* is 'to thresh'. *Debulhar se em lágrimas* is to thresh yourself (or dissolve) into tears. Emigration had emptied the village and nothing would fill it with life. Once set firmly down in a loop of the Ponsul with the river defending it on three sides, now it rattled around in Roman walls several sizes too large.

The archway at the north gate opened into a dig, a grand archaeological site where people lived and scratched a living. In a cobbled square where the Manueline *pelourhino* stood I found a café half-open. A woman with a fly-whisk battled to repel insects besieging her tired pastries and served me a half-warm *galão* or milky coffee in a tall glass. Outside, by a table and four ill-assorted empty chairs, a bar-football table slumped drunkenly and silently, like a memorial to vanished youth. Brownstone houses had quoins of granite blocks that looked far too big, as though they'd been cut for grander buildings. The place was full of memories but had been struck dumb. Someone had forgotten to hire the actors. There were a handful of bit parts of course. A man tugged a bottle of wine out of a crate in a truck and grinned at me as he walked past. The driver snatched it back with a guffaw. He was parked under an official blue banner celebrating patrimony and 'the Future of the Past'.

Igaeditania was sacked and burnt by the Swabians in 420. The Visigoths rebuilt it a century or so later. Their Egitânia was created a diocese in 599 and had a mint licensed to coin gold *trientes*. I clambered among the footings of the bishop's palace beside the small basilica. The faith for which the Sé now stood was faith in the past. I glimpsed Roman inscriptions and raw archaeological riches through a chink in one locked door. Another had a steeply pointed moulding above it, framing the crucifix, armillary sphere and arms of a later Portugal, but at the south end a marble bath and associated niches preserved under a corrugated shack were the substantial remains of its sixth- or seventh-century baptistry. At least in legend, Egitânia was the birthplace of King Wamba who, as you may remember, was elected in 672 but given a hard time by Basques and Gauls, and then by his own nobles and churchmen after he called clergy up for military service. He was shaved, deposed and banished. The Moors sacked the city in 713 and called it Idanha.

Washing hung beside the Templars' Tower. Its chunky granite was all in proportion and founded on the podium of a Roman temple which tradition ascribes to Venus. Love, prayer and war. Unlike Wamba's clergy the Knights Templar were the sword in Christ's hand, monks with a military vocation. Alfonso III of León had taken Idanha during the *Reconquista*; it was set in the county (not yet country) of Portucale that Alfonso IV gave to Count Henry of Burgundy as part of his wife's dowry. Their son Afonso Henriques, *o Conquistador*, gave it to the Templars for safekeeping. Dom Sancho II gave it a charter in 1229, and Dom Manuel I would give it another one in 1510. Still the inhabitants moved away from their city of bad luck to Monsanto or Idanha-a-Nova. But why? After its bishopric was removed to Guarda in 1199 it fell victim, so the story goes, to a plague of ants which lasted a hundred years. This metaphor for a protracted curse may be illuminated by knowing that the ant has always been a form taken by *bruxas*, witches. Well, if you can't find a reason, you have to invent one.

There was no door at ground level into the Templars' Tower. I climbed a plank and got in at a pointed window. There was nothing more than naked stone inside. What did I expect? After the Frankish king persuaded the pope to ban the Templars in 1312, Dom Dinis gave Idanha and other Templar holdings to his newly-created Order of Christ. He believed in continuity. The pope turned a blind eye. Through the simple, transparently self-supporting arch of the town's south gate, a paved road led directly to a grove where women picked up olives from the ground between trees. A half-roofed barn within the walls contained a heap of cut stones, fallen joists and a great granite basin with a trio of stone pressing-wheels ready to roll. I wanted to hear that rumble, that crushing sound. I wanted the boys and girls to come back from fields and distant factories, or wherever else they were hiding, to come home and play table-football and pop music and make babies. Information published by the town council – that of Idanha-a-Nova (Idanha-the-New), ten miles away, under whose jurisdiction Idanha-the-Old has been since 1811 – claimed that 'the efforts being made by archaeologists, ethnologists and other specialists in the various relevant scientific areas, backed up by properly structured and financed projects, should restore the village of Idanha-a-Velha to its undeniable value in terms of history and heritage.'

It was a site, a dig, all the eerier for being half-alive. As I found my way towards the Roman bridge a huge noise started up. A drill driven by a thudding compressor rattled within the sounding-box of a stone house. A man in dungarees wheeled a barrow up two old doors on planks and tipped rubble into the back of a lorry. It was a relief, a joyful din. On the high plinth of granite blocks on which houses facing the river perched, two old men in black hats gossiped. One had little sight, a stick, an Adidas sweatshirt. Beside the Roman bridge a mattock sliced – shoink, shoink! – into dark earth. The woman who wielded it had her bulging apron on backwards. She smiled up at me.

'This is rich soil,' she said, 'but our village is very poor.'

High on its holy mountain, just three miles away as the crow flies, squats the town of Monsanto. I caught an early bus to it a few days later. We drove out of the warm dark through dawn mists clinging to contours and snaking above streams. Granite boulders material- ised. A gypsy woman slept with her bundles on the seats. A smart young woman with tightly bound hair got off, together with some of her raucous pupils, at school in Idanha-a-Nova. As an old man alighted he tweaked the ear of a silver-haired woman in the front seat, then tweaked it again. The bus rocked with mirth. Soon the bus was almost empty and driving through medieval Portugal, between pomegranates and vines, tight town walls and bent bal- conies, or above drops to lush plots and pocket-handkerchief fields watered by wells. Donkeys with panniers or bundles of hay slowed us. We circled around the hill of rocks, its skirts of olive groves hooped and gathered by dry-stone walls, then climbed.

The Spanish Civil War, hatched in Estoril, began in July 1936. At the end of September the Portuguese Legion was formed. We are, remember, in Salazar's New State. In October, Portuguese Youth put seven- to fourteen-year-olds in forage caps, green shirts and belts with S on the metal buckle. S for Salazar. S for Sebastião. It drilled its members in the use of wooden guns and the fascist salute. German air force officers trained in Portugal for Franco's service. Matériel from German freighters was forwarded daily from Lisbon by rail. A Portuguese expeditionary force, called *viriatos* after the Lusitanian hero Viriato who repelled the Romans between 147 and 139 BC, served alongside Italian divisions and the German force. Arms stockpiled in Spain by Portuguese democrats for use against Salazar were urgently appropriated. Franco's rebellion, they say, defeated both Spanish and Portuguese democracy at a stroke. Though dissident Portuguese volunteers fought against Franco, Portugal itself was to be insulated from free Europe for a long time. It recognised Franco's government in Burgos in 1938, the same year that a beauty contest was organised for Portuguese villages. Of nine finalists, Monsanto was declared 'the most Portuguese village in Portugal'. It still boasts this title. But how can it be so Portuguese when there's nowhere else like it in the country? Maybe Portugal has shrunk to the size of a hill of boulders whose unique village thus merits the accolade 'most Portuguese'. In 1938 Monsanto's population was three thousand. Now, it's not even two hundred. 'Once we were so great, now we are so small.' But still proud. How Portuguese!

A silver cockerel on Monsanto's church-tower pirouetted in the breeze. One moment it looked down to a distant hazy plain, the next it turned to face a boulder as tall as the church. A row of houses seemed ordinary enough, except that one was a hulk of granite overshadowing the street. Here a house crouched between stones, two walls of masonry, two of solid rock, a frail human-scale home between Scylla and Charybdis. There worn steps climbed past a warm grey house with green doors to a lichen-covered boulder poised to roll downhill, and hens cooped behind wire in the crevice beneath it. That's how the place is, pinched shadows between granite globes, elegant townhouses, small courts of herbs and flowering trees, steep stairs between rocks and cottage doors, claustrophobic alleys weighed down under the sense of impending mass, sheer drops and gulps of air.

At a viewpoint, where cannon pointed their snouts over a dwarf village below and towards the mountains, three workmen prised up setts and dug trenches to bury electricity-supply cables. All poles and pylons were to be felled, they said, all wires were going underground. Since 1938 the threads of power had become horribly tangled in Monsanto's maze, and patrimony demanded that the town should look primitive in a pristine kind of way. For tourists, naturally. For them old buildings had been demolished to make way for a new *pousada*.

'A crime,' said a workmen, 'pulling down anything for that!'

It was built in granite, sure, but granite employed like breeze-blocks, framing a self-consciously classy entrance and topped with a range of gymnasium-style windows.

'A crime,' he breathed, more vehemently the second time.

Polythene bags full of water hung in many picturesque doorways. I asked the workman what this meant.

'It's a habit that's spread from the Alentejo,' he laughed, 'to keep away flies. I don't believe in it.'

How Portuguese! Upwards I heard water trickling into a rocky basin. The elemental plumbing looked unaccountably twee, though a notice announced: 'Water from this Spring Quenched the Thirst of Obscure Heroes.' I was thirsty and chilly. I found the workmen again in the one open bar in town. We were the only customers. I wanted breakfast.

'Have you bread rolls?' I asked the gloomy patron. He looked doubtful. 'Or a sandwich? Pastries or cakes?'

He looked at his wife. She was feeding their daughter on a high stool behind the counter with something like porridge from a spoon. The girl was a woman of about twenty. Her navy blue tracksuit bulged with a nappy. As spoon reached mouth, her head twitched sideways. Her staring eyes were fierce and her hands were clenched. Arms and legs danced an involuntary jig. Her mother glanced up and shook her head.

'No,' he said, 'no bread or pastries or cakes.'

I was thinking, what Portuguese café does not overflow with an abundance of these basic luxuries? And, how good it is not to hide your adult child with cerebral palsy in a back room but to let her live where the life is, where customers can like it or lump it. And again, what patron has to ask his wife whether he has bread? All thought was cut short when he served me a steaming hot *galão*, or rather threw it at me. That is, he thrust it forward onto the counter with more momentum than was strictly necessary. Pure accident. The tall glass tipped and coffee sluiced out in an arc. I jumped. It mostly missed. He quietly apologised and half-heartedly wiped the counter while he made me another. His wife hectored him and grumbled to herself as she thoroughly mopped floor-tiles and counter-front.

There were good paintings on the walls and bold ceramics on a big table. Were some of them the patron's own work? He looked

160

more artist than caterer. He nodded, grudgingly. Books by Dr Fernando Namora filled a bookstand. Namora is perhaps the most widely-known Portuguese writer and was the patron's friend until his death in 1989. A notice in town had pointed me to his house. It was a shrine. As a young newly-qualified doctor he practised here and married a Monsanto bride. One of his books, *Retalhos da Vida de um Médico*, is published in English as *Mountain Doctor*. In *Domingo á Tarde* ('Sunday Afternoon') he examines the small print of a doctor's contract with death. Here in Monsanto he had worked alongside the magic arts – both 'sympathetic' and 'contagious' – as practised by local *bruxas*. Here too, for sale in the café, were instruments of women's work: square tambourine-like drums called *adufes*, and *marafonas*, faceless dolls built on wooden crosses.

Something to eat was what I wanted. I tried to find an open shop. It was early Friday morning, it shouldn't have been difficult. But invisible bread and flying coffee made me question my luck. It was in the first hours of Tuesdays and Fridays, after all, that witches stripped naked, anointed their skins with unguent kept under the hearth-stone, pronounced the spell *'Por cima de silvais/E por baixo de olivais'* ('Over dog roses and beneath olive trees'), disappeared up their chimneys and met together at convenient crossroads. Nothing was quite right. I began to feel a bit like the man in the Portuguese and Basque tale who overheard the words, but spoke them in the wrong order – 'Beneath dog roses . . .' – and fetched up at the coven in tatters. I found myself in the depths of a small shop that called itself a supermarket. Nothing took my fancy. In desperation I bought biscuits and persimmons. Outside I drew breath.

'Did you get the right change?' a man whispered. 'You have to watch that one. He discovered a pot of gold here, I'm sure of that, though he denies it, and sells off the coins one by one.'

If this was the end of the rainbow I wanted to go back to the beginning. An old woman took my arm and led me into a gap between houses. She had a basket hidden there, covered with a cloth. She drew back the shroud to reveal a grubby blank-faced *marafona* like the ones I'd seen in the bar.

'I am willing to sell it to you,' she said.

Maybe she was a genuine *bruxa* and the doll's grubbiness a sign of authenticity. *Bruxa* is 'witch' first and 'rag-doll' second. *Marafona* means 'rag-doll', then 'harridan' or 'whore'. The language is loaded against strong wise women, or foolish ones.

Up slippery steps and a steep path I came to pigsties, each a low turf-covered stone hut and a wall of heaped rocks enclosing a granite trough. A millennium hence, serious archaeologists will pronounce them shrines. Pigs, awaiting sacrifice on Martinmas, greeted me with snuffling chortles which set dogs off who didn't share their sense of humour. In a pen beyond they whined and howled and wailed as if I were some misbegotten sprite.

A bleak grotto between boulders had been unconvincingly sanctified with a cross. Above it a man sat by the track with dried figs, unripe fresh ones and pomegranates for sale. He was engrossed in stitching the upper to the sole of a new shoe. Was he a prophet too, like the cobbler of Trancoso? What future, what fifth empire fermented in his mind? His friend, who materialised beside him, had very clear plans. He would guide me to the castle. He had Chinese eyes and an African mouth. He was not exactly fat, but fleshy, and more, too fleshly, out of kilter in Manichaean terms. His flesh/spirit balance was upset.

'He is two sexes,' a woman told me later, 'and has forty cats.'

'Ah,' I said, 'that explains it.'

'He returned here after many years,' she said, 'to sell up his family house. It was summer, so he saw all the tourists who are not here today, thanks be to God, and he said, My life is here. He doesn't sleep. If he hears someone in the early hours he fixes them with his torch and says, Do you want a guide?'

He fixed me with an unnerving gaze. I said no. Not over or under the dog roses. Not behind the boulders. I insisted. No.

As I climbed the atmosphere grew heavier. It was warmer but I felt clammy. The town that had seemed so high up looked like a grey-and-terracotta model village among pebbles below. Lidless keyhole-shaped sarcophagi lay beside the roofless ruin of the church of São Miguel among remains of the old village. An archway incised with runes led up into the crown of granite, part natural, part fashioned, that the holy mountain wore. Masonry that would have looked massive anywhere else was daintily fitted between colossal rocks and neatly pieced together upon gigantic fragments, to make walls, castellations, stairways and gates. In a bleak court a newly-roofed chapel squatted, its doors barred. A vast boulder poised at the brink of a well. Had it toppled the well would have choked on it. Here overlaid were a Lusitanian hill town, a Roman stronghold, a Visigothic fortress and this Templar castle rebuilt by Dom Dinis. I sat on a plinth of rock at the highest point, 2,500 feet. Black-and-tan goats with hobbled hooves clambered and grazed. Birds flew below. Clouds swept in from the south-east dragging skirts of rain. Plains spread away to dimly-lit *serras*. It should have been exhilarating. It was forbidding. I should have risen above the oppressive town and the weight of the hill itself, but up here on the peak it was as though the mass of the mountain and its inner darkness hung like a volcanic cloud above my head and relentlessly bore down.

On 3 May each year, at the Festa das Cruzes (crosses), women chant songs to the rhythm of square *adufe* drums as they are beaten up to the summit. Pitchers of flowers and a floral calf are tossed from the heights to commemorate the lifting of a legendary siege. The defenders fed their last corn to their last beast and, in a gesture of prodigal deceit, threw the fatted calf over the battlements. Their besiegers gave up and went home. Now, at the *festa*, the oldest women sing a triumphant dirge to celebrate those obscure heroes and dance with *marafonas*, the faceless ones who give protection against thunderstorms. I could see that the bruised clouds were going to bypass the hill today, not wet or strike this castle. In 1815 the stronghold was still complete. Then on Christmas Eve the governor forbade the traditional burning of the cork-oak trunk before the church. He burnt it in his own hearth. His impertinence was rewarded with a spectacular thunderstorm. One bolt of lightning, and this is for sure, hit the castle's powder magazine. The explosion ripped out the castle's heart and, so the story goes, made fire-irons fly from the hearth and strike the governor dead.

Someone must have had good cause to curse him: *Raios te partam!* 'May thunderbolts cleave you!' Thunderbolts are rocks which hit the earth and bury themselves seven metres deep, then rise up through the soil a metre a year until, after seven years, they surface. Placed on house roofs they are specifics against lightning strikes. You'd think Monsanto should be safe enough by that reckoning, for the whole place might as well be made of thunderbolts. But the coveted *pedras de raio* are not boulders. They turn out to be small prehistoric arrowheads or hammer stones. Sympathetic magic has become tangled with atavistic half-memories. On this unquiet peak my mood was low. The holy mountain belied its name. It felt bad-spirited, unholy. I felt as though I perched on an anvil. I ate my biscuits and sliced into a persimmon that looked succulent but dried my mouth instantly as a blast of breath from a forge does, or a gust of fear.

I left the fruit for goats or ravens. Down in the bar the glum patron served me a beer with no mistake, but there were still no pastries or sandwiches. A big-framed handsome man drew me aside and introduced himself, the first person here to do so.

'José Reinaldo,' he shook hands firmly. 'I'm in the merchant marine but love this place. I survive long periods at sea. There you have to have an inner life. I first came here to show two Swedish girls the real Portugal. It was my first visit of course. Naturally I fell in love and now I have four houses here.'

Every Portuguese is supposed to be susceptible to the call of the sea, and every sailor has his *saudades* for his native soil. This one had four footholds on an adopted holy hill.

He leant closer. 'But the patron, he is a good man. Today he is shocked, he is not himself because there's bad trouble.'

'Trouble?' I said.

'Last night he was threatened with a gun.'

'Why?'

'Oh, some argument, you know, but in such a peaceful place . . .'

'Who with?'

'The baker came in with a handgun and said he'd shoot him.'

I'd seen the bakehouse. Now the bar's lack of bread, pastries and cakes made sense. The sailor's paradise had been sullied. My unholy mountain had been demythologised.

The bus had brought me uphill, but to be carried away from this place I had to walk down and catch it at the bottom. I met a woman and a donkey laden with firewood and cloth-wrapped bundles. A cloak was cowled over her black hat. She had bushy eyebrows above dark eyes that glared at me with understandable resentment or inexplicable malevolence.

Smoke rose from the roadside. A woman with her hat on top of her scarf led a dappled grey mule by the head collar backwards and forwards, to and from a bonfire of scrub among the olive trees. Her man walked behind, one hand and his weight on a plough bobbing and jerking through stony soil, his free hand wielding a switch. Furrows were short and shaved olive trunks. At each headland she turned the blinkered mule while he manhandled the plough so that its share would bite and cut true. Above them Monsanto rose to its full height, a huddle of dwellings high on its rocks and half-hidden between boulders.

But I was out of its shadow. In the village at its foot I ate a big ham roll in a dark café while women and boys came in to make payments to the woman at the counter. She took money, stamped documents heavily and handed them back with weary resignation. I was carefree. In the airy square a piebald dog came at me, growling, but was called off by a man up a ladder. He was shaking down olives which two women were picking off the cobbles and heaping into plastic bowls. A third woman with two teeth grinned gaily at me from her seat on a horizontal lamp standard. It was a new concrete one waiting to be erected. She patted it and I sat down to wait. The man came down his ladder and told me that all the olive trees in the *praça* were his. He had worked in the electrical goods business in Lisbon.

'This place,' he said sadly, 'is now no use to anyone.'

'The young ones have gone to Lisbon,' said one of the women, 'for the money.' They rubbed thumbs and forefingers.

On cue a squat creature with hat, scarf, apron and woollen leggings hobbled past weighed down by bulky bags. She might have hopped off a misericord. All at once everyone shouted and waved at the bus. I waved back at them as I boarded it with the creature and another elderly woman. We paid our fares to the driver who was young and fat and sweaty. The second woman sat on his briefcase by mistake when the bus lurched forward. He shouted at her and screamed abuse at them both as he flung us round corners and thugged through narrow lanes with no regard for donkey-carts or pedestrians carrying loads on their heads. He was crazed. They got off two villages later.

After that he drove calmly and steadily. I was his only passenger.

165

He turned to me, lifted eyes to heaven and clicked his tongue as if to say, 'God, how Portuguese! Doesn't it get you down, doesn't all this olde worlde stuff get on your tits?'

14

A LITTLE ALENTEJO

Pego and Évora

TRACHEOTOMY may or may not be a common surgical procedure in Portugal, but I saw several men with hoarse muscular voices and flaps of quivering gauze fixed to their throats by sticking-plaster hinges. One such man stood on the station platform at Castelo Branco. He looked like a small powdered dummy gone apoplectic. I was on my way from the province of Beira Baixa, with its Portuguesest of all villages, to the Ribatejo and a place on the Tagus's south bank nicknamed 'a little Alentejo in the Ribatejo'. I was moving from claustrophobia to the wide spaces. The small man's arms flung about him with alarming violence. Had they connected with anything beyond his own wound-up body they would have done damage. He ached to shout but could only gulp imprecations and wheeze out a huge frustration whose immediate object was a large wife who moved luggage about silently while he raved. He clutched a handkerchief to the hole in his throat and heaved up sputum.

The shift in latitude I was anticipating was psychic rather than geographical, superficially southwards, yes, but more deeply towards the 'south'. The metaphysical south on the heart's map. A blonde woman in a plump plaid suit recruited a team of tame men who sprang into action when the train pulled in; they ordered all her packages on luggage racks or under seats and then reordered them according to further instructions. Outside, unreeling and meshing dry-stone fences. Walled wells with long levers. Pine trees and heathers. Long views across sunken plains to the Serra da Estrêla. Cultivated gardens among ruins. Swathes of spiky, charred forest.

Stench of caramelised sap. My neighbour was a gentleman whose Roman nose, sensuously-sculpted lips and splendid head thatched with short white hair surely qualified him for a toga, not the fawn-and-cream tweed jacket, morning-suit trousers and grey suede brothel-creepers he actually wore. He was a lively peasant, full of twinkles and chatter about food and foreigners and high prices. He must have broken hearts. He sliced the corner off a carton with a pocket knife against his great thumb and poured milk down his throat in an arc like wine from a skin. Dry stream-beds and steep ravines gave way, as we dropped, to fields on the hills. One figure, a slender African woman with a twist of purple cloth round her head and gold earrings swinging, bent to her mattock.

At Vila Velha de Ródão I should have been alert for the Tagus but my eye was taken by a girl who got in and sat on the other side of the carriage. She had cropped yellow hair and a face almost fine, but coarse, with an aura that might have been fey or brute. I caught the Portas de Ródão and, below them, the dancers of stone amongst olive trees, stolid monoliths and sharp shards, little inlets full of dead trees, steep tiers of shimmering eucalyptus. As the river broadened and deepened, I thought about the rock art under water. At Fratel a middle-aged man got on, inspected us all and took the seat facing the yellow-haired girl. He gave her a long, sourly self-indulgent glance, slid his tie from his collar and folded it tight. She put booted feet on the seat beside her, curled up and shut her eyes. Below Fratel's hydroelectric dam there was a big drop, the water fast and boiling like hot syrup, sluicing, erupting, spinning with counter-currents between jagged reefs. The man shed his emerald-and-gold tweed jacket. He swivelled the waistband of his sage-green trousers and reassembled his genitals between wide-spread thighs. The tumultuous Tagus swirled round islands of trees. Herons rose in numbers from gravelly cliffs. Egrets lifted from sheeps' backs with a flickering of wings. The man unbuttoned his blue-striped shirt to reveal a white vest, unfurled a handkerchief – a blue-and-white floral one – and mopped his armpits thoroughly. On the rugged height above Belver station a fairy-tale castle was decked with flags and banners. It was held by the Order of Hospitallers of St John of Jerusalem and was rebuilt in 1390 by Nuno Álvares Pereira, the Holy Constable. My fellow passenger slowly raked the sleeping girl head to toe, toe to head with his eyes and meditated, holding the crumpled handkerchief before his face for a long time. Above Belver dam unhealthily bright slicks of algae clung along banks and weirs. Below it, the south bank of the river began to flatten like a dying wave, to flatten and spread south, 'south'. The man buttoned his shirt and checked his assets: gold watch, gold spectacles, wad of banknotes, notepad, gold pen. A colossus rose above the far bank, the chimney of the generating plant called Central de Pego. An inlet station stood in the river, a still temple. Cooling water cascaded down concrete ledges opposite the ruins of an old quay. The man stretched his beige cotton cap and fitted it on. Having undressed and ravished the yellow-haired girl several times over, it was time to stand up, stretch himself and prepare to alight. She opened her eyes.

Pego's red-and-white-banded chimney rises high above a pair of curvaceous cooling towers which themselves dwarf the rest of the thermo-electric power station. Black smoke, white steam. Water returned to the river by pipeline and cascade is supposed to be barely two degrees warmer than when it was drawn out. Two coal trains a day, each drawn by two diesel locomotives, feed the plant. A pile of European money is going into automated signalling and electrification of the line from Lisbon which will permit four trains a day to satisfy Pego's appetite. The plant will burn the coal to heat the river to produce the steam to generate the power to drive the trains to carry the coal . . .

It was on St John's Eve that I first visited Pego proper. The power station that had borrowed its name loomed like a visitor from a future world, but far enough off, beyond woods to the east. It was burning hot, and hard to look at the low white houses with walls, windows and doorways framed in ochre or azure or gold, and decorated with imitation bas-relief. Between them riotous cabbages, onions, feverfew, iris and marigold fought for space around the feet of olive, fig and vine. Dark figures moved on the shadowy sides of streets and wide spaces, some with rectangular wooden trays on their heads. Women with flagons at the pump hid their faces under hat brims. Their uniform was black and blue and grey, the sleeves long, the stockings woollen. A young woman in baggy T-shirt and shorts gossiped with them, leaning on a baby-buggy. From under its canopy and a cute baseball cap an infant peered out, waving hands and red-socked feet at me. A donkey-cart with a shaggy load of hay on rubber tyres clep-clepped down the broad main road. An articulated wagon with asthmatic air brakes and bad breath snaked past it at high speed and shuddered the small shops. The honest proportions of the old buildings contrasted with a street of new houses, also one-storey but busy with flimsy arches and porches, twee garden walls and balustrades, pastel pebbledash and tasteless tiles. Inside, some women still worked traditional carpets, sumptu-ous rag-rugs and embroidery. An ancient woman in a solid doorway – a deep, yellow-bordered niche framing a worn green door – stepped out of the frame to meet me. I greeted her, a tiny shadow in the glare, and she grasped me with both bony hands. Her skin was marvellously crumpled and she had bruised patches beneath glittering eyes as if she did battle with bad dreams and long memory, and won.

'I am the oldest person in Pego,' she announced with a truly beautiful smile, 'I am one hundred and two.'

She probably was. She was begging in the nicest possible way. I gave her something. Survival demands recognition. I bought lus-cious plums at a row of stalls by the hose-damp public garden. Building labourers stood on the flat roof of a new villa under the high noon sun drinking beer from bottles. A brash café, Trottbar, was filling up with men and music.

This is south, only just, but beyond the Tagus, *além do Tejo*: a 'little Alentejo' just ten miles from the real thing. I slake my thirst inside a low bar where a cicada sings behind a pink door in a tiny plastic cage. It has a leaf to chew on and there is no telling whether its incessant chirping is complaint or celebration. Still, I want to let it out. I should be drinking more against the dry heat but I'm impatient to get down to the river. The sun and the scents on the stony track are intoxicating. Pine resin on the air transports me to childhood. Cork oaks' vivid wounds please my eye and my fingertips. Blackened boles and leafless branches give off that thin fragrance which time refines from the reek of fire. The shapely skeletons among new growth stand for resilience, not death. A green wagon drawn by a tan pony bounces uphill on its leaf springs. The aged driver's brown cap and his passengers' straw hats and check blouses seem festive after so much dark felt and cloth in the village. There is a gateway, beehives, and a grand *quinta*, but most of all there are flowers: scrub meadow rife with purple and pink, white and yellow, lavender and blue. There are butterflies doing brilliant semaphore and cicadas, free ones, sending unintelligible morse. They take me sixty miles south, and seven years back, to fields near Évora. Then I lay among grass and herbs outside the capital of Alto Alentejo on the eve of another Feast of St John.

Évora is the place to go for the *Feira de São João*. The Lusitanian town of Ebora Cerealis became the fortified Liberalitas Julia under the Romans. The temple, dedicated to Diana by tradition if nothing else, dates from the second or third century; its podium, partial architrave and fourteen granite columns, with bases and Corinthian capitals of local marble, survive only because it was a slaughterhouse until 1870. By the twelfth century, along with Alcántara, Alcácer, Badajoz and Mérida, Évora comprised the Moorish province of al-Qasr, one third of the southern land called al-Andalus. Then in 1159 it was taken by Afonso Henriques, the first king of Portugal, but held for only two years. Penetrated by the knight Giraldo Sem-Pavor (Gerald the Fearless), it was assailed by scaling ladders in 1165 and never reverted to Muslim hands. Alone among Afonso's conquests south of the Tagus, Évora held out against the Almohad invasion from Morocco in 1191.

Évora is *the* place to be for St John's Eve. Then its Moorish, Mudejar, Gothic, Manueline and Renaissance buildings, its marvellous aqueduct encrusted with limpet-like houses, all its close-packed planes of white against white within tight walls, its gates and arches, arcades and balconies are voice-boxes and sounding-boards for the thrum of drums, squeal of pipes, clack of clogs, skirl of accordions, throb of hollow jugs, chink of bells, smack of hands and the plain or frantic chanting of insistent phrases by which the people's soul relieves itself:

> Alentejo has no shade
> But what comes from the sky.
> Shelter yourself here girl
> Underneath my hat.

Or:

> As the wind is to fire
> So is absence to love;
> If it's little, it puts it out;
> If great it fans it higher.

And again:

> To love you I lost God;
> Through your love I lost myself,
> Now look at me, alone,
> Without God, without love, without you.

The devastating richness of simple words sung with emphatic cadences flows strongly, then ebbs amongst the swirl of music. In *Praça do Giraldo* successive groups of musicians gather and dance on their way to the fairground. Every week farmers strike bargains on trust in this square, with no stock in sight. Within days of St John's Fair, 1484, the Duque de Bragança's head was struck off here, guilty on twenty-two counts of treason against João II, Lord of All the Secrets. Évora was a favourite seat of the House of Avis. Cardinal Dom Henrique founded the city's Jesuit University of the Holy Ghost when the 'longed-for' Infante Sebastião was five years old. In the wake of King Sebastião's defeat at Alcácer-Quebir and the cardinal's own brief reign, Philip of Castile passed through Évora three days after the Feast of St John, 1580, on his progress to Lisbon and the throne of Portugal. On the restoration of the Portuguese monarchy, João IV established his court here. Évora yielded to Castilian forces on 22 May 1663 but, after the Spaniards' crushing defeat at Ameixial just a month later, it was retaken on 24 June, the very day dedicated to St John.

The folk-dancers in breeches and scarves, shawls and swirling skirts, the sloe-eyed gypsies, the soberly-dressed but intoxicated farmers and their families were, when I saw them, variously celebrating not-Spain, long days, love, fire and water. Love, because John the Baptist is, perhaps through conflation with John the Beloved, the lovers' patron saint. Water is John the Baptist's own, and his dawn's dew heals the sick. Fire, like water, is a mystery in his gift by inheritance from the gods of pagan Midsummer. I found no bonfire, if there was one, though at Chaves in the north I once saw a blaze by the castle keep and brave souls leaping over it for St John's sake. Sebastião himself gazed into the flames here in 1573. The fires he watched were not *fogueirinhas* (little bonfires) *de São João*. The nineteen-year-old king, unruly and zealous, filled his pale eyes with the glimmer and flare of an *auto-da-fé*. If souls leapt, they leapt clean out of charred bodies. That particular day just seventeen Jews were burnt for their sins.

The Chapel of Bones seemed closed when I tried the door under the main dormitory of the Franciscan monastery. The royal church of São Francisco and the nearby palace were built for Dom Manuel the Fortunate, but it wasn't the commonplace grandeur of Moorish-Gothic Manueline architecture I'd come here to savour. I wanted to see if the later *Capela dos Ossos* lived up to its reputation. After some moments of suitable suspense the door opened and the custodian invited me inside. I read the matter-of-fact rhyming motto over the entrance, *Nós ossos que aqui estamos pelos vossos esperamos* ('We bones that are here wait for yours'). What sixteenth-century monk masterminded this, the most famous bone room in Portugal? What morbidity is here, or what triumph of the spirit? And what a conjunction of painted ceilings with pillars and walls: above my head, three vaulted baroque nave roofs glorifying, and prettifying, the Passion of Christ; below, the architecture of mortality. Its building blocks were the bits of five thousand disarticulated skeletons gathered, so the story goes, from thirty-two monasteries and forty-eight churches.

'Are you staying long?' asked the custodian.

'Not too long,' I said.

'Fifteen minutes?'

'Yes, fine.'

He went out, locking the door behind him. The clunk, and the rattle of the key's withdrawal, was pure Hammer Horror. He'd left the lights on, bless him. Jawless skulls, fleshless cheek by jowl, each one's top teeth gnawing another's cranium, did not merely stare sightlessly from the walls. They were the walls. Pillars were clad with long bones, horizontal ones, wattle awaiting clay. Arches and niches made much of small bones, and macabre heraldry out of pelvises and death's heads. I imagined the monkish quantity surveyor as he ordered building supplies from his resurrection men, supervised sorters who sifted through heaps of disinterred stiffs, dismembered them, arranged bones according to type and graded them for size. I could see the cunning precision with which each had been bedded in mortar. I smiled at neat parodies of carved stone, and at graffiti that rebels and young lovers had scratched on skulls. I thought of the Architect's displeasure at that, and of almighty chaos at the sound of the Last Trump when all this work would be undone, the chapel dismantling itself, each bone seeking its fellows, mortar unsetting, deliquescing, reverting to sloppy clay, to flesh which should reclothe the reassembled multitude.

It was a long fifteen minutes. The chaos I pictured would be, in fact (if such could ever be fact), the very antithesis of chaos. Entropy in reverse. Hope. Two corpses, a man's and a boy's, hung at the chapel's west end, relatively intact, said to have been the objects of a wife and mother's revenge. On her death bed she cursed her persecutors, conjuring flesh not to fall from bones, as if mummification by malediction would disqualify them from resurrection. It hadn't worked. Entropy had not been halted, just slowed down. Flesh clung to bone, sure enough, but only in bits, and leathery. The custodian unlocked the door and let in air, daylight, a sussurus of banal sound and a crocodile of devout sightseers. Dusty braids of women's hair hung at the entrance, my exit, one an offering 'from Rita Batista when she had a bad headache', others from brides who hoped against hope for love, long-lived love, and again, for long life.

That night I entered the *Museu dos Fenômenos*. It was a sideshow in the great fairground beyond Dom Manuel's palace and the city walls. After stalls of crafts and souvenirs, bars for drink and food and more drink, showcases for farm implements and produce, stands of government propaganda, racks of new clothes fit for an emperor, after luckless games and risky rides, tinny PA exhortations and raucous pop, after a power cut which stopped everything – lights, bumper cars, Muzak, official videos, big wheel and all – everything except oil lamps, tallow flares, lecherous laughter and passionate gypsy *flamenco* . . . after all that the Museum of Prodigies was an oasis. The power cut had left me on the threshold of a fair somewhere between the middle ages and the nineteenth century. I crossed that threshold into the museum.

One of a modest queue of the credulous, I stared at misshapen, misbegotten embryos in bottles. A live lamb with six legs baa'd in Portuguese. A stuffed two-headed dog snarled stiffly, silently, but twice. A one-headed dog with two bodies balanced the equation. We gazed at abortions and oddities, the four-footed chicken and the stuffed cow whose fifth leg hung from its spine like an empty sleeve, and there was soon nothing to say. Dumbly I handed my ticket in, to an eight-foot-tall Moçambican with a stooping smile and hands like shovels.

This was anthropology, not political correctness. Outside the circus next door three bears danced a tortured dance, fur quivering. Inside, two acrobats dressed like bank clerks did the best man-handling act I've seen. Clowns ate fire on St John's Eve. Girls pirouetted and climbed ramps on big balls. A parrot tightrope walked and picked up prizes with nothing less than disdain in its eye, its caw. For a glittering finale, for John the Baptist, a nervous glamour-girl stabbed keyboards to make water music in the ring. Fountains played high and low, refracted coloured lights but never coincided with her fingering. That was not the worst. Before the girls on balls, and just as the firm floor they needed was being laid on the sawdust, a trapeze act glittered high in the tent's dark. Spangles, skill, sweat. They swung, she flew, he caught. And then he didn't. They lost their grip and she dropped frozen-faced. I can see it now. She crumped onto the boards and lay still, extinct, a human out of Bosch or Breughel. They gathered her up and carried her out twitching while the brave girls balancing on balls rolled in. It seemed an age before the siren.

I walked outside, beyond the soiled straw, trampled grass and stink of diesel. I lay among flowers, looked at stars in the big big top and considered the great bear, contortionists, dry bones. That was sixty miles south. On a later St John's Eve, I am parched and walking through a little Alentejo in the Ribatejo. Under the fizz of cicadas I sense a pulse, a shimmering sound. A woman slashes at bamboo and her husband stacks bundles on a station wagon's roof. Through the bamboo grove, water. Clear pools of the Tagus aquiver with young fish. A wagtail on a boulder. A red kite's spread primaries, high up. Downriver, a pall of smoke beyond the golden town of Abrantes.

15

QUEST FOR THE *MORANGO FIZZ*

Abrantes and Constância

A SLICK OF BLACK SMOKE announces Abrantes. Just downriver from town on the right bank the municipal rubbish tip burns fitfully, smoulders and slips towards the Tagus. It never goes out. 'It's our visiting card,' a nurse told me. The new hospital is another one: a brown block below the horizon, a blot on the townscape. And, by the tourist hotel, the Telecom tower is an etiolated multi-storey mushroom. I'd heard good things about Abrantes from a woman who was born there, idyllic childhood memories. What kind of bad medicine has it taken since?

Abrantes is promoted as 'a city of flowers', and whenever a tourist office or a planning department starts on about flowers you know there's something wrong. The westbound train quails when it sniffs the scent of smoke and flowers, or because it sees the castle and town so high on their hill, and dives across-river to the south bank.

At the station of Rossio ao Sul do Tejo ('the Square to the south of the Tagus') I bought a beer and took a handful of *tremoços* from a dish on the bar. They fulfil the rôle of peanuts, but they're yellowish beans, wet and salt and slippery. Pressed between finger and thumb they jump out of their skins into your mouth. They tasted disappointing but were addictive all the same. The nurse was concerned with bad habits.

'The Portuguese smoke too much, drink too much and eat too much. Too many of the dishes they love are fatty,' he said, dissociating himself from his nation by his use of the third person. I remembered, with no nostalgia whatever, the *Cozido à Portuguesa*

I'd been served in Santarém. 'They suffer many cerebro-vascular accidents, many diseases of the liver and pancreas. The rhythm of drink and hot weather brings on seasonal complaints. Alcoholism is a big problem.'

I'd started this by asking about the smoke. He went on.

'Now, suddenly it seems, we have drugs in Abrantes. So there is crime. There's unemployment of course, but if anyone really wants a job they can find one. I hope to go abroad, to Scotland, to get more qualifications. We each have a c.v. which is added to, added to, added to from school onwards.'

He pointed at his Rapido train ticket as though it were his papers. It had been printed out at the computer terminal in the ticket office. It specified class, carriage and seat number. After all he'd said I was glad to see 'não fumadores' on his c.v.

'If an employer sees foreign qualifications there, immediately he says, Ah! very good.' He smiled ruefully, 'It is all very Portuguese, very Third World, just like the rubbish that may slip any time into the river. It is a primitive solution to the problem. You see, the Portuguese are a little lazy, a little disorganised.'

A glistening green streamlined train drew in precisely on time. Doors opened with a sucking sound. The nurse passed from the bar through the heat into an air-conditioned aircraft-style interior. He adjusted the angle of his plush green seat and arranged text books on the table in front of him. I waved him off from his home town and went in search of it.

The tremoços had made me thirsty. On my way to the road bridge I stopped for a lolly. For months I'd asked in vain for one of Olá's cheapest, a straight ice lolly without an ice-cream heart or a nut-and-chocolate carapace. I asked for it, the strawberry one called Morango Fizz. But there were none. This did not surprise me. I hadn't discovered one in captivity yet. All the cheap varieties were marked with a biro'd 'N' on this glossy chart. N for 'Não tem', 'Don't have.' So I didn't. Instead, as I walked, I developed the theology of sublime effervescence.

Faith in fizz, I decided, should be a basic doctrine of the millenarian morango cult, the cryogenic creed peddled by ice-cream vendors. The sun overheats our bodies, I theorised, sweating. Overheated bodies incubate parched spirits which need slaking.

Need gives rise to hope, hope fostered by mouth-watering icons but never fulfilled because the leap of faith, the plunge into the freezer cannot, despite all our rummaging in the chill dark of unrequited faith, come up with the advertised flavour. That much-vaunted tingle on the proffered tongue, that fruity solace is a mirage. *Morango Fizz* had promised everything to my hot dry soul. It was the one-so-longed-for.

It was a hot dry walk across the bridge, over a low, turbid river Tagus. A fisherman with a long rod stood by a moored *barco* in the road's shadow. On a bank littered with flotsam and overhung by willows he wound in a silver fish. The stretch of railway between Santarém and Rossio ao Sul do Tejo was opened in 1862. It pressed on to Badajoz or to Madrid. Then in 1870 this road bridge linked Abrantes with Rossio. I could see the rail bridge of 1891 that took the line on up the Tagus. Together they symbolised the passing of a river trade that had once been international. In the sixteenth century Abrantes and district had been one of the most densely populated regions of Portugal and jealous Santarém had protested to Parliament about its upriver rival. But the Tagus had never been made navigable as far as Toledo, despite the hopes of Spanish kings. Abrantes's population dwindled. Road and rail ended its life as a port. When at last it was raised to the status of city in 1916 it was only, they say, because as a republican hotbed it had helped to plot the 1910 revolution, the end of monarchy.

St John seemed to tiptoe through carnations while dancers from Pego pounded the boards with their clogs. A handsome bearded figure with a lamb and a book in his hand, the saint was clothed not in raiment of camel's hair but of gold lined with crimson. Half life-size, he stood on a draped table among the flowers, *cravos encarnados*, blood-red 'nails'. It was St John's Eve in Abrantes. The carnations were crepe paper, but stuck into pots of living basil. They had little flags flying from their stalks inscribed with mottoes. *Cravos* stand, as I've said, for the Passion and for passion. I bought a pot. Its message read:

> If the laurel didn't have
> so many middle branches

from my window I'd see
the eyes of my dear love.

A plump woman in a pale dress jumped up and down, clapped out of time, shrieked and applauded madly at the end of the dance. She ran recklessly through the crowd, along with small children who had the freedom of the courtyard, and fell on the neck of an aged young man. She kissed him and patted his head. A group were singing a sentimental pop song now, but the human music-stand-cum-page-turner lost concentration, wandered off the stage, then stared at what he held in his hands and ran back to his stiff pose. Improvisation was in the air, and good humour. We were in the grounds of Santa Casa da Misericórdia, halfway through their week of brotherhood.

Santa Casa da Misericórdia can be translated as 'saintly house of mercy'. There are four hundred or so around the country, local charitable institutions belonging to a five-hundred-year-old union. Misericórdias were almshouses and charity hospitals. Today they manage old people's homes, aid programmes for people with handicaps, crèches and other causes. They get government grant-aid and exemption from value added tax. They raise some money from events and private donations, but millions of *contos* (hundreds of millions of pounds) annually from football pools and lotteries. Misericórdias are big saintly business. Their controversial holding company invests in, among other things, the hospital and funeral industries.

Old people sat on a line of chairs set against the long wall of their home, the hospital of 1532. At one end of the courtyard men sprinkled themselves with bottled water as they sweated over barbecues in split oil-drums, fanned charcoal, grilled sardines. Behind the staging at the other end stood the church of Misericórdia. On the fourth side land fell steeply away to dusk in the Tagus valley. By now I could see where I was, beyond the ugly new hospital and the smoke that got in my eyes. The old town was, as the guide books had hinted, more delightful and less gentrified than Santarém. Its steep streets of flower-laden houses looked gratifyingly unselfconscious.

I'd tasted the *tigeladas* (sweet egg puddings, literally 'bowlfuls') and *palha de Abrantes* (egg 'straw') for which the city is famous. In the café where I'd been told the students hung out I met well-coifed matrons and young couples introducing their babies to one another. A grey-haired man devoted his complete attention to a winsome black girl while his thickly-made-up wife beamed upon them both. Armed with a bundle of long bamboos frayed at one end, a short woman in an overall dusted down a tall street door. The Renaissance south doorway and steps of Misericórdia were washed and brushed up for the feast by a raucous sisterhood. Inside the church six rococo panels painted by the 'master of Abrantes' told the old tale. In his 'Visitation', the Virgin in a stylish gown arrives at sixteenth-century Abrantes, followed by gossips discussing the fashion statement she's making, to inspect a devout Elizabeth in matronly habit and gravid with the saint we're celebrating. At the story's far end, the 'Deposition in the Tomb', Christ's carcass is clumsily carried beneath the Marys' meddlesome gaze. The smart man taking the weight of his legs must be Joseph of Arimathea, with a sharp eye for a heavenly photo-opportunity.

John the Baptist stood aloof now, head still on his shoulders but feet awash with red carnations and flickering candlelight. Old people sat. Children ran and screamed. The simple-minded stood, or danced, clutching one another like bulky packages. Two stanzas of a poem by Fernando Pessoa (here lacking the original's exact rhymes) hint at the night's potential everywhere:

> At the ball where everyone dances,
> someone lingers without dancing.
> Better not to go to the ball
> than to be there, without being there.
>
> The basil plant and the banner
> that's on the paper carnation –
> all this fills the entire night,
> O mouth of blood and honey.

My mouth was stuffed with sardines. I'd started with classic *caldo verde* (cabbage soup) at the food stall, followed by grilled *sardinhas* washed down with a tumbler of wine. More sardines were put in front of me, unbidden. A man at the bar grinned and wished me *Bom apetite!* I had had enough, but I took his hospitality on board with reasonably good grace. Then more sardines. I protested good-humouredly.

'No, you must eat,' he said. 'Don't worry, I am controlling it.'

Aaaagh! I thanked him, but my good humour entirely evaporated. So did I, into the crowd and the noise. I found an appreciative home for my overloaded plate. The musicians and dancers of Rancho do Pego were stamping out a little Alentejo on the boards. One of the girls spun her white skirt wildly, but her white blouse was buttoned high at her throat. The scarf that hid her hair was crimson, her flushed face dark, eyes black and fixed on her partner. The boy's flannel breeches and short tweed jacket with bottle-green collar, cuffs and elbow patches were worn as if they were cloth-of-gold. From under his *campino*'s cap he glared at the girl with a passion. Then the dance tore them apart, threaded them through other arms and drew them back together. It looked the way young love should look. An elderly black woman bounced a white baby on her knees and gazed at them with almost painful longing in her eyes.

The *pensão* was a mistake. I'd chosen it for its charm. At first I found no one within, then I found the outside bell. A dubious expostulation drew me up narrow stairs through a half-door to a dusky interior containing dusty plants and a skeletal man called Artur with an angry boil on his neck. On the wall hung a large cracked canvas he'd brought back from military service in Africa on which some Portuguese had daubed a wide-eyed *nganga*, or medicine man, leading acolytes in ritual leaping over a fire. St John's Eve in Angola, I thought, but decided not even to attempt irony in my poor Portuguese. The ochre landscape and the black figures in it might have been fine if they had not been warped, just, by racist handling of the paint.

Many keys rattled in the darkness. The room was grim but clean and quiet. I threw back the shutters and propped the sash window open with a coathanger. I had to have light and air even if the heat came too. For four nights I stuck it, and the ants that emerged from a crack in the wall, climbed the bed leg and processed across my pillow and face. I dreamt of Central Africa but here there were no rats, cockroaches or snakes. Nearby there was a bar with ranch-style doors and customers to match. The patron beamed a shiny welcome. His cowed son wiped glasses and fetched my lunch. One loud girl with a blouse under strain slapped her lumbering boyfriend's face in pure fun. A *bombeiro* (fireman) with a prodigious arse in blue overalls punched his way through the doors – waff-waff-waf-waf-waf! – and tugged her hair. She went frighteningly quiet then. Two older women, primped and permed, had stepped in from another film. They watched me earnestly over their coffee cups and, as they left, implored me to have a good stay.

A double-decker bus debouched picnickers from a town in the north onto the open space beside the castle. The ground fell precipitously away. A man in a straw boater and a linen suit was staring upriver towards a hazy Central de Pego.

'I love castles,' he offered. 'I've travelled all over the world and I've seen many castles – I've seen the Tower of London too – but none can compare with the castle of Abrantes.'

He had cold eyes and a small but sensuous mouth. Death in Abrantes, I couldn't help thinking. See Abrantes and die. I realised soon enough that he had nothing to do with the tourists. They wanted to see Abrantes and eat. They didn't even follow me into the castle. The custodian did, in his car, just in time to unlock the main gate. The round bastions and ranked arches that punctuated the castle's inner wall had looked impressive from outside. Inside there were flagrant jacarandas and mulberry trees on crutches in a shabby formal garden, a rusty child's tricycle and fading decorations in a once-grand chamber. See Abrantes and decay. I climbed springy iron stairs to the top of the square keep that served as a belvedere. Now I could see far up and down the Tagus valley, back to the mountains and across the plains. I could see how important this castle once was. The Almohads had besieged it fruitlessly in a rearguard action against the Christian reconquest. Dom Afonso Henriques gave the town a charter. Dom Dinis gave it to his queen, St Isabel. In June 1385 Dom Nuno Álvares Pereira and Dom João I joined forces here to march on Aljubarrota and rout Castile. With this under his boater, a Portuguese heart in his suit and eyes gazing towards Spain as our man's had been, his feeling for this formidable shell made perfect sense. For centuries Abrantes remained the key to central Portugal. Junot captured it in 1807 and Napoleon created him Duc d'Abrantes for his trouble. Wellesley retook it two years later, shortly before he was made Viscount Wellington, and made it his HQ:

> *Quartel Geral em Abrantes*
> *Tudo com dantes.*

'Headquarters at Abrantes, everything as before,' runs the cynical proverb. Now, a livid cloud advanced out of a vast sky.

Warm rain hit the hot stairway and went up in puffs of steam. I ran for the whitewashed museum in thirteenth-century Santa Maria do Castelo. It used to be the castle church. Before that it had been a Moorish mosque, probably a Visigothic church and, certainly, a Roman temple. Decimus Junius Brutus took the hill town from Iberian Celts in 130 BC. Its name was refined, so it's said, from gold found in the sandy strata of the riverbank. Those *barreiras* are still 'golden' – *aurantes* in Latin. A headless Roman statue retained a comically pompous air. A pulpit with a twirl at the base hung at the wall like a granite ice-cream cone. Tombs of stone lace, flashy and intricate, fêted three illustrious Almeidas, Counts of Abrantes, whose family furnished Portuguese India with its first viceroy and the home country with a conspirator against Spanish rule. Glorified figures levitated in a black space made of drapes and spotlights. An almond-eyed Virgin proffered her extrovert toddler to a sturdy and all-comprehending Most Holy Trinity. Under the eye of soulful St Francis, a monkish child clung to the Virgin of Milk's clothes, his mouth stopped by her proud breast.

A four-foot snake slid across my path, a steep one running down between tortured olive trees above fields of sunflowers, just east of the castle walls. No one believed me about the snake. Between the inner and perimeter walls women planted out lobelias in a well-stocked, well-watered Eden. At the castle's prow, high above the Tagus, stood a tall cross and a monument like a spiky chapel to the momentous meeting of Nun'Álvares and Dom João. Some of its stained glass was shot. It glittered on the paving in a dank corner beside a pair of discarded knickers.

Between those knickers and proud Dom Francisco de Almeida,

first viceroy of India on his plinth, a glossy raven blinked at sky and river from a tiny cage. It made me angry. Ravens fed St Vincent before his martyrdom in the days of Emperor Diocletian. They accompanied his body on the voyage from Valencia to his burial-place on Europe's south-westernmost cape, *fim do mundo*, end of the world, called Cabo de São Vicente. When his remains were trans-ferred to Lisbon in the twelfth century, ravens again escorted the ship. São Vicente was made Lisbon's patron saint and a pair of ravens took their place, with the ship they guard, on the city's crest. Cram mythic ravens into the devout imagination, or onto heraldic escutcheons, but don't confine a real one in a cage where it can't stretch its wings. I examined the padlock, the hinges, the bars. I thought about getting hold of some bar-cutters and climbing into the castle gardens at night. I'm sorry I didn't do it.

Together with the castle, the heavily-buttressed early baroque church of São Vicente dominates the city. Of all its wonders – glitzy side chapels, spiralling pulpit stairs, exuberant altars, gilded bishops – the most famous are two panels of *azulejos* that, high up in a church full of tiles, you might easily miss; rare ones, in limpid and dense blues, the saint's galleons and ravens.

But it was the church of São João, founded in 1300 by the Queen Santa Isabel, that contained my favourite wonder. Outside it, the big show: an ivory Mercedes, with a primrose bow masking the radiator grill, waited for an exultant bride and a frightened groom to enjoy and endure the bearhugs, the tearful kisses, the salvoes of confetti, the guffaws and giggles of a crush of relatives. Inside, a sour-faced verger had already set to, clearing candle-ends and scrap-ing at wax. Coy Christ stood on an altar by the door, covered in too much blood as if made up for amateur melodramatics. His was a church sideshow made, I thought, by a woodcarver more used to fairground organs, embellished as it was with garish scrollwork and fruit and birds. At each side a big face with buck teeth and bulbous eyes stared from hair and a beard of writhing foliage: a deeply-wounded Jesus flanked by two Green Men, large as life. The dying king, sap in the bud, blood on the sheets.

The painter stood in her atelier. It was cool there. The walls were white, her blouse was blue silk. I had tried to reach her that afternoon from a glass phone-box like a sauna. Gasping, I'd explained who I was and why I thought we ought to meet. I'd walked past the façade of the mansion of the Albuquerques, site of the royal palace where Manuel I lived while plague ravaged Lisbon, and across the top of town from where, it seemed, a king could supervise his kingdom. Sirens screamed and *bombeiros* hung at an engine loosed from red fire-station doors. I'd stuck to a black leather chair in the foyer of the tourist hotel where Maria Lucília Moita and I had arranged to meet. When she'd first appeared she looked like a woman you might find at an embassy party, for her face was refined, with luxuriant hair held back from it in a disciplined coif.

She drove me the few yards to her home and studio. It was mercifully airy and she offered me whisky, bread and quince jelly, almond tart. Their colours were the colours of her work. Some early paintings had the ripeness of fruit or stained glass, but those of the last twenty-five years were muted in tone, not intensity. Their palate was of whites and blacks, golds and ochres, the colours of winter, but winter heavy with spring. They held the weight of masses, geological and architectural, the fluidity of trees and water, the lightness of wind. They looked cool, as white heat looks cool.

We shared our passion for the river. She could paint the river beneath the river, *o rio por baixo do rio*; I was searching for the words. Here was the inner journey, its stations, canvas by canvas, for which journeys in the world are a metaphor or, at worst, a poor substitute. Here was the earth, abstract and palpable, here the private life of rock, here water under a bridge of stone, here despoiled houses, here a charcoal face of Christ *antes de Ressuscitar*, 'before rising again'.

'Time moves on and I move in time,' she said. 'I grasp lessons and memories which have stayed in me and become *saudade*.'

Life had stopped in Abrantes. The snake went on its belly out of Eden. While nuptials raged the bloodstained god stood by in the green wood. The count who ruled India was neighbour to the bird of death in chains. And, in the heat, Artur's *pensão* had the scent of Mbandaka, a town on the Equator beside the Zaïre River where I once felt I'd like to die. Maria Lucília ended that train of thought. She gave me a sight of the unseeable destination. I'd had it, going upriver against the current, but going with the flow lulled me, blinded me for a while and made me forget. I was aiming for the end of the world.

But first, to dinner with new friends. José had vision, but no sight at all. His friend António guided him around the obstacles that prevent most of us taking a long view. He brought him upstairs to a table in the restaurant called *O Fumeiro*, the Chimney. We laughed a lot. Suddenly they were Zé and Tó. Then Zé invited me to stay in his flat. And leave Artur after only four nights?! Yes please.

Artur had been in Angola at the time of the 1974 'revolution'. So had Zé, in the town of Salazar, listening to the BBC with his father on 25 April. In Lisbon President Caetano was bargaining for a helicopter to fly him out of trouble. He'd read *Portugal e o Futuro* by General Spínola, ex-governor of Guiné Bissau, even before the book was published in February 1974. Spínola could not remain loyal to the government's African policy, so Caetano sacked him as deputy chief of staff on 14 March and was relieved to see a coup in the general's support fizzle out two days later. But Spínola knew that Portugal could not win her colonial wars, especially since ground-to-air missiles were in African hands. Both men knew what was destined to happen at home. Africa – Angola, Moçambique and Guiné Bissau where, of 100,000 Portuguese soldiers who served in the wars, 26,000 had been maimed or injured and more than 8,000 killed – Africa would bring Caetano down, as it had Sebastião.

Zé was one-quarter African. His mother's mother had been an Angolan. His father had had four wives and eleven children. One of Zé's sisters was a teacher. She discovered that she was being paid less than her colleagues and asked the headmaster why. He read out a law which explained away the apparent unfairness. Later she and her brother questioned it in the capital, Luanda. The law was a fiction. The headmaster had made it up on the spot. She was paid the difference.

'That's what woke me up to politics,' said Zé, 'to the arbitrariness of power.'

I had swapped permanent dusk, soldier ants and African musk for Zé's bright flat: all marble, tiles, polished wood and balconies overlooking the lower city and the Tagus valley. Artur was regretful, but took a philosophical view of life's disappointments. The boil on his neck had not yet burst. Zé enjoyed seeing his home through my enthusiasm for it. Headquarters at Abrantes, everything completely different. Tó left on a school trip to the lush mountains and lakes of Gerês in the north, so when we walked to the cafés Zé rested his hand on my shoulder. Everywhere I asked in vain for a *Morango Fizz*. In Pelicano the post-punk waitress was coolly solicitous. In Chave d'Ouro the gossip was hot. In Tutti Frutti, Vasco the waiter teased Zé and whispered '*Bimbo!*' in his ear. It means 'bumpkin', 'rustic'. I explained its English meaning. Suddenly all brainless blondes had straw in their hair, all bucolic matrons had wasp-waists and boobs like melons. In a nearby bar, when Célia served Miguel the midget he might have been Superman, but she wept on Zé's shoulder about the café's ignorant new proprietors.

'Every humble person dreams of owning a bar,' Zé told me, 'they think it's El Dorado.'

We talked about hopes and fears. Zé recalled the idealism of the late sixties when he was at Salazar's old university, Coimbra. Salazar had fallen off his chair by then, but lived on, unaware that Caetano had assumed the presidency. Hopes, and Coimbra, were shaken by an earthquake of 7.3 on the Richter Scale.

'We have a saying,' said Zé, '*Quem tem cu, tem mêdo!* – He who has an arse has fear. I put my arm round my aunt's neck – she had God on her lips – and the door bang-bang-banged. It seemed the floor would open up. Things fell off the walls.'

Natalya, Zé's cleaner, could be trusted to leave everything in its place. She was a classic Mrs Mop but she wore a big badge on her apron, 'Lose Weight Now, Ask Me How'. Once we were so great, now we are so small. She wanted to supplement her 400 escudos per hour and knew that *bimbos* dreamed of being bimbos.

'Now we think dreams are made in Brussels,' Zé shrugged. 'I don't think so. I have a black view of our future in Europe.'

Luís Vaz de Camões sat, with a manuscript on his lap, beside a heap of loudspeakers and a tangle of cable on a concrete bench overlooking the confluence of his 'sweet Tagus' with the Zêzere river at Constância. A young man loaded the PA system from the weekend's fair into a van and I sat beside the bronze poet, maker of the myth of Vasco da Gama, Dom Sebastião's bard. Tradition has it that Camões lived here and, just as Dom Manuel escaped the Lisbon plague by lodging in Abrantes, so Sebastião came to Constância to take refuge from a later epidemic.

Travelling is too often escapism, running away from threats or everyday reality at home. Even if only to face new threats, fresh reality. Some scholars argue that Sebastião ran away to Morocco to avoid marriage, sex, the obligation to father an heir. Commonly, we run off to get away from ourselves, though self is the one piece of baggage we can't leave behind. Unless, like Sebastião, we leave it for dead. Let's hope Camões made a short voyage up the Tagus to escape rats, thugs, women, or the displeasure of Sebastião's grandfather, Dom João the Pious.

According to his contemporary Diogo de Couto, Camões was 'a man with a terrible nature'. He may have been banished here for that, but whatever Constância's natives thought of him then, they love him now. They've given him a garden and rebuilt his house, if it ever was his house, on the medieval quay. Thanks to the possibility that Camões really did live here for a time, Constância has awarded itself the title 'poem town', *Vila Poema*. Mad Queen Maria II decreed it a 'notable town' in 1836. Later poets lived here too: Vasco de Lima Couto, who left his house to the town as a museum, and Alexandre O'Neill, descended from wild Irish O'Neills who settled in Portugal in the eighteenth century. The town guide offers *a evasão num ambiente poético*, 'escape in a poetic atmosphere'. Good poetry evades nothing, nothing escapes it, but I'd escape here any time to rest and meditate and work. For that it's the perfect town. In a sombre bar I drank beer and ate *tremoços* with a pipe-smoking poet who took me home to a timbered room where, with his partner, a translator, we shared coffee and talked books.

The Camoniano Garden aspires to cultivate all the plants mentioned in Camões's verses around an amphitheatre paved with Ptolemy's earth-centred planetarium. Walls like white scrolls unfurl around a pool of water-lilies and an oriental pavilion with a peaked roof of green tiles. From banks of polled willows, to which boats decked with flags and flowers come each Easter Monday to be sprinkled and scoured of evil in the name of Our Lady of the Good Voyage, the town of white houses embowered in bougainvillea and hibiscus clambers uphill, ever more exquisite, to a cobbled tree-shaded courtyard before the mother church that is its summit.

I climbed to it several times one day in the hope of finding the doors unlocked. And back down to the *pelourinho* topped by an armillary sphere in Praça Alexandre Herculano where the bar, as usual, had not one *Morango Fizz*. Or, again, all the way down to Misericórdia church, open; greenish tiles gave its nave a submarine feel; the multi-layered arch behind the altar was a cavernous maw thick with bone-coloured carving that could have been coral; in the holy-water stoup I found a brown corduroy cap that must have belonged to a drowned mariner. Or, yet another descent, through an arcade of trees, under an arch and down a narrow street of steps, Rua do Arco, to the quay and the ancient ruin called Casa dos Arcos, now topped up with brick and concrete and labelled Casa Memória de Camões. Banishment here would have been a promise not a threat.

An outboard-powered *barco* ran a ferry service from the quay across Camões's limpid Tagus. Except that it wasn't limpid. Scabs of brown scum floated on its surface and the far bank was dominated by the CAIMA paper factory belching steam.

'They built it here,' explained a woman who sensed my dismay, 'because it must have a supply of pure water.'

Poems, as I have said, cannot evade reality.

'Clean water is needed for the wood-cleaning process. Now, when it's pumped out, it's polluted.'

Poets need paper. Helicon is a sullied spring. A man in swim-shorts washed himself in the shallows directly opposite the factory. The counter-current took a flotilla of scum upriver under his nose. He bent, cupped hands and drank. An insect made him jump, then pursued him until he dived in.

I thought of my friend's memories of the river at Abrantes.

'When we first moved to the house by the river we could swim and spend delicious days in the fine sand,' she told me. 'That was fourteen years ago, or fifteen. Over the years it has become more and more dangerous, fast, dirty. Emptier as well. The last time I went in I could only wet my feet and return to muddy sand.'

I imagined Camões with his one good eye gazing at the river from his house here. A far cry from the River Mekong, off the mouth of which he was shipwrecked, barely saving himself and the manuscript of *Os Lusiadas* by swimming ashore, but losing, if tradition is true, his beloved Chinese mistress.

Now he has abandoned the house for a bench above the Zêzere. I stood on the road bridge that crosses it. It ran clear and fast. It rippled over gravelly beds and ran into the Tagus with little fuss. The marriage of the two rivers used to be a turbulent one, for Constância was once called Punhete, from *Pugna-Tage*, 'struggle of the Tagus'.

From the bridge I climbed back up to the mother church which was supposed to open for mass at 6.30 p.m. On the way I stopped at a small cash-and-carry for bottled water to rehydrate myself. The air-conditioned chrome-plated neon-lit cave was a sudden shocking sanctuary. It contained a freezer full of ice-cream cones and lollies in bulk.

'Sorry, no, we have no *Morango Fizz* . . .'

The white church that had been shut tight all day was adorned with stone scrollwork and a sumptuous bell-tower. A pigeon sat in a niche beside the sanctus bell. Two rivers glinted far below. The paper factory fumed. The priest emerged from his house on time and unlocked the west door with a great key. Inside, the church was more ballroom than holy place: all fine plasterwork, gilding and chandeliers. The chancel's vaulted ceiling was panelled in pink and blue marble, and above the nave was the painting I'd been hoping to see. It had all the confidence and blandness of the eighteenth century. I wished I could stare up at it with an innocent eye.

Three chubby pink babies on the left stretch a scroll between them, '*Vila Nova de Constância*'. A fourth child grasps fronds of dill and rosemary. On the right two babies' heads poke from clouds and whisper in one another's ears. The ceiling's focus is a fine woman in a billowing blue cloak. An old man with a lyre in one hand points her out to a young man who is quite naked. Beneath their feet, a town like a little heavenly city is painted at the perfect union of two rivers.

I wanted the earth, the pulse of water, the intimacy of rock, the face of Christ before rising again. I wanted the poet to speak out of his terrible nature. As I left the priest alone at his altar he began to intone the rite, far back in his throat, far back in a building overloaded with meaning and, empty, utterly meaningless. Ah, the terror of the intercessor who finds himself lost between nobody and no one.

16

FAIRY-TALE MANOEUVRES

Tomar and Almourol

AN UNSOLICITED LETTER was forwarded to me from an old address as I began to write this book. It had been sent by the Chancellor of the Order of the Holy Grail. He announced himself also as Chancellor of the Lofsensic Ursinius Order, and Grand Prior of the Templars. He offered me a bewildering range of memberships, baronies and knighthoods.

'The honours are free of charge as honours should be. A modest handling fee, however, is charged . . .'. I scanned the duplicated page: '. . . the Order of the Templars is founded in 1118, and is still active.' I thought it had been formed in Jerusalem by Hugh de Payns, and eight other French knights dedicated to protecting pilgrims from Muslim muggers, in late 1119 or early 1120, but what's a year or so. 'Knights or Dames receive two large diplomas, one in the English and one in the German language, and a medal with band.' The diplomas would be in full colour and plasticised, the medal a Maltese Cross. 'Also an Identity Card confirming the Diplomatic Immunity. Fee US $140, necessary as well: three passport photos and these data: date of birth, weight and height, colour of eyes and hair.'

Though I could always use diplomatic immunity, I sent no money or personal data, just a request for Templar contacts. Knights Templar first arrived in Portugal with Crusaders who made landfall *en route* for Palestine in 1128. The Grand Prior swiftly responded with a handwritten note: 'I know that the Order is going strong in Portugal but I have no addresses anymore. *Sic transit gloria mundi.* Yours sincerely . . .'

Some graffito artist at Praia do Ribatejo, just west of Constância, had gouged a name into the metal beneath the orange paintwork of a bus shelter: 'GUALDIM PAIS'. I saw it on my way to the castle of Almourol that squats or floats, depending on the weather conditions and your state of mind, on a magical island in the middle of the Tagus midway between the Atlantic and Spain, between Lisbon's Alcântara port and Alcántara's Roman bridge. On my travels up and down the Tagus, Almourol always appeared suddenly and, even the first time, with a shock of recognition, as though turning the page in a medieval manuscript I'd come upon the Platonic idea of a castle vividly illuminated on a page of text. It was real enough. Gualdim Pais, Grand Master of the Knights Templar, ordered the rebuilding of that island fortress in 1171.

'The Templars are back,' I'd been told in Lisbon. 'People love that sort of thing, grandiose investitures and noble missions like serving Christ's poor and crusading against practices that offend His people. Plenty of scope. Dangerous scope.'

The Templar Order officially re-registered itself in Portugal in 1984, getting on for seven centuries since it was banned. Graffiti in a bus shelter suggested that its heroes were not simply the property of an élite. Perhaps, even in Praia do Ribatejo's salubrious surroundings, there were roaming bands of Templar skins with blood-red crosses on their black T-shirts.

Gualdim Pais had attended at the birth of the nation. He was the companion-at-arms of Dom Afonso Henriques, Portugal's first king. As Templar Grand Master, Pais was a part of that impulse that persuaded Rome to permit, and sponsor, not only crusades to the Levant but also the western crusade or *Reconquista* in the Iberian Peninsula. In 1160 he ordered an astonishing castle-church to be built at Tomar, a metaphor in masonry for the medieval mind that forged this country, a metaphor that long outlived its appropriateness, a mind that persisted within the armoured skull of King Dom Sebastião. The One-so-longed-for held court here in 1569. The stones still live, in suspended animation as if today might be the twelfth century, or the sixteenth, or somewhere in between. The Templar castle and its heart, the Convent of Christ, hovers amid the drone of cicadas high above Tomar's old town.

To get to Tomar I took a bus through contemporary Portugal.

I risk sounding stupid to express how it felt. The Tupperware
factory, a little bit of Salt Lake City. Mighty works between
Abrantes and Entroncamento, a swathe of dishevelled land through
pine and eucalyptus forest, the new east–west road that links the
Lisbon–Porto highway with Spain. Montalvo, a notable parish swallowed up by development, with estates of villas on the outskirts,
the sort that boast brash tiles, pebbledash and lions on gateposts.
When the bus filled up a peasant woman moved her bundle on to
her lap but no one would sit beside her. Out of place among pale
faces, shoulder pads, terylene blouses, thigh-hugging skirts and
high-heeled shoes, she looked about her for company. No one met
her eyes. After crossing the Zêzere the bus turned up a minor road
over wooded hills and put her down on the fringe of a half-hidden
village, then dropped to a paper factory, the Nabão river and a
main road flanked by an odd mixture of crops and villas, greenhouses
and factories all the way to Tomar.

It was in seventh-century Tomar, then called Nabantia, that
Santa Iria was so foully murdered and tossed into the river. The
Nabão swept her corpse into the Zêzere, then down the Tagus to a
miraculous watery grave below Scallabis, renamed for her, Santarém.
Hers is a story of godly virtue versus devil-inspired lust set before
the Moorish occupation in Christian Visigothic times. A chapel
near the east end of Tomar's old bridge marks the traditional site
of Iria's martyrdom. A luxuriant island basks in midstream, just
upriver from the bridge and the king's watermills. Once it was a
sandbank. Now it is a garden offering tourists delicious sanctuary
beneath aspens, elms and poplars. I hadn't seen tourists in quantity,
or matching sets of schoolchildren in distinctive colours, since I
left Lisbon. Here they were well catered for. There were cafés and
ice-cream stalls, but still no *Morango Fizz*. The island's Santa Iria
Inn faced the Templars' Hotel on the far bank: names separated by
yards of water, by five hundred years.

A great free-standing waterwheel with earthenware pots lashed
to its fins turned relentlessly beside the footbridge from the old
town. Known as Moorish Wheels, or else *Tardo Romanas*, many of
them used to irrigate the valley. The secret of their construction
and perpetual motion, the sentimentalists say, has been lost in time.
Here, the difference in water level above and below the weir was

a foot or so. We all stared at pots filling and emptying, at the hefty wheel revolving amongst shimmering weeping willows, as if it was a miracle. It got close.

In the old Jewish quarter, empty earthenware flagons are discreetly embedded in the walls of the synagogue, open mouths pointing downwards so that each can pour its bellyful of sound back over the heads of the congregation. Four fine columns support a high vaulted roof, but the natural acoustic has been augmented by the pots to give the cantor's chant an other-worldly resonance, an unearthly fullness.

Luís Vasco had invited me into the synagogue and given me a skullcap to cover my head. He showed me the original ogee-arched entrance doorway, the excavation of the ancient ritual bath, and scrolls of the law within an ark like a plain wardrobe.

Rabbi Joseph of Tomar died, according to the inscription on his gravestone, in Faro in 1315. We can be sure there was a Jewish community in his native town before that time, but this synagogue was built in about 1438 when Infante Dom Henrique, Henry the Navigator, was Grand Master of the Order of Christ which had superseded the Templars. The Order dominated the town and fuelled the discovery of an ever-expanding world. At home, not just Christians but Jews, Muslims and newly 'discovered' Bantus from central Africa were welcome at Dom Henrique's court. Here in Tomar he encouraged a thriving Jewish community. But time, and tolerance, was short. In 1496 Dom Manuel ordered Jews to leave Portugal or convert. This synagogue became a public prison, but one in which, after the charter of 1516 extended their privileges, no 'New Christians' could be locked up. Subsequently it became São Bartolomeu's chapel and after that a hay loft, cellar and grocery warehouse. It was declared a national monument in 1921. Now it houses the Luso-Hebraic Museum named after Abraham Zacuto, the astronomer from Salamanca whose work enabled Portuguese mariners to calculate latitude at sea. He, who was a refugee from the Spanish Inquisition, refused to be baptised as a New Christian simply to escape the attentions of the Portuguese Holy Office. Tomar witnessed just two *autos-da-fé*, in 1543 and 1544. It's only recently that the street outside has been renamed Rua da Judearia.

'In 1992,' said Luís Vasco, 'we celebrated the first Yom Kippur in this synagogue for almost five hundred years.'

The Talmud prescribes that a synagogue should be sited on the heights of the city. In Tomar that position was taken by the Templars. Romans and Visigoths had proved the strategic spot, and Gualdim Pais's builders employed remnants of their masonry in constructing the Tower of Homage and the walls that embrace the citadel. More stone was brought from the ruins of nearby Roman Selium. The marvellous core of the work that Pais commissioned remains. It is a high crown of stone, topped with bells to point the mass within and warn of threats without. At once a castle keep and a circular temple, it sanctified the defence of the road to Santarém and Lisbon and focused the prayer that powered the reconquest of Estremadura, Beira and Alentejo. Its design was inspired, following the Order's custom, by the Church of the Holy Sepulchre in Jerusalem. The Templars' full title is, after all, the Poor Knights of Christ and of the Temple of Solomon.

Around a table on which sacrifice was enacted the world revolves. That altar, from which the body of God is dispensed, stands at the heart of a two-storey *charola* whose eight close-set pillars make eight narrow arches, surmounted by eight lancets. The word *charola* means a 'litter' on which sacred images are carried in religious procession, it means 'niche', and *levar em charola* is to fête someone by carrying them on the shoulders of the crowd. Within the prism of masonry at the temple's core the host was raised to heaven, and Christ the King glimpsed. The octagonal *charola* is surrounded by a sixteen-sided ambulatory pierced by sixteen arches framing deep alcoves high enough for the Templars to have attended mass mounted on horseback. Each man focused inwards upon the rite before leaving the shelter of those niches and riding out of the church door into the world. Starting from the mystery of God, two elements on a square table, then pressing outwards through the *charola* and the ambulatory arches – one, two, four, eight, sixteen – it cannot have seemed so very far to infinity.

The temple was roped and barricaded off when I was last there, in the middle of a decade of restoration work. I couldn't feel it from within, but power still radiated from it. It has often been suggested that the Templars went in for occult practices. Concentric rings of stone, rather than of charcoal or flour, might be the magic circle of the Grimoires, fortified with holy names and symbols, framed within an angular figure and potentised by prayers, adjurations and spells of knowledge. A bird fluttered around the *charola* like an unquiet soul. For me there was no soaring of the spirit here, rather a strong sense of weight, a centripetal force pulling inwards to the earth, intimations of magma, the molten womb. The temple felt magical.

Feelings do not prove that the Templars were followers of Simon Magus, despite the charges of gnosticism and of the worship of Baphomet that have been levelled against them. Their official rule was Benedictine, with special teaching furnished by St Bernard, the mellifluous doctor, in *De laude novae militiae*, to reconcile the spiritual and military vocations. However, some suspect that a secret rule based upon hidden knowledge (occult gnosis) was practised by an inner order of initiates. These winks and nudges, and the Temple of Jerusalem connection, have also hinted at common ground with Freemasonry. Such seductive trains of thought and feeling are, like their manifestations in the coven and the lodge, both sentimental and dangerous. They are truly captivating, in the sense that they make us slaves.

Though it's entertaining to manufacture mysteries, there's enough romance and hard-nosed passion in taking the Templars at face value. Charges against the Poor Knights of Christ were fomented when rulers grew jealous of their wealth and influence in the Europe of 1300. Kings banked with them, and Muslim caliphs too, for they were rock-solid. Philippe-le-Bel of France entrusted them more than once with his gold, but turned against them with the backing of Pope Clement V and initiated a squalid process of interrogation and confession, recanting and denial, imprisonment, torture and burning as heretics. Predictable accusations, such as those of sodomy among the knights and of secret alliances with the Moors, were nothing to the charge that initiates were obliged to spit on the crucifix and deny Christ.

The Order of Knights Templar was suppressed throughout Christendom in 1312. In Portugal it was quickly reinvented by King Dom Dinis as the Order of Christ. Infante Dom Henrique was its Grand Master from 1418 until his death in 1460. The

Order's wealth was annexed to Portuguese foreign policy and fuelled the prince's crusading ambition for new lands to be won in Christ's name. The discoveries swelled the Order's coffers through trade in gold, sugar and slaves. Henrique built himself a palace within Tomar's castle walls and added two cloisters to the Romanesque rotunda. Inside the convent I saw an exhibition of every possible image of Henry the Navigator, from the grandiose to the comic-strip. His is the icon, with the compulsory big hat and far-horizon gaze, that cannot but say, 'Once we were so great . . .'. Rui Cunha's sculpture of 1993, the Infante in scrap-metal armour, with internal cogs and pipes, has a spring for a neck and glass eyes in place of vision. Michael Barret's painting of the same year is entitled *O Infante Pessoa*: the poet of intellectual empire dressed in Henrique's clothes, under a broad-brimmed hat instead of a fedora.

High on a corner of the church there's a figure thought to be that of the prince, with the wings of a predatory eagle flattened over his crown and the peak of his helm in its beak. The sheer ferocity of that joint gaze made me nervous. Behind the eyes, the tender unanimity of man and bird made me nervous too. The scale and ambition of this place made me nervous, not because of its mystery but because of its certainty. It made me nervous because it's got a nerve. Or had one.

Manuel the Fortunate capitalised on it. He added a nave to the round church, trimmed it with flamboyant stone lacework and gave it a deeply carved doorway within a towering porch iced with all the symbols of discovery and empire. After him, Dom João III converted knights back into monks and built the greater part of the Renaissance monastery or convent of Christ. In all there are seven cloisters, from the latest two-storey Palladian one of 1557, the year Sebastião acceded, with its pompous fountain and sinuous spiral staircases of heart-wringing delicacy, to one of the very earli-est, the airy Cemetery Cloister tiled in Moorish style and scented by roses and orange trees in raised beds walled with blue and saffron *azulejos*. In an arcade of pointed arches lies the coffin of Baltasar de Faria who brought the Inquisition to Portugal. Once you could glare at his corpse through glass. Now he's been hidden under stone.

Stone conceals and reveals. Like any other work of man carving tells the truth and it lies. From the delightful cloister terrace of Santa Bárbara I looked at the chapter-house windows and gasped. They light the choir where the Order's business was enacted. Photographs of them are reproduced everywhere to illustrate the quintessence of Manueline architecture, but to see the real thing – I almost said, and will say, to see these stones in the flesh – is to witness Portugal at its apogee gazing, infatuated, at itself. Like baroque frames around small mirrors, the carvings that border the windows are rich and strange, shadowed and gilded with lichen. The upper rose window sits deep within bellying shapes defined by ropes and encircled by mouldings; to look into it is to stare through the aperture in a camera's iris diaphragm. The lower window is rectangular, filled with an austere grille but flanked by exuberant columns, here fluted, here dense with polyps, here draped with seaweed, knotted with cables, chained to vegetable forms or moored to the wall by ropes and rings. Crowned armillary spheres hover high at each side. Above the window coral gives way to visceral shapes like carved ivory, then to the Order of the Garter bestowed on the Infante, surmounted by the shield of Portugal and the cross of Christ. Below, something like the roots of an amputated tree or the stipe of a mighty weed from the Sargasso Sea weighs heavy on the shoulders of a bearded, behatted man whose fine hands hold on tight while his body of rope unravels. He is bearing all the wonders of new oceans and new worlds, the rich burden and the terrible glory of conquered nature.

Across the Nabão, twenty-two Grand Masters of both Orders are buried within Santa Maria do Olival's walls. If Tomar is Portugal's geographical and spiritual heart, then its church of St Mary of the Olive Grove, with a history of holy miracles and skirmishes with the infidel, and relics of the Order of Christ, claims to be the mother of all the churches in Africa, Asia and America. For some it is the centre of the world.

'Santa Maria do Olival,' a devout tourist told me, 'is the very soul of our faith and our national epic.'

Tomar is laid out in the form of a cross aligned with the cardinal points, with the Praça da República at its centre. There Gualdim Pais stands on a plinth with his back to the town hall and his eyes on the church of St John the Baptist. Infante Dom Henrique poses before a creeper-shrouded gateway to a clipped garden, gazing pensively at the tourist office. On the barren open space misleadingly called *Várzea Grande* (Big Meadow) in front of the Palace of Justice the cross of Christ stands high on an attenuated column, while on the hill behind it the Templars' battlements are dwarfed only by cypresses like black flames. This is how it was, and is. I remember three soldiers in the foreground carrying their kitbags towards the railway station.

Two ranks of soldiers in forage caps pounded down from the fairy-tale castle of Almourol, broke step as they reached the island's shore and clattered in single file over a temporary footbridge laid across flat-bottomed pontoons. On the Tagus's north bank they re-formed without a pause, fell into step and ran up to where I stood beside their commanding officer. A boat with an outboard motor and a full complement of troops screamed, bucking, from the bridge right around the island to the bridge's far side, drawing an almost-complete and widening circle of wake. The Portuguese flag flew high on the keep.

'This is a very pleasant exercise,' said the commanding officer.

Pleasant if you're watching, I thought, on a sunny Sunday afternoon. The conscripts were sweating. The officer and I had to shout at one another because the air was full of moronic macho chanting designed, presumably, to make you forget what exactly you're doing. It's called discipline.

'Morale-raising stuff,' he mouthed, 'and a good day out.'

He told me that his troops were stationed at Tancos Militar. I'd got off the bus outside the gates of the army camp there and walked along a melting tarmac road to a turning down a rough track which brought me, eventually, to the river and beneath the railway track that runs beside it. At this, the halfway point of my journey from Spain back to the ocean, I'd expected an island set like a jewel in the river crowned with the castle out of medieval legend that I'd glimpsed many times. Until today I had no real-time, real-place context in which to imagine it. I hadn't expected Knights Templar in shining armour, nor young men and women in prosaic khaki.

Of all the castles in Portugal Almourol is said to be the only one with no history. The island is conventionally described as diamond-shaped. It's a rough one. I paid the ferryman to row me around it in his *barco* and land me on a sandy beach at the far side. From dense tree-shade I emerged into sunlight, prickly-pear thickets and hard-edged shadows cast by massive boulders. The castle's stonework was founded on them. Strabo wrote about this island two thousand years ago, and the castle that has no history was once the site of a Lusitanian settlement taken and fortified by the Romans, some of whose work remains in the lower walls. They left coins on the island which later occupiers, Visigoths and Moors, didn't pick up. Christians took possession of Almourol in the course of the *Reconquista* and Knights Templar had the citadel rebuilt. Its walls, punctuated by ten round towers, snugly fit the steep contours and are equipped with all the turrets, arrow-slits and battlements that a fairy-tale castle needs. Trippers have carved their grey names into fleshy green cactus stems. Over the castle's round entrance arch is inscribed the date 1171 and the name Gualdim Pais. They say it has no history because it never saw military action, unless you count a little exercise on a pontoon bridge as action.

By the whipping flag on top of the keep I could see mile after deserted mile and cool off. Below, troops dismantled assault equipment and loaded trailers. On an embankment above the khaki trucks a long train drawn by a pair of orange locomotives sizzled up the line loaded with coal for the Pego power station. A pair of storks flapped over the castle. Higher, an eagle cruised, light on its head, straight wings with dark tips and a wedge of tail. A pied wagtail hopped along the battlements. Below, fish jumped in the river. Before I realised it the army had driven off, the island was an island once more. The castle had a river for a moat, one which flowed past for ever and left it, if you wanted it that way, with no past at all.

Castles are like dead beetles or crabs. The exoskeleton remains long after the viscera have gone. Here, strong ramparts protected hints of living quarters. I clambered about the walls and inner terraces, all the levels on which the organism had operated in life. I saw the remnants of a tunnel said to have connected the castle to the shore. Facilities of that kind are obligatory in fairy-tale castles. I thought of the stories that cling like lichen or shift like shadows on Almourol's stones.

Almourol was a fearsome giant who guarded the princesses Mira-
guarda and Polinarda. Once upon a time Palmeirim, a Crusader
from England on his way to Constantinople, put in at Porto and
heard of the two beautiful ladies. In the manner of fairy-tale knights
he fell in love with the idea of them, or, to be perfectly chivalrous,
with the idea of one of them, and made his way to the Tagus. He
defeated Almourol and stole Polinarda away. Or, if you prefer,
Almourol defeated him, only to be vanquished himself by another
giant called Dramusiando. Fairy-tales are histories of the heart with
optional endings.

Beatriz was the daughter of Dom Ramiro, the castle's constable.
He had murdered the mother and sister of a Moorish boy whom
he took to Almourol as his slave. Naturally Beatriz fell in love with
the beautiful Moor. One night they made a perilous descent of the
castle walls, crossed the river without the help of a pontoon bridge
and eloped together. While they lived happily ever after Dom
Ramiro died of a broken heart. Or, Beatriz plunged to her death
from the battlements, rather than wed the husband Dom Ramiro
had chosen for her, followed by the lovesick slave. Either way, the
ghosts of Beatriz and the Moor haunt the castle every St John's
Eve. Or her shape walks here alone and sighing on nights of the
full moon.

I re-entered the real world gently, courtesy of the ferryman and
a slow walk along the tracks, not to Tancos Militar and the barracks,
but to the village of Tancos. From its beautiful waterfront I looked
back at the legend, picked out and illuminated by the late sun. A
long beer in a small bar revived me. Card-players, including one
like Popeye in a baseball cap, roared and fell silent, then roared
again. They told me no, no, there would be no bus now today, not
Sunday. An African Grey parrot understood my Portuguese. The
little woman all in black behind the bar talked copiously to both
of us. No bus, no train, not this time on Sunday. Then her daughter,
son-in-law and their children came to say goodbye after their weekend in the sticks. As the text-book middle-class family drove off
towards Lisbon in their Seat, the woman in black waved and waved
and called quietly, tearfully after them, 'Adios.' I felt I was watching
old Portugal say farewell to its future.

Whatever anyone had told me the bus came on time. It was

empty but for the driver, me and folkloric music at full volume. He was fast. In a lurching echo-chamber I sped towards the setting sun.

17

BACK TO THE BIG LETTUCE

Lisbon

UNDER ITS DOME the Mercado Ribeira gets down to business before dawn. Scents of massed flowers and heaps of pristine fruits and vegetables fill the upper storey of the riverside market. Downstairs butchers like warriors in white coats hack at carcasses. Fishwives gut the sea's harvest and set it out like jewellery. They screech at and laugh with one another as they work. They break into snatches of song. The catch has declined and they no longer cry glittering wares, balanced on their heads, around the streets, but it is still to them, so romantics say, that the *fado* belongs.

> She's a *varina*, she wears slippers,
> She has the movements of a cat.
> In her basket, the caravel;
> In her heart, the frigate . . .

Varinas take their title from the coastal town of Ovar. There, and at Aveiro, there's a strong strain in both blood and custom of the Phoenicians who once settled up and down the coast.

> Instead of ravens, on her shawl
> Seagulls come to roost . . .
> When the wind tempts her to dance
> She dances in the dance with the sea . . .

Now the ocean which laps its length means much less to Portugal. Wealth – Eastern spices, African slaves and Brazilian gold – all came by way of the ocean. Today the prestigious oceanarium is to the east of Lisbon's centre and money flows downriver from the EU. But still, in bars and shops all over the city, the recorded voice of the great *fadista* Amália Rodrigues sustains the old romance.

> Her dress is of seashells,
> She has seaweed in her hair,
> And in her veins the throbbing
> Of the engine of a trawler . . .

It's a modern *fado*, but it's full of *saudade*. Amália wrings the fringes of her raven-black shawl. Ai! Remember how, in the nineteenth century, the Count of Vimioso fell scandalously in love with Maria Severa, exotic beauty and legendary *fadista*, whose father was a gypsy and whose mother, from Ovar, once kept a tavern in the fishwives' quarter of Lisbon. Could there be a better pedigree for the song that belongs to this city?

> She sells dreams and sea-tang,
> Tempests are her street-cry;
> Her first name: Maria . . .
> Her surname: Lisboa.

On the tram to Alfama a woman sits behind and beneath a huge polythene bag full of fresh lettuces. Like *Alfama* the word for lettuce, *alface*, is Arabic in origin. Lisbon's inhabitants are nicknamed *alfac-inhas*, 'little lettuces'. We whine to a halt, clang the bell. This morning some little lettuce has parked his car too close to the tramlines just below the Sé (cathedral). The driver does all he can to nudge his tram through the gap but can't pass. He gets out and climbs the Sé's steps. Perhaps prayer will help.

I follow him into this hefty castle of a church. The door's set beneath a rose window between towers. There's a Romanesque wedding in progress. A late guest has abandoned his car and rushed in. The tram-driver recruits three men dressed up like bitches' dinners. The four of them tumble down the steps and bounce the car out of the way. I wave the driver goodbye and follow the dinners inside, like turning up at a film premiere in dungarees. The priest's vestments are classy, but nobody notices his words, they're too busy eyeing each other, preening and whispering. Yellow gold, varnished jowls, tinted contact lenses. The smell of incense is overpowered by perfume and aftershave. Cheap soap. A scene from a cheap Brazilian soap.

In the wonderfully bare chapels of the apse I find peace with stiff effigies of real snobs, long out of it. The beautiful cloister is a dig. There's a plank leading up out of a trench into the Mother of God's lap. Our Lady of the Wheelbarrow. The verger looks as a verger should, virgin-pecked but intimate with, if not God, at least with His ironmongery and stoneware.

'There was a pretty garden here,' he says.

'Yes,' I reply, 'I've walked around it.'

'Then there was some subsidence so we dug, and we dug.'

There are walls down there, steps, pits, grindstones and mystery masonry surrounded by the gothic arches and rose windows of the ambulatory. All this, focused beneath the Sé's defensive bulk, details under the weight of God's fortress.

'These are Moorish baths,' explains the verger, 'and before that a Roman villa.'

'And where are the ravens,' I dare to ask, 'that used to guard St Vincent's relics?'

The two ravens that escorted the ship in which Dom Afonso Henriques brought São Vicente's remains to Lisbon in 1173 bred here. The great earthquake dispersed the saint's ashes, all but a few relics now kept in the sacristy, but the ravens stuck to their post, guaranteeing the safety of the realm as the Tower of London's ravens preserve the British crown.

'Despite the sacristan's care,' the verger takes the weight of my question, sighing, 'the last descendant died in 1978.'

Apparently, ravens disapprove of revolution.

The Rua da Saudade climbs towards the castle. It must be climbed in the present tense but it leads to the past perfect. I took my time weaving through the imperfect past, up the alleys and steps of Alfama. Cages hung by windows, prisons for canaries or finches. Washing hung between buildings, over roofs, on balconies bright with flowerpots. Plants sat on sills between shutters too, between the outer world and interiors glinting with brass and glass and modest chandeliers. Exteriors were on a different plane. Stucco cracked and scabbed and fell. Ox-blood wash faded to sensuous damask. Moss sprouted in pantiles and guttering. Lichen clung as firmly to back walls as *azulejos* to front. Every so often between houses I glimpsed thin blue distances, the Arrábida hills, river, docks, bleached monuments, a crazy ochre roofscape, exposed and secretive and spiky with aerials, and the startling white dome of Santa Engrácia. It's a church rebuilt on terrible history, after alleged profanation by a 'New Christian', and a byword for a task never done, 'the works of Santa Engrácia'. Commissioned by a hundred nobles of the Brotherhood of Slaves of the Most Holy Sacrament in 1632, it was not completed until 1966, its soaring dome finally topped off to mark the fortieth anniversary of the New State. Now the National Pantheon, it's an airy wonder, a phantom pregnancy gravid with the hopes of heroes.

Lunch-time curry was fragrant in the Goanese restaurant close to the gate of the Castelo de São Jorge. St George slew primal dragons for Portuguese as well as English, and his castle here is a heavily-restored puzzle of stone, set on Roman-Visigothic-Moorish foundations, inlaid with trees and water. One moment I stood exposed on a battlemented terrace with the atmosphere of a village square, whose cannon like bulky trinkets threatened the city and waterfront with nothing more than open mouths. The next I enjoyed delicious shade within the maze where waterspouts spewed into stone troughs, flamingos stood in small lakes, black swans glided, peacocks and guinea fowl strutted the banks. Why does the exotic misplaced become mere garden ornament? Screeches ricocheted around the masonry. The heads of eighty Moors from Almada were stuck on poles outside this castle when Christians besieged it for seventeen weeks in 1147. Why does blood leave no lasting stain? Here the hero Martim Moniz held the gate open for Afonso Henriques's forces even as he was hacked to pieces. Here berserk Crusaders forgot all Afonso's guarantees to Lisbon's inhabitants and massacred them indiscriminately.

Heroic youths with sticks tormented swans. Mangy cats slunk spitting in the undergrowth. From the battlements I saw the city laid open. Trams and buses came and went in the square called Martim Moniz. One side was crumbly old layer-cake Lisbon, the

The *Portas de Ródão*, or 'gates' of the Tagus below the town of Vila Velha de Ródão.

Second-century Roman bridge across the Tagus below the Moorish walls of Alcántara in Spain. Arabic, *al-kantara*, 'the bridge'.

The not-so-holy mountain: boulders and dwellings at Monsanto.

Left: Manoeuvres on the island of Almourol.

Below: Heat and shade in Constância, the poets' town.

Ploughing at the foot of Monsanto.

Above: Bearing new oceans and new worlds, the rich burden and terrible glory of conquered nature. Detail, the chapterhouse window, Tomar.

Left: Aspiring staircase in the Convent of Christ, Tomar.

Above: The Paço Real, Sintra, where Sebastião dreamed of his Moroccan crusade. From this site, Moorish governors once ruled their Portuguese province.

Cabo da Roca, westernmost point of Europe, 'where the earth ends and the sea begins'.

other a Big Lettuce of sheer façades and multi-storey mirrors. Sprouting sunlit from the horizon like a pop-up toytown was Amoreiras's postmodern shopping and office complex whose purpose is as simple and deadly as this castle's was, power and money. I turned inwards to look for ravens. I'd made a pilgrimage to their cage in the past and spoken with them. They'd hopped from perch to perch with the gravity of undertakers and 'crrarked' at me with gratifying candour.

Now they were missing. Who now would speak to me of Valencia and Cape St Vincent, of the compass called the rose of winds at the end of the world, launchpad for the discoveries? Demoralised pheasants fussed in the old raven enclosure, targets for little boys with stones. On whose wings could I travel? That's why I climb to this castle, to take off from its labyrinth. Tradition has the *Voador*, 'flier', Bartolomeu de Gusmão lifting off in 1709 from the village of Santa Cruz within the castle walls. He's commemorated at the airport by a statue outside the post office and a mural above the escalator that lifts you to Departures. Why isn't he known outside Portugal? Should we remember Charles Lindbergh for his solo flight across the Atlantic in 1927, but not Sacadura Cabral and Gago Coutinho? Five years before Lindbergh, with incredible boldness, they flew from Lisbon across the South Atlantic to Rio de Janeiro in the biplane *Santa Cruz*.

In the absence of that small hydroplane, of Gusmão's 'big bird' or of funereal ravens, the fired imagination takes me up from the cranium's confines. From these turrets I touch down and walk the castle walls of Bragança in the north and Silves in the south. Lisbon's seven hills shimmer, their buildings all at once reduced to stone huts and paved roads like those of prehistoric Citânia de Briteiros, on its own hill not far from the palace of the Dukes of Bragança at Guimarães. Monuments simplify, become phallic giants, pierced pigs, mythic bulls that up there survived the tide of monotheism. Christian Belém and miraculous Jerónimos, that survived the 1755 earthquake, speak of Henry the Navigator's town, that didn't, by Cape St Vincent. The Marquês de Pombal's chillingly humanist reconstruction orders the Baixa. Alfama's shrines and streets of steps echo the enormous penance of Bom Jesus.

Like Father Gusmão, I came down to earth in the Rossio. At the

Nicola coffee house I had a drink and talked politics, the conservative pious north versus the radical 'African' south with its Moorish indifference to religiosity. The Nicola is the place to join the nightly toast to the poet Bocage (1765–1805), son of a Setúbal lawyer, who scandalised Goa with his stormy impiety and deserted to Macão. Famous in Lisbon for ripe satire and raunchy improvised verse, his finest works are sonnets which anticipate the Romantics: their strict form holds intense personal feeling, as bars contain a wild beast.

The novelist Almeida Faria, an Alentejan with sympathy for Bocage's temperament, pointed out the pictures on Nicola's walls which illustrate episodes from the poet's life, including an officially-sponsored attempt on it. Bocage extemporised:

> *Sou o poeta Bocage*
> *Venho do café Nicola*
> *E vou para o outro mundo*
> *Se disparas a pistola.*

'I am the poet Bocage, I come from the café Nicola and go to the other world if you fire your pistol.' The Inquisition confined him in 1797 for preaching atheism and revolution. Once they might have burnt him. As it was, at forty he burnt himself out.

Almeida Faria had been a great friend of the late Alexandre O'Neill, one of the Irish family who came to Portugal in the eighteenth century, and a poet in the Bocage tradition.

'He suffered a stroke,' said the novelist. 'Then we were asked to go to Brazil together. We both loved what Brazilian writers were doing with the Portuguese language. I still do. I went with him to the doctor and asked, Should he go? Yes, said the doctor, because it will be his last journey. And it was.'

Almeida Faria wanted to show me the Casa do Alentejo. We walked up Portas de Santo Antão. Nick Cave and the Bad Seeds were on that night at the Coliseum. Kids in studied black cruised in shoals with slogans on their T-shirts: *Nirvana*, *Eraserhead*, and *No Name Boys*. A seventeen-year-old Sporting Lisbon fan had just been stabbed to death by one of Benfica's No Name Boys. We passed the passage, Pátio de Tronco, tiled with modern *azulejos*: ten portraits of the poet Camões above, 'Portugal' to the right, 'Sempre' to the left – Portugal for ever! – and an inscription stating that on 16 July 1552 (eighteen months before Sebastião was born) Luís Vaz de Camões was arrested at the Portas de Santo Antão for his part in a brawl (the gang mugging of a palace official) and brought to Tronco municipal gaol ... Unlike the No Name Boys he had friends, or lovers, at court to win him a pardon on the grounds that he was off on the king's service to India (and Macão and Moçambique and the rest of his life).

Almeida Faria liked the mad guys – the Camõeses, Bocages, O'Neills – liked that strain in the national character. In 1990 he stirred up the Portuguese psyche with his novel *O Conquistador* in which Sebastião is reborn in 1954 and grows up to be a sexual conqueror, rather than the passionate and fanatical but chaste young king of history who died fighting the Moors.

'Sebastião, like almost all crazy men, is much more fascinating than a good king,' he said. 'And this crazy battle, and all the crazy things he did, are appealing. Especially for young people. In the last twenty years the myth of King Sebastião is getting bigger and bigger every day.'

I wanted to follow that up, but we'd reached the Casa do Alentejo. We climbed steps and entered a Moorish-style confection. Stairs climbed to landings around a central covered court, giving ever new views of its over-egged elegance. It should have been empty and brilliant. It was dark and cluttered with detail. I tried to take in its paintings and tiles and statuary. I do remember two things. A room named Sala de Olivença after that still raw wound, that bite out of Alentejo that for almost two hundred years has been Spanish Olivenza. The room screamed, 'Not-Spain!' Then, in a dining-room, a vulgar food bar, chrome and glass, quite out of keeping and proportion with the ponderous grandeur of the space.

'Ah, you see,' said Almeida Faria, 'it's so very Portuguese.'

Alone, a few steps down the road, I entered the even more extravagant fastness of the Lisbon Geographical Society. Some years ago I'd stood on the steep bank of the River Zaïre, where the Yelala Falls end above Matadi in Camões's 'mighty kingdom of Congo', and read what Diogo Cão's expedition had cut in the rocks there in 1487: *Aqy chegaram os navios* ... 'Here arrived the ships of the illustrious King Dom João the Second of Portugal. Diogo Cão. Pêro Anes. Pêro da Costa.' It was beautiful and melancholy. Men landed small fish from the great river and pounded groundnuts in a rocky mortar beside their cave. The inscription could have been carved yesterday. Now, in Lisbon, I wanted to see the remains of the pillar of stone, *padrão*, that Cão had set at the mouth of the Congo river in 1482. For my benefit a cleaner flicked switches that lit up a big map of the discoveries. The museum had no other visitors. Its treasures, or plunder, was irrelevant. Portugal had Europe on its mind. The *padrão* had been used for target practice by a British man-o'-war, its fragments cherished by Angolans as powerful fetishes. Now, with perfect irony, it's back in Lisbon among other waymarks once proudly planted on West African shores. I stroked the battered stones and shivered.

Hawkers draped with sashes of lottery tickets tempt your fate: 'Here's the big chance,' 'Brings happy days,' 'The wheel spins tomorrow.' Down in the metrô a young man rocks on his haunches as, from the warped saw he holds like a violin under his chin, his bow drags an ethereal music which fills and haunts the subways. An old soldier exposes the stump of his thigh, his false leg in a laced boot standing on the pavement in front of him. A girl with healed-up scars where eyes should be squats with a money-box slung round her neck. A knife-grinder wheels his bicycle through the crowds, playing his signature tune on pan pipes. A showman enchants a group of us with a levitating toy man. He stamps on it, jumps on it, but still it rises, dances. It's a parable, of course. It's called Sebastião. A policeman has a ragged boy by his scruff. The boy's father leaves the pitch where he and his sorry wife sell wallets and purses, empty ones. The boy's younger brother follows, but father curses, orders him back to the square of cardboard in the doorway where he sleeps. Cowed, he curls up on it, one knowing eye open. It watches father beat little big brother for the policeman's pleasure.

At the bottom of the broad wooden stairs leading up six flights to my *pensão*, gypsy women block the way with flowers and sleeping children. Barrowloads of wild flowers have been wheeled into the city's heart for Ascension Thursday, *Dia da Espiga*, Day of the Ear of Corn. The gypsies part to let me by without meeting my eye.

Flowers wilt in the heat: an olive twig for peace, lavender for faith, marigolds for wealth, poppies for happiness, wheat for abundance. A group of such women, the buzz goes, have stocked up at a supermarket and offered not money at the checkout but sharp knives. At the first turn of the stairs a youth sits poring over lists of figures and a wad of banknotes as he does every day. He never looks up. At the next a finance committee of middle-aged men is sorting out lottery takings. We exchange greetings as usual. On the second floor the defunct firm, Fernandes & Martins, has a letter-box with the flap neatly welded shut in three places.

From my room I look across the Rossio to the Bairro Alto and Carmo's ruins. Below me a fat man, his bare torso protected by a cardboard breastplate and backplate both labelled with a crudely drawn '6', is chanting in a high-pitched voice. A thin scholar is setting up his telescope, as on every summer night, with a neatly-written notice about the moons of Jupiter. He's a streetwise Galileo funding his studies. He'll show passers-by the celestial bodies for just 100 escudos. In Figueira the bodies on offer are strictly terrestrial. They meet the eyes of men and say seductive things like 'Fucky-fuck?'

On the eve of Portugal Day snack stalls and the Electro Tombola were going full belt in Praça de Camões. Tomorrow, 10 June, official speeches would stress national identity, dust off the notion of *Portugalidade* and invoke the name of the poet. Portugal Day is also Camões Day. Spain has its day of *Hispanidade*, Columbus Day. That day, and every other, Spanish TV shows two kinds of map in its weather forecasts. One is the whole Iberian Peninsula with no Spanish/Portuguese border at all. The other is the Peninsula *minus* Portugal, as if the Atlantic had neatly swallowed all land as far as the Spanish frontier. That's *Hispanidade*, that's how the Spanish regard, or disregard, their neighbour. I once asked a Spanish friend what jokes they told about the Portuguese.

'You won't believe it, but I don't know any,' she said after a long pause. 'We simply don't think about them.'

Tomorrow the Portuguese may think about themselves: the ones who never left, the ones returned after revolution waved a brisk goodbye to the colonies, the black Portuguese who came from Africa or the Cape Verde Islands or half the globe, the white diaspora that withdraws and shifts to Europe, backwards out of the big world. They may think of what Camões said, that if Spain is the head of Europe, then Portugal is the crown.

Now, on the eve of Portugal Day, the front of the church of São Cristavão in Alfama was hung with garlands and Chinese lanterns. A parade of girls in floral dresses and boys in white with white guitars sang out charming *marchas* under garlanded arches and escorted tinsel-decked portraits of St Christopher, St Lawrence and St Anthony to and fro. Then *fadistas* took over the church steps and roused the neighbourhood with old favourites. A woman dragged the corners of her black shawl down over her full pink blouse while the pair of seated musicians that flanked her intertwined the thrum and jangle of *viola* and *guitarra* and underpinned the words.

> Whenever Lisbon sings
> I don't know if she sings or she prays
> For when Lisbon sings
> She sings the *fado*, for sure.

A man in jeans and waistcoat set his face firmly to the horizon of memory and self-knowledge, the threshold of destiny.

> And we went! Our fatherland's a tree
> With roots and trunk and branches.
> Because we went, is why we are!
> Because we are, is why we go!

The next night, in the early hours following Camões Day in the Bairro Alto, eleven black Portuguese were seriously injured and one, of Cape Verdean origin, went into coma and died from multiple fractures of the spine and skull caused, a doctor at São José hospital confirmed, by extreme violence. About fifty white 'skins' in cult gear and armed with knives, knuckledusters, iron bars and bottles, had launched a running attack on every black person they saw. Spokesmen talked of 'unprecedented racist violence' that blemished the country's 'tradition of tolerance and hospitality'. Myths die hard. In 1995 a survey found that half the population (compared with a third in the rest of Europe) felt there were too many 'residents of a different ethnic origin'. I thought of fifteenth-century slaves dumped in cesspits, and of the Minister for the Army who urged on his troops in the African 'provinces' with the words, 'We are going to fight savages. We are going to fight wild beasts – wild beasts who are not Portuguese, because they obey orders from international Communism.' That was in 1961, when Portugal Day was still officially known as *Dia da Raça* – Day of the Race.

Hard on its heels come the feasts of the popular saints. St Anthony, 13 June. St John, the twenty-fourth. St Peter, the twenty-ninth. In 1195 the infant St Anthony was baptised in Lisbon's Sé. The font's still there and the room where he was born, across the road, was eventually incorporated into the small church of Santo António da Sé. To the world he's St Anthony of Padua. Here, and especially on his feast, he's known as Santo António of Lisbon, wonder-worker, saint-of-saints and patron saint of lovers.

> This latticed window
> Makes my life a Calvary,
> Because you won't allow
> It to be my confessional.

This *fado* mixes the powerful cocktail of Passion and passion while the next begs forgiveness with its tongue in its cheek:

> Santo António, a thousand pardons,
> Because we all, without thinking,
> Went up today to your altar
> To get candles for the balloons.

On St Anthony's Eve Lisbon's *bairros* (quarters) enter teams of marchers for a mighty parade of lights, costumes and bands down the Avenida da Liberdade. The sacred *marchas* of Lisbon went to Brazil and, in the days when Dom Pedro IV was emperor, came back from the shanty towns of Rio de Janeiro as supercharged *marchinhas*, the dances of Carnival. Oh for a touch of Carmen Miranda, their most celebrated Portuguese exponent, today. There were ordinary high spirits, but none of the outrageous exuberance, the anarchic sensuality of Rio. Later, though, it seemed all Lisbon crammed into Alfama and pressed up to the castle, the bonfires, stench of grilled sardines, trestle bars, singers, street dances, a tide – with its small flotsam of broken glass, fists, blood – that carried me towards dawn.

A girl plucks the carnation from the pot of basil her boyfriend gave her and replaces it with a wild artichoke which, in liturgical purple, represents St George's shoulderplates, gauntlets and lance. The carnation she puts in her hair or at her breast, depending how passionate she is, or wants to show she is. The artichoke she singes with flame and if in time it flowers again it signifies requited love and resurrection. If not:

> There is, in the *guitarra* I hold,
> So much pain that I even suppose
> It made of the self-same wood
> On which they nailed Jesus.

Not that you have to take it all so seriously:

> My love – no one disputes it –
> Is no saint, but all in all,
> Taking away what's no good,
> Leaves nothing at all.

Eve of the Feast of St Peter. Mouraria, the 'Moorish quarter'. He might have been the big fisherman himself, the man dancing in Rua da Mouraria. We celebrated in a makeshift arena of stalls at the foot of the Escadinhas da Saúde, or 'little stairways of health', supposedly named for Nossa Senhora da Saúde but really so called because you feel a lot healthier climbing down them than up. The dancer was too drunk to think about it. And wild, in the desert of his head. Maybe he was John the Baptist, sweating in religious ecstasy, though he wasn't wearing a camelhair coat. Or eating locusts and wild honey. No, no, it was sardines and red wine again. Ah, forget the sardines.

On temporary staging the band was black and coffee-coloured, blowing up samba and salsa, plucking out cadences of *fado*. A young woman, one of the Marys, with a concave figure and a weathered brown face, came and slouched beside me at the bar, smoking. The apostle flung his arms to the stars, lunged at a mate. A blond guy in a very white shirt sashayed across the mosaic cobbles, dancing with no one but a carrier bag and blowing camp kisses at all the butch men. He was outrageous, enjoying it almost too much. The skill of the stoned dancers was extraordinarily touching. Their gestures were loving, mad, threatening. Smart young couples danced among them, then left them to their life. I climbed the Escadinhas, met a roaming pye-dog and gazed back downstairs with him, breathing hard.

> They ask me about the *fado*? I knew him!
> He was a drunkard, he was a bum
> Who tramped about Mouraria;
> Perhaps a little leaner than a greyhound,
> Saying that he was blue-blooded
> Because he hung around with the gentry . . .

18

THE CELESTIAL BULL

Campo Pequeno

. . . His father was a poor bastard
Who even took himself aboard
The caravels of da Gama;
An ill-dressed one, and dirty,
More quarrelsome than a sailor
From the old alleys of Alfama . . .

He went to *Esperas* for bulls,
Became a renowned horseman,
Was the rage in the Carnival!
In that reckless lifetime
He – who came from nothing –
Being nothing, was everything!

You ask me about *fado*? I knew him.

I heard Alcindo de Carvalho sing this biography of *fado*. He had
sung it for forty years. He was smart in houndstooth tweed, while
the *guitarra* and *viola* players either side of him were dressed as
bank managers. But the voice! It rose in a crescendo of pain and fell
into intimate dialogue with the *guitarra*, the pear-shaped Portuguese
guitar tuned and fingered like a twelve-string cittern. Lyrical and
bell-like, or jangling and tearing, the *guitarra* led, answered and
provoked Alcindo while the rhythm and harmonics that held the
song together were provided by the *viola*, or Spanish guitar.
Not that the Portuguese say 'Spanish'. To them it's the English
guitar.

Fado means 'fate' and fate, they say, is Portugal. And here it was: *fado* in a suit, white-collar *fado*. But then, in Parreirinha de Alfama, the *casa de fado* she has run for forty years, Argentina Santos stood still under an arch with her heavy coiled hair, her black lace, her strong expressive hands, her pure dark voice, and at once I was in the Lisbon of gypsies and fishwives.

> To the canary, the crystal throat;
> To the nightingale, the presumption of an artist;
> You shouldn't envy, sparrow, you have more:
> A bohemian spirit . . . You are a *fadista*.

At number 13 Rua da Atalaia, in the Bairro Alto, a young man whacked glasses and bottles down on rough tables, moved customers up, and rearranged stools and beer crates to seat the young people pressing in. He wore a shaggy short coat and an expression of infinite sadness. From behind the bar he made sour asides, commentary on the *fados* being sung, and sometimes he moved to the front to stand beneath the red light, the only one apart from candles on the tables. With pinned-up pictures of singers and instruments at his back, and a lad playing a mean *guitarra* at his side, he allowed a doleful song to slip from the corner of his bent mouth. Before the last phrase was out of it the small bar erupted with applause that shocked the candle flames. We were all conspirators.

Anyone who spoke during a song was severely reproved with looks and hisses. A swarthy man with a close blue shave, glossy ponytail, mocha-coffee-coloured suit, gold studs, cufflinks and chains, kept his seat at the table and sang like a *mafioso* making a difficult confession. When he'd finished, everyone burst into loud chatter, in relief from suspense.

'This song started in Lisbon,' said my friend Helder, 'sung by the common people before it became a fashion, by women to begin with. Now they say it came from Brazil: from Africa to Brazil and from Brazil to Lisbon.'

A young man stood up to sing, frail and ragged. His eyes were moist. He had a harsh voice and bad teeth. Everything about him made him seem old, except his youth. His regrets were too big for him, but at least his yearning had a future.

'They say that the *fofa* and *lundum* dances from the black community of Alfama mixed with ballads and bred a lascivious song and dance tradition that enraged poets like Bocage, and somehow created the *fado*,' Helder continued, 'but I don't know. I think it came more directly, from the middle ages, from the platonic *Cantigas de Amigo*, Songs of a Lover.'

A sharp-featured young woman with henna-coloured hair turned, in the singing, to a luminous beauty. Her neck strained upwards and her lyrical timbre crossed the border into wildness. A man with perfect romantic film-star looks had a trespassing voice whose depth and abrasiveness scoured the soul.

'This man is a Spaniard,' said Helder, 'but a Spaniard who prefers *fado* to *flamenco*. His Portuguese is good and he has, as we say, a beautiful mouth.'

Uma bôca bonita, a pretty mouth, the mouth of a gypsy, the throat of a medieval troubadour whose ear had filled with Moorish cadences. That quaver, those arabesques.

'Somehow *fado* happened, out of many influences we cannot disentangle,' Helder knotted his hands, 'so that by the beginning of the nineteenth century – only then, in a form half as old again as the blues – we have songs reverting to an older, purer tradition which became known as *fados castiços*.'

Helder pinched the lobe of his right ear between thumb and forefinger. Caste *fados*, pure-bred, the real thing that the Count of Vimioso, himself an amateur *fadista*, fell in love with when he fell for Maria Severa. Her mother – *A Barbuda*, 'the bearded lady' – gave up her tavern in Madrugoa and moved with her daughter to Mouraria's notorious red-light district, Rua do Capelão, popularly known as Rua Suja, 'dirty street', where Maria learned the trade, and to sing and dance *fado*. If the art-form was debased at that time, as many suppose, what was it that elevated it through her artistry to the heights that the Severa myth claims? Her first love committed a *crime passionnel* for which he was banished to Africa. Here was fuel for a fire of yearning, for *saudade*, the exile's nostalgia for home and love, the loser's idealisation of the lost, the traveller's longing for a past too far into the future ever to be reached.

The related Spanish word *soledad* came to mean only 'solitude' and 'loneliness' and left the burden of 'nostalgia' and 'sense of loss', with all the baggage of homesickness, pining and yearning they imply, to a term of Catalan origin, *añoranza*. *Saudade* still holds the lot. It's a shame the English can't borrow the Welsh *hieryth* which has more strong feeling than sentiment in it. And it's sad that neither *hieryth* nor nostalgia has any future. You can only hope for hope in Portuguese.

'There's no translation for *saudade*,' said Helder, 'that's what I've learned since I was a child.'

The fifteenth-century king Dom Duarte wrote in his book *Leal Conselheiro* (Loyal Counsellor): 'it seems to me this term *suydade* is so very fitting that neither Latin nor any other language has a similar term for such feeling'. In Camões's lyrics *saudade* is the love-sickness which destroys *saúde* (health). In Dirty Street the same disease, that willed affliction, had its own gloss, but was strong and honest enough to imbue Severa's singing with fascinating power. The Count of Vimioso, the *fado*-singing, bullfighting aristocrat with a love of low life, was seduced by her passionate nature and hearty appetites. The word *fadista*, please note, also means 'ruffian' (masculine) and 'prostitute' (feminine). The Severa myth – romantic, sordid, tempestuous – stands as an icon on the high altar of *fado* because it mixes the sacred ingredients of *varina* and gypsy, aristocrat and troubadour, siren and whore, alley and bullring, bohemia and high society. The literary legend has her dying wanly of poetic consumption. Tuberculosis. Popular history kills her more realistically with full-blooded over-consumption: too much pigeon and red wine. She died of a surfeit in 1846, aged twenty-six. Her lover was distracted:

> On the arm of his *guitarra*
> A black crepe bow he tied
> When they came to tell him:
> Severa's just expired!
>
> The Count of Vimioso –
> *Ai!* – almost became mad
> When they went to tell him:
> Severa has just died!

Ai! is the cry of *saudade*. It regrets and pines for the past. I heard it in number 13. It longs for a future and becomes respectable in *casas de fado* where you must pay a lot for your drink and your dinner. Because *fado* is passive, and despite its breeding, it became one of a trinity of soporifics during Salazar's dictatorship: the F words, *Fado, Fátima e Futebol*.

'It's very bad to say it,' said Helder, 'but *fado* is hopeless. That was OK before the revolution because it was seen as a song accepting everything, not trying to change anything. *Fado* can be a song of resignation, it's true, but on the other hand it can demand. It can accept everything as though it was written down from the very beginning before we were born, resigned to fate, or it can be a song of revolt, claiming something, looking to find our destiny.'

So it's both, though sentimental *fados* tend to express not active rebellion but wistful resignation. Lisbon's *fados castiços* are bleaker than the more lyrical Coimbra *fados* which have their roots in the man's medieval song called *Cantiga de Amor*. Rodney Gallop describes the Coimbra *fado* as 'the song of those who still retain and cherish their illusions, not of those who have irretrievably lost them.' Loss belongs to the Lisbon *fado*.

The Count of Vimioso irretrievably lost Severa, but at last he lifted himself out of passivity, the unhinged grief into which he'd fallen, and made for the insane activity of the bullring.

> Here, for me, the trinity
> Of good things Portuguese
> Are the *fado* and *saudade*,
> And a *pega* taken toughly.

I'd argue that the earliest account of the *pega* – bull-catching – is found in the Gilgamesh epic, written down in Mesopotamia early in the second millennium BC. Ishtar, goddess of love, had desired Gilgamesh, the Sumerians' 'old hero', and sent seven years' drought to punish him for his rejection of her. This drought was personified by the Celestial Bull, created by Anu for Ishtar his daughter only when she threatened to break down the doors of hell and bring up the dead to eat with the living. The Bull of Heaven fell upon the earth. His first two hot snorts slaughtered men by the hundreds,

and with the third he charged Gilgamesh's companion Enkidu.
Enkidu leapt on the beast:

> and took hold of the Bull by the horns and the great bull
>   head
> thrashed over him and the reeking bull slobber poured
> over his face and Enkidu fought the Bull
> and the foul tail of the Bull brushed over his face . . .
> 'Two people, companions, they can prevail together,'
> and Enkidu seized the Bull by the reeking tail
> and Gilgamesh thrust his sword with the skill of a butcher
> between the shoulders and horns, and they killed the Bull.

I am riding the immaculate metrô to an ancient ritual. Think of
Cretan bull games. Think of the seventh labour of Hercules. There
will be blood, yes, but not much. In Portugal the bull is not killed
in the ring. I have seen men hurt, tossed, or crushed between the
bull's head and the wooden wall of the arena, the ambulance's siren
whooping above the roar of the crowd, but a *cavaleiro* (horseman)
who lets the bull so much as touch his horse is booed, and the bull,
in the end, is simply stopped by men on foot and empty-handed,
without capes or weapons.

Celt Iberians astonished the great powers – Carthage and Rome
– by defeating Hamilcar Barca in 228 BC; in defence of blockaded
Ilici they unleashed a herd of horned beasts dragging incendiary
carts. Strabo wrote of the Lusitani and their sport: 'the peoples of
the coastline, fond of meeting on horseback the ferocious Hispanian
bulls'. Minoan art depicts the *pega*, as well as the snow-white bull
the sea-god Poseidon gave King Minos, and the Minotaur at the
heart of the labyrinth that can be identified with the Phoenicians'
bull-headed Baal Moloch, who was also fed with human sacrifices.
The bull cult was widespread and it's likely that the ritual of
seizing the bull bare-handed was introduced to the Lusitanos by
the Visigoths. In the third century it was probably a wild *aurochs*,
the bull's extinct ancestor, and not a dragon, that St George lanced.
Moorish horsemanship modified the bull games of the Peninsula,
but in Portugal it never extinguished the *pega*.

Upriver in the Ribatejo, *campinos* have plucked the bulls they want from the herd and transported them to the bullring in lorries. They used to be driven through the streets. Stories are legion of *esperas de gado* in Lisbon and of *largadas* (releases) which got out of hand. Back in 1954 a bull broke out of its lorry in Praça de Pombal and gave the Avenida da Liberdade a new meaning as it trampled its way to the Chiado, a poor exchange for the *campo* or open country. It damaged two trams, scattered numerous café chairs and tables, and injured a number of people before it was stopped. That took twenty-five bullets. I surfaced at the metrô station called Campo Pequeno (Little Field). Not far up Avenida de Berna, beyond the Calouste Gulbenkian Foundation and Galleries, there was a new mosque with a mighty crescent-topped dome and, for the *muezzin*, a minaret like a helter-skelter. More venerable, but just as surprising, Campo Pequeno's bullring of 1892 was a Moorish-style confection in red brick with onion domes.

Its arena, the *campo pequeno* that mattered, is surrounded by banks of step-like concrete seats that hold 8,500 spectators. I hired a cushion. People packed in around me with bread and sausage, fresh crab and plenty of bottles. Hawkers sold beer, ice-creams, Sintra cakes and souvenir *bandarilhas*, barbed, beribboned darts. From the cheap seats opposite, spectators squinted into the evening sun. To avoid the *sol* I'd paid for *sombra*. Recorded music gave way to the live brass band, the president of the *corrida* and his party filed into their box and, to a whinnying fanfare, the cast for the night's drama assembled on the sand. *Campinos* in red waistcoats, glittering matadors in suits of lights, amateur *forcados* in flowery jackets ready to catch the bull and, astride superb Lusitano stallions, *cavaleiros* in frogged, embroidered satin coats and lace ruffs who doffed their tricorne hats to the president. The eighteenth-century costumes were completed by a black ribbon on the back in memory of the Count of Arcos, disembowelled at Salvaterra de Magos in 1799. Later, Severa would sing:

> For me the biggest fun
> Is to beat the *fado*;
> To see fight with a bull – alone –
> The Count of Vimioso.

Now, I am not Ernest Hemingway or Roy Campbell or any other artist who compromised a fine sensibility with *machismo*, who smothered *anima* with animus. I don't like blood sports, but sitting there I knew, however politically incorrect it was, that I was gazing into the heart of the labyrinth. Tonight, Theseus and Enkidu were arrayed in courtly clothes, as befitted a sport of kings that schooled princes for war. King Dom Sancho had lanced bulls, from one flank or the other, in the thirteenth-century manner. When a bull appeared in the path of the royal carriage, João II had despatched it with a sword thrust before the eyes of the queen and his retainers. In 1634 the Duke of Bragança obtained, for the Infanta's birthday, a brave lion which took on a bull and killed it. The same duke once shipped a rhinoceros to the pope. It smashed through the hull and sunk the vessel. But the bullfight was more rite than sport, deeper in the blood than games for the rich barbarians we call rulers. King Minos spared the white bull he should have sacrificed. He satisfied the Minotaur with man-morsels. Here in the ring, the first victim may not be the bull. Here in the maze, on our behalf, acolytes offer themselves up to the Baal-beast.

The bullfighter is death's bridegroom. Dom Sebastião fought on horseback in the arena before embarking for Morocco and the battle of Alcácer-Quibir. Belmonte, the Andalusian who revolutionised the fight in Spain, danced closer to the horns than anyone thought possible. Gored more than fifty times, he chose in the end to die by his own hand.

The president's trumpeter called for the first bull. It was released into the ring with a flurry of sand and excitement, full of hot power, its horns encased in leather. The first *cavaleiro* tempted it with precise and risky dressage, a balletic dance at which the bull charged.

'*Toiro! Oi, oi, oi, toiro!*'

The horse shifted a gear, the bull's horns often inches from its flank. Again and again rider and stallion confronted the bull. Men in the crowd roared, women grew wet with passion. Applause and whistles registered the spectators' approval or distaste for a joust conducted according to the noblest rules. When the bull came at the horse, horns level with the stirrup, the *cavaleiro* planted a *bandarilha* vertically between the shoulders into the *morrilho*, or fleshy part of the neck.

Blood glittered thickly on the beast's black hide and trickled down its forequarters. If ever he missed, the horseman saluted the bull, the *bandarilha* held before his face like a sword. At last he raised two fingers and, once granted permission by the president, rode high-stepping, no hands on the reins, and simultaneously planted two darts.

> Noble and bold *cavaleiro*,
> Bearing refined and valiant!
> In your art of *toireiro*
> With the bull at your front
> You recall the tradition
> Of our ancient nobility
> Who bequeathed us, for blazon,
> The Portuguese-style bullfight.

Between the fight's phases, between fanfares, matadors caught the bull's eye with flourishes of the *capa de brega*, the yellow-and-magenta cape, to play it, make passes, lead it into the desired area of the ring. Each successive bull settled into a different patch on the sand, its *querência* (liking), the 'home sweet home' that it made its own. It had to be challenged and drawn out. For the climactic phase of each fight, eight *moços de forcado* entered the arena while matadors distracted the bull. Then one *forcado* drew a *campino*'s green stocking-cap onto his head and stepped forward, hands outstretched.

'*Toiro! Eh, toiro!*'

He called the bull and, hands on hips, postured proudly while his colleagues marshalled themselves in two lines at his back. The bull pawed the ground, flung up sand, snorted.

'*Toiro! Toiro! Eh, toiro!*'

The bull snorted and charged with terrifying momentum. As it reached him the leading *forcado* launched himself into the air, leapt onto its head and was taken between the horns. He tried to lock his arms around them and hang on. *Pegar* is 'to catch'. This is the *pega*, the struggle to seize the bull.

'*À unha, à unha, à cernelha!*'

Bare-handed! By the withers! A *forcado* is a two-pronged fork with balled points mounted on a rod that *campinos* use for stopping

226

the bull. It's also a 'pitchfork'. It was the human pitchfork, not the beast, who was tossed like a bale and trampled. The bull's hooves flailed over his prone body. A matador flared his cape and seduced the bull. The *forcado* got up manfully from the pitted sand. He tried again.

> When in the sand of the ring
> I see a valiant *forcado*
> Calling a thoroughbred bull,
> Clapping hands in its face;
> When one man defies
> All the bravura of a bull –
> All of that heroism
> Touches the frontiers of madness.

He held on this time. His team grabbed haunches, legs, and the biggest *forcado* hung on to the tail. They were dragged across the ring. But the bull stopped. They stopped him. They jumped off, jumped away, all but the man on the tail who twirled the bull round, one complete turn before letting go.

The band brayed crazily. The *pega* was over. The leading *forcado* was bloody but bright-eyed. Steers with chiming bells round their necks were driven in to pacify the bull and gather him up. The crowd exulted. Man had taken on fate, the Celestial Bull, and won. He had acknowledged and defied death.

You ask me about *fado*? I knew him,

> He went to *Esperas de gado*,
> Became a renowned *cavaleiro*,
> Was the rage in the Carnival!
> In that abandoned lifetime
> He – who came from nothing –
> Being nothing, was everything!

19

GLORIOUS EDEN

Serra de Sintra

KING SEBASTIÃO stands in full sun, fresh-faced and armoured, in the niche between two mock-Manueline horseshoe arches that interlock on the façade of Lisbon's Rossio station. Hardly anyone seems to notice him standing just above their heads as they pass. If they look up on entering the station it's not to catch his naive fanatical eye, to savour heraldic architectural details or to consider the armillary spheres that hover like impending destiny above the second-floor windows. It's to check the clock that stands between pinnacles above the roofline's fretted masonry.

I've a few minutes to spare before my train leaves for one of Sebastião's favourite oases, the summer palace of the kings of Portugal. It's not that there aren't oases in Lisbon itself. There are many. The steep Botanical Gardens with plumbed-in irrigation and illuminated marble mushrooms beneath palms and forest trees. The high Praça do Príncipe Real, that changed its name to Praça do Rio de Janeiro and back again, with limes, elms, silver maples and a famous cedar like a pergola spreading enormous shade beneath the ironwork frame on which it rests. The Martyrs' Garden beside the statue of the 'ever-popular and continuously effective Dr Sousa Martins'. The delicious Estufa Fria ('cold hot-house'!) where jungle paths zig-zag between pools, humid groves, waterfalls and grottoes, all set in a corner of the Parque Eduardo VII. England's Edward VII, that is, who renewed the 1385 Treaty of Windsor between the oldest allies. There in the park, Major Sidónio Pais dug in with regiments of the Lisbon garrison and overthrew the government in December 1917. One man's oasis is another's last ditch.

Trains leave from the station's second floor, where President Sidónio Pais was assassinated in December 1918. I've saluted Sebastião in his niche and bought a ticket to Sintra. It's an escape to the picturesque. Sintra is a laboratory of Portuguese psychopathology. A retreat and a penance. A landscape of dreams and nightmares, gold and blood and madness. It's 'the place where the Winter has chosen to spend the Summer', along with crazy kings. If he'd had any sense, Sebastião would have stayed in his pretty oasis, not got lost in the real desert.

My train left from the second floor and plunged into a tunnel beneath a hill. If you know Lisbon you'll understand. Within a few moments I was in a burrow below the Botanical Gardens. Last night, deep in the dimness of 'the Alley', the *casa de fado* A Viela, I listened to Celeste Rodrigues, Amália's sister. The walls were covered with silhouetted scenes of old Lisbon by a mural painter who had loaded his brush with *saudade*. In the corner was a lamp-post. João and Hermes, the musicians, sat behind it in grey suits. Celeste, like a black raven, arched her neck beneath the light and kneaded the fringes of her shawl. The shawl, and the black, had been given fetish status by her sister.

> I went from alley to alley;
> In one of them I chanced on her
> And remained as if entranced.
> Under the light of a street-lamp
> There stood the *fado* itself,
> For all of her was *fado*.

A man at the next table echoed the verse in a bass rumble as the *guitarra* sang and everyone joined in. I sensed the tension, in the *fadista*, between song and silence; in the bullfighter, between daring and death; in the sailor, between exploration and isolation; in the figure of Dom Sebastião, between *saudade* and hope. I knew I was sitting in a new democracy, so recently shorn of its world of colonies and still poised, after a decade, between the Atlantic and the European Union. The British, I decided, might learn a lot about loss of glory, about nostalgia, about a radical look at the future, if they faced this music.

> Songs of the Portuguese
> Are like ships on the sea:
> They come from one soul to another
> At risk of being shipwrecked.

So wrote Fernando Pessoa. Next, Arminda da Conceição was standing, a dramatic strain warping her body and tugging eloquent
anguish up from her guts. Such husky regret, such deep pain, such
longing in a stance so upright and proud.

'All poetry – and song is an aided poetry – reflects what the soul
lacks,' Pessoa whispered in my ear from the darkness. 'So the songs
of sad peoples are cheerful while the songs of cheerful peoples are
sad. The *fado*, though, is neither cheerful nor sad.' He leant closer.
'In the *fado* the rightful gods return from afar. That's the second
meaning of the figure of Dom Sebastião.'

> O *fado* who *fado* was,
> O *fado* who is to come,
> *Fado* of the king-so-longed-for,
> *Fado* of Alcácer-Quibir!
> You go to war hidden
> In the knapsack of the soldier.

My train was throbbing through sunlight thrown off Lego-style
apartment blocks beside the striding Aqueduct of Free Waters. It's
just what you want in a desert. I thought of the matter-of-fact
verses that João Roiz de Castelo Branco addressed to a knight of
Alcácer-Sequer serving in North Africa:

> While, there, you breach the walls
> And stockades of the Moors
> We here run with the bulls
> And make great festivals.

For the poets of a small country, distance and difference are
inexhaustible themes. We passed through the station with the
legendary football name of Benfica, home of the No Name Boys
and site of the only palace in the Lisbon area not to be destroyed

230

by the great earthquake. A palace, incidentally, never entered by Salazar's PIDE, a safe house in which to plot revolution. In the year 2003 Dom Sebastião makes his return here, if you can believe Manuel da Costa's *El-Rei Desejado Cavalga Ondas de Luz* ('The King-So-Longed-For Rides Waves of Light'), a 1990 sci-fi fantasy. His space capsule descends into Benfica's stadium and lands on the pitch in the middle of a match between the teams of Benfica and Belém. The mathematical tables at the back of the book prove it possible beyond the shadow of a doubt. Did you doubt it? No. How better could *o Encoberto*, the hidden one, make an entrance, his glittering re-entry?

Across the gangway a perspiring mother was trying to roll down and button her boy's shirt-sleeves.

'You can't arrive there looking like a bumpkin,' she said. 'D'you want them to think you're a *bimbo?*'

He resisted her again and again, and won. He might have been five years old. He was at least twenty.

Perhaps because it was Sunday, and election day for the European Parliament, we had to change at Cacém. It was a long wait, stranded in hot sun on a platform like a sandbar. A tall girl, about twenty-five, was cared for by wary parents as if she was not a doll, but a feral cat. Her haughty mouth was full of strong white teeth. Her fingernails were long but unpainted. Whichever way she turned, outstanding breasts and buttocks had a life of their own within a drab brown dress.

At last, from the second train, I saw the landmarks I was looking for: a fantastic palace and a sober castle perched on what Lord Byron called the 'horrid crags' of 'Cintra's glorious Eden'. More than once, fuelled by Eugénia de Jesus's fine Sintra cakes, I've clambered about up there. The Moorish castle's mighty walls hang and twist like garlands of stone between mightier natural pinnacles and boulders. They hold remnants of its vital cistern, of its pre-1147 mosque and its post-1147 chapel. The date 1147 is, of course, that of Lisbon's 'liberation' from the Moors by Afonso Henriques, though Snorri Sturluson's *The Saga of Sigurd Jorsalafari* tells how Norway's King Sigurd, 'Jerusalem-farer', took this castle out of Moslem hands in about 1107 on his way to the Crusades and eventual madness. Its square tower dominates a plain whose horizon is lost in heat haze, in flexing images of Mafra, the lines of Torres Vedras, the river Tagus and the Atlantic Ocean. But the castle is itself supervised by a high cross and a palace whose domes and pinnacles, turrets, towers and machicolated castellations look as if they have sprung from the imagination of mad King Ludwig. Indeed, the landscape of Sintra might have popped up whole and gothick out of a Victorian book of fairy-tales.

The Palace of Pena really was a maggot in the brain of a Bavarian king, Ferdinand (Fernando) of Saxe Coburg-Gotha, cousin of Prince Albert (Queen Victoria's consort) and second husband of the Portuguese queen Maria da Glória. In 1839 he bought the abandoned mountain monastery of Nossa Senhora da Pena that had been built by Manuel the Fortunate. The story goes that while hunting on these peaks in 1499 Dom Manuel had glimpsed Vasco da Gama's fleet returning from India and vowed there and then to build the monastery. Dom Fernando commissioned the Prussian engineer Ludwig von Eschwege to develop and expand it from a vertiginous house of prayer into a strenuously whimsical dream. It's Moroccan Scottish Baronial out of Grimm, frozen in time, just as it was left, they claim, when the royal family abandoned it in 1910. It's stuffed with sumptuous frippery, gilt, cement 'woodwork', porcelain, papier-mâché, *trompe-l'oeil*, all revolving around a miniature Manueline double cloister and a chapel containing a French high altar of 1532, in alabaster and black marble, and a crucifixion scene sculpted in Nottingham alabaster with hints of old pigment clinging to it. The palace's main tower is a replica of the Torre de Belém. King Fernando lived up there in the clouds with his mistress long after the death in childbirth – the eleventh child – of thirty-four-year-old Queen Maria.

The king was also responsible for the restoration, the over-restoration, of the Moorish castle, and for afforestation of the hills – pine, cork oak, chestnut, walnut, rhododendron, giant ferns and mosses – which both sets off and softens old stones and new, giving Sintra town a backdrop of grandeur and playfulness worthy of a high-class pantomime set. Nevertheless, Ferdinand's work would have pleased Robert Southey who regretted, back in 1801, that Portuguese merchants were buying up properties 'so that they will one day dispossess the English, and this I do not like. Cintra is too good a place for the Portuguese. It is only fit for us Goths – for Germans or English.'

Regrettable that Sintra is part of Portugal at all. Eh?! They say that everyone finds in Sintra a part of their own fatherland. The versatility of the landscape, of which Almeida Garrett says 'here is Spring enthroned,' accounts for the proliferation of palaces and mansions and villas built by the international rich. Even the pollution of opulence, with its invariable vulgarity, hardly spoils the Serra de Sintra. I didn't have to go far to find myself in my home county of Devon. In woodland among granite boulders that might have been a valley on the fringe of Dartmoor, I entered a monastery that could not be in starker contrast to self-glorifying grandeur. After first coming here, to the Convento dos Capuchos, I remembered no details at all. I knew that I'd ducked my head and passed through successive close and serious glooms hacked out of the rock in the sixteenth century. The district had then been notable not only for palaces but for religious houses and penitential retreats. The Marquis of Pombal's post-earthquake survey noted more than forty hermits' cells hereabouts. If it's not a contradiction in terms, this convent was a communal hermitage. Embedded here, I felt ambiguous spiritual foci, towards aspiration and morbidity. I sensed spiritual motion, upward and downward.

When I revisited the Capuchins' house I noticed the arches and small courts, spring water trickling into a stone basin, a dwarf chapter-house, a rude refectory and a tiny chapel, facilities of the foundation built in 1560 to fulfil a vow of the last great Viceroy of India, Dom João de Castro, by his son. Its small community followed the reformed Franciscan rule of São Pedro of Alcántara. Now, in my mind, in his Spanish home town, I could see the saint's sinewy figure with arms upstretched. But what persuaded me, once again, of the austere and other-worldly devotion that had possessed the place, was its dozen cells. They were small, dank and atmospheric, full of different qualities of darkness rather than of light. Doors, shutters and ceilings were covered with rough cork which stilled the silence that otherwise vibrated in the man-made caves. It was warm to touch, though the air on my face was chill and damp. I squeezed through a narrow doorway. Stupid to say it out loud, but I told myself that however romantic the convent seemed, confinement here would have been unbearably claustrophobic had it not been for a species of invisible luminosity. I eased the cell's window-shutters apart and saw lichen-covered boulders and the lightweight shadows of trees.

When Sebastião visited these cells, from his summer palace in Sintra, they were almost new but hardly more comfortable. Here the young king shed glory and esteem, together with the body he loved to renounce and risk. Here he took on self-denial and penitence, and if possible stripped himself down to pure spirit. Here he knelt at the feet of his confessor, full of ambition. He came from luxury to austerity in order to gather himself, all his energies, his redeemed and dangerous soul for the push, the attack he would make on Africa.

Hadn't the Navigator gained a string of forts along the North African coast, now shamefully reduced? How better could Sebastião repay the infidel, who held sway for so long in the domains that were now his, than by claiming their lands for Christ? Shouldn't the Serra de Sintra nurture holy ambition, a zealous dream that would take him to the mountains of Atlas? From there would he not look out upon all the kingdoms of the world, the empire of the spirit, that fifth empire for the winning of which Portugal was destined to be the Almighty's glorious, humble instrument? Did not the deposed Moroccan king Mulai Mohammed even now cry out, invoking his aid against the usurper Abd al-Malek? And had not Mohammed promised free rein to the Church of Christ in his restored kingdom? What better moment then, given of His grace by God himself, to mount a last decisive Crusade against the forces of the evil one?

'My son, you are the desired one whose desire rests in God, and is of God, to fulfil the will of God. Go in peace.'

And in the bulky royal palace at the heart of Sintra proper, the ex-Governor of India could not restrain himself from speaking his mind on the subject of El-Rei Dom Sebastião's African plans. It was always dangerous to air your thoughts in a headstrong ruler's hearing. He did not whisper his considered opinion.

'Aren't raving lunatics usually tied up?' he shouted. 'Why then have they let this one loose?'

The royal palace, or Paço Real, is a sonorous building and I like to think this story is true. The kitchen, a cavernous half-tiled chamber, gives the palace its most famous features: two conical chimneys that are the full width of the room at the base and rise like oast-houses or elegant kilns, each to a narrow neck ringed by a pair of raised rims and a fine lip that a master potter might have turned on his wheel. Think of rumour reverberating in those organ pipes and seeping out with the smoke. The Sala das Pêgas (Room of Magpies) was already accustomed to scandal. When Philippa of Lancaster caught her husband, Dom João I, kissing one of the ladies-in-waiting, the whole court twittered. King João had the ceiling painted with a flock of magpies to satirise their gossip. Each bird holds the legend 'Por bem' in its beak: 'in honour' or 'for the good'. Kings do everything for the best, naturally, and from the very best of motives in the best of all possible worlds.

This king had expanded the Moorish palace that he found here in the early fifteenth century. From it the *walis* (governors) once ruled their Portuguese province. Dom João had ordered more tiled rooms and courtyards from Moorish craftsmen who still lived in Christian Portugal and excelled in the Mudéjar art of *azulejos*. Some of the earliest tiles, rare black ones, surround the door in the Sala das Sereias (Room of Sirens) on whose ceiling a ship is lured to its doom upon a painted ocean. In the middle of the Sala de Jantar dos Mouros (The Moors' Dining-Room) stands a fountain surrounded by half-tiled walls of rippling blue, green and white and splendidly glazed doorways. Dom Sebastião's bedroom is similarly tiled but with utterly different feeling. Here he lay in splendour, chaste and certain. Maybe it was in this chamber that Dom João de Mascarenhas spoke boldly but quietly against the king's African adventure.

'Be sure to carry with you a shroud,' he hissed, 'in which to bury the kingdom.'

Sebastião may have told him that he had different luggage on his mind, talismans for mission: the sword Portugal's first king carried to victory at Ourique, a sacred banner blessed by the pope, one of the arrows that pierced St Sebastian, and a crown ready for the head of the first Christian emperor of Morocco.

In the souvenir shop I asked officials whether I could see the patio on which the poet Camões spoke his epic for Sebastião's delectation. They were gruff and unforthcoming. But as I went round the palace the compulsory guide was human, humorous even. In the grand Sala dos Brasões (Room of Blazons) she pointed out blue-and-white-tiled scenes and grotesques around its four-square walls, then asked us to count the coats of arms on upper walls that formed a panelled octagon capped by a coffered ceiling. A dark medieval hall seemed to hover above the airy chamber. It has, says Cedric Salter, 'something of Arthur and the Round Table about it'. Up there were blazons of all the country's leading families. Well, all bar one. The Marquis de Pombal had ordered that the arms of Távora be wiped out, and the family itself, following an attempt on the life of King José 'the Reformer'.

In the bedroom prison, where Pedro 'the Peaceful' confined his brother Afonso 'the Victorious' for six years until he died insane during mass, our guide indicated the furrow the prisoner's feet had worn in the tiled floor. Earlier still, Pedro 'the Just' never regained his sanity after the murder of his lover Inês de Castro. He worked obsessively, as insomniacs do, on codifying Portuguese law, or danced all night in the streets, but flew into furies at the strains of strings, insisting on hearing nothing but wind instruments of silver. The guide asked, rhetorically, whether the throb of strings tugged too painfully at his memory of Inês's voice. And in the long, luxurious Sala dos Cisnes (Room of Swans), she caught my eye and winked at the portrait, hung between panels of green and white diamond tiles, of young Dom Sebastião in full armour.

'Wait,' she whispered.

She led the rest of her charges away, returned with a key, unlocked a door and let me out. All at once I was walking on the Patio of the Audience: a red-tiled floor perhaps twenty feet square, low walls of azure, aquamarine and gold, then gardens and trees, crags and sky. On one side there was a canopy of masonry supported by pillars. Beneath it, I sat down on the tiled throne where Sebastião once sat, with a bench of tiles on his left, to listen to the prematurely-aged, one-eyed poet half-reading, half-reciting the newly-minted matter of Portugal that he had dedicated to the eighteen-year-old king and published in 1572, *Os Lusiadas*, 'the sons of Lusus', the Portuguese.

Camões had forebodings about Portugal, about the young mon-

236

arch's idealism and madness, his chastity and wildness, his fanatic piety. For all that, he starts his epic, which mythologises the Portuguese and puts Vasco da Gama in Aeneas' shoes, by addressing the king as the 'new terror of the Moors', and in its coda prophesies deeds worth celebrating: Mount Atlas fearing the very sight of him, Marrakesh and Taroudant sacked, and all mankind seeing in Sebastião a second Alexander the Great with, ahem!, no cause to envy Achilles' luck in being hymned by Homer. Camões got his pension. A small one, but still.

Camões had seen Sebastião shifting from palace to palace and examining the graves of his ancestors. In Alcobáça, where Pedro will rise to face Inês at the last day, he tried to pre-empt the resurrection by opening the king's sarcophagus. Scandal stopped him. At Batalha in 1574 he exhumed João II from the tomb where he had lain for eighty years. The young king held the illustrious corpse to his own body and measured himself against 'the Perfect Prince and lord of all secrets'.

'Behold!' he exclaimed, 'the best officer of our kingly office.'

Then he ordered the Duke of Aveiro to kiss the corpse's hand. Already, Sebastião was a resurrection man.

I'd chased him around Portugal, but it was in the silent, claustrophobic dusk of the cork convent, and here, on this patio's echoing brightness, that I came closest to him. Though what an Englishman from Devon could have to do with a crazy Portuguese king, God knows.

My indulgent guide hustled me onwards. We could hear the next tour's small hubbub. I looked out of a window into the town square and couldn't believe my eyes. Really. Honest. There, on the day of elections for the European Parliament, gaudily caparisoned horses trotted by with riders in full armour under a banner announcing *El-Rei Artur* . . . 'King Arthur and the Knights of the Round Table'. It seemed that British Celts, not Southey's English or German Goths, had retaken Sintra from the Portuguese. Queen Guinevere rode in one of the open carriages that take tourists round the sights. Lancelot had the hots for her as usual. Arthur had Excalibur unsheathed.

That day, voters had the choice of at least a dozen parties and coalitions, from Communists through Greens and Social Democrats to the Democratic Party of the Atlantic or the Popular Monarchists. If I'd been of the latter persuasion, I'd have been sorely tempted to make my cross and send the Once-and-Future King to Brussels. If we could only wake him from his sleep under the hill, under the desert dune, wouldn't we all?

20

SEBASTIÃO'S BEST MAN

Affeton and Alcácer-Quibir

CAMÕES MAY have underestimated the power of his words. I'm struggling to find him some excuse for so irresponsibly reinforcing Sebastião's sense of destiny. If the poet ever doubted that the pen is mightier than the sword he certainly believed in that proud premise of Portuguese imperialism: the penis mightier than the sword. When he employed the Actaeon myth to warn the presumptuous king against counsellors who would devour him like dogs, he urged him to go and gaze at the naked goddess Diana. Perhaps Sebastião just couldn't get it up.

Tom Stucley could. Known to his friends as 'Lusty' Stucley, he was an Englishman who got involved by accident with the crazy Portuguese king. I'd been fascinated by *sebastianismo* for a long time without discovering the connection. Then I went to interview the president of the National Library in Lisbon, Maria Leonor Machado de Sousa, and she mentioned Sir Thomas Stucley. Stucley, I thought. That sounds like home. And it was. The Stucley family house is in Devon, a dozen miles from where I live. Reduced to a gate tower of *circa* 1480, it's still called Affeton Castle. Officially, Thomas was the third son of Sir Hugh Stucley of Affeton. Unofficially, he was rumoured to be one of Henry VIII's bastards. What's for sure is that he wanted to be a king himself. As a double agent, he played European monarchs off one against another and, when he enters our story, a veteran adventurer of fifty-three, he was on his way to Ireland with a force raised from the pope in order to reclaim it for the Catholic Church. He was already known in Europe as the Marquis of Leinster, but he would be king of the Emerald Isle once he'd taken it from Queen Elizabeth I.

His brother, Lewis Stucley, was the queen's standard-bearer and must have heard the news about court – intelligence was good – that his scandalous brother was making for Lisbon, with Madrid's money and Rome's troops behind him it seemed, *en route* for a commotion in England or Ireland for which he was bound to recruit King Sebastião's aid.

Sebastião had had letters from the pope entreating him to speed Stucley's progress to Ireland, but the Holy See's consul-general in Lisbon knew that the king had his own crusade, also blessed by His Holiness, to think about. The pope's veteran mercenaries were just the reinforcements Sebastião could do with on his forthcoming Moroccan adventure. The consul-general tried to warn Stucley not to enter the Tagus. He sent a horseman post-haste to Cádis. He dispatched a pinnace to intercept Stucley at sea. He posted Stucley's own secretary at Cascais to keep watch over the approaches. They all missed him. Somehow on the night of 18 April 1578 Stucley's vessel, the *San Giovanni*, had limped towards the mouth of the river and stood off, with twelve feet of water in her hold and troops ready to mutiny, awaiting a pilot. She could face no more ocean without re-caulking. The grandiose Marquis of Leinster would be staying. Oh, what comings and goings, intrigues and brave faces, high living and low cunning. Dom Sebastião agreed to give Tom Stucley audience at eight o'clock on the evening of the nineteenth. Fate was unkind to bode so well. The king, who spent much of the first half of this year moving between Sintra, Évora, Salvaterra de Magos, Coruche and Almeirim, was at that moment staying right on the waterfront, in the Monastery of Jerónimos at Belém, for the obsequies of his grandmother Caterina, the stern mentor who with the Jesuits had brought him up. His father had died eighteen days before Sebastião was born. His mother had returned to Spain soon afterwards. Now, at the age of twenty-four, Sebastião had lost the only real parent he'd ever had, and hated. He prepared for a rite of passage.

It was not to be marriage. The Portuguese are not known for lack of libido, so it's of interest that two of their most important figures,

Dom Sebastião and Fernando Pessoa, seem to have been more or less asexual. Not to mention Salazar. Pessoa was thirty-two when he fell in love with Ophélia Queiros, a platonic affair. Was he homosexual? One critic, through close analysis of the texts, has concluded that Pessoa was not, but that two of his heteronyms, Ricardo Reis and Álvaro de Campos, were. Above all, Pessoa was an intellectual who wrote laughable love letters. Sebastião, by contrast, was by no means cold. He always looked for action and trouble. But hunting, riding and fighting exhausted him and he sometimes fell into paroxysms. This tendency, together with asymmetrical oddness and congenital sexual problems, was a result of royal interbreeding. He was strong but alone. He never loved anyone except, as he thought, God. At birth he had been *o Desejado*, the desired one, and now the pressure was on him to produce an heir. He, for complex reasons, was absurdly proud of his virginity.

'Sebastião had a mysterious sexual life, or no sexual life at all,' Almeida Faria told me, 'maybe he was gay, maybe he had a venereal disease. He didn't want to get married, that's the real point of his life. I think he died because he didn't want to get married. He went to this absurd battle in August, in the desert, with a medieval army, with horses already tired from the trip, soldiers not at all interested in fighting, the poor Arabs who didn't attack us, so there was no reason for it at all. But he was completely obsessed with the battle, which I think, deeply, was a way to avoid the great problem of getting married.'

In his poem *D. Sebastião* Miguel Torga puts it like this:

> He who goes to seek the bride in the noise of war
> Dies without bride and without love, quite alone.

Sebastião looked for a best man to escort him to the wedding. On that night in the spring of 1578 he waited for him in Jerónimos. In May 1995 Dom Duarte, Duke of Bragança and pretender to the throne, waited there on the eve of his fiftieth birthday for the hand of twenty-eight-year-old Isabel Inês de Castro Curvello de Herédia. Monarchists had long despaired of an heir to the non-existent throne. Glossies strained to glimpse recipients of His Royal Highness's glad eye. The previous year, when I discussed *Sebastianismo* with him, I heard the usual speculation about his sexuality. Then the media went wild about his engagement. And his bride's names: Isabel, Portugal's queen-saint, and Inês de Castro, victim of illicit royal passion.

The day before the wedding, the first 'royal' one for more than a century, police arrived outside Jerónimos to evict demonstrators camping in front of the archaeological museum that adjoins the church. The peaceful demonstration had been mounted against the hydroelectric scheme at Foz Côa which threatened the prehistoric rock carvings. The electricity company's hired experts said they were recent, well, recentish, and best preserved under water anyway, if they weren't cut away from the rock face and put in a nice museum. Anything to shut protestors up. Police shifted one of nine tents but the demonstrators held their ground. Dom Duarte turned up and spoke to them.

'I agree with your fight to preserve the rock engravings.'

A government minister pronounced it 'unthinkable that the Foz Côa dam and reservoir would not be built'. Then the Socialists won the general election in October 1995 and stopped the electricity company in its caterpillar tracks. The carvings were saved. The blighted valley was destined to be an Archaeological Park. The past was given a future.

As the Socialists came to power it was announced that Dona Isabel was pregnant. A boy, for sure. An heir. And, if tabloid rumours were true, the boy would be called José or Sebastião. He was born by caesarean section on 25 March 1996 and baptised Alfonso de Santa Maria. The newspaper *Expresso* did not hesitate to proclaim him *o Desejado*. It was just ten months since Dom Duarte's bride, watched on TV by millions, passed through the great sea-cave of the church between the sarcophagi of Luís de Camões and his hero Vasco da Gama. In the south transept Sebastião's remains rode a marble elephant, *si vera est fama*, if rumour is true. If a more powerful rumour is true, he wasn't there at all.

Stucley waited in the miraculous cloisters until the refectory doors opened and he was beckoned into the presence of the monkish king. The mature, worldly-wise operator was flattered and cajoled, was offered billets for his men in Cascais and facilities in port for his ship's refit, but given no final promise of aid by the Machiavellian youth. Soon after, on St George's Day, Tom Stucley was still dreaming of an Irish crown when he returned to parley with the autocrat and, over a barrel, or a shivered hull, found himself suddenly compelled to enlist with all his force to serve under El-Rei Dom Sebastião in Africa.

An image comes to me: the young man I had watched on the compass – 'rose of the winds' – set in paving beside the Monument to the Discoveries, sailing his radio-controlled land-yacht across the map of the world. Famous words come to me, that Camões put into the mouth of the old man of Belém who attacked Vasco da Gama's ambition just as he set sail for India:

> You let the enemy breed at the gate
> Because you seek another far away
> For whom you depopulate the ancient state
> Enfeebling it, making it waste away!
> You look for an uncertain, unknown fate
> So fame may puff you up with flattery . . .
> Oh! Cursed be the first man in the world
> Who set sail on the waves in a frail bark.

Lack of funds, not confidence, had prevented Sebastião's crusade for years. He warded off doubt by surrounding himself with like minds, glory boys who rejected the counsel of mature statesmen. In 1574 he made a preliminary reconnaissance to Ceuta which should have taught him something. At last, against the advice of his uncle Philip II of Spain and his great-uncle the Grand Inquisitor Cardinal Henry, he spent every last *cruzado* he could raise on mercenaries and on outfitting his troops.

On glorious, pious Corpus Christi he processed through packed Lisbon, with the Host under its cloth-of-gold canopy and to cannonfire from St George's Castle, accompanied by the standard of St George that stood for the old alliance, the blood-bond between the royal house of Avis and the house of John of Gaunt. With Sebastião went the archbishop, bishops, nobles and dignitaries including the Marquis of Leinster, Tom Stucley, bearing the standard of Ireland to the Sé. High mass was celebrated there and the

Imperial Standard dedicated, already emblazoned, as if to tempt fate, with the crown of Morocco.

This show hid a bear-pit of dissent over arms and money and frail loyalties. Fine plumage hid unease in the pit of Stucley's stomach. Aside from his own troubles he worried about Portuguese nobles who decked themselves out with etched and gilded armour, pretty weapons, silks, gaudy pavilions and coaches as if they were off to a joust, not a real battle in the desert. A parade suit of armour of Dom Sebastião's survives in Madrid, blued, embossed and damascened by Anton Peffenhauser of Augsburg according to the latest fashion. Art and prestige combined to let armour outlive its usefulness – or uselessness in the face of gunpowder – by several centuries. Sebastião may have been king of Portugal and lord of Brazil, the Azores, Goa and the spice islands, but he had no money to spare and no ear for Tom Stucley. The Marquis of Leinster was not consulted about the battle plan. In any case, the king despised strategy and tactics as cowardice. He denied the possibility of retreat and had no plan for it. Defeat was unthinkable.

At the Terreiro do Paço on 14 June Sebastião embarked. But for ten days contrary weather kept the royal galley at her berth. The king did not disembark again except to hear feast-day masses and he slept in his clothes. On the twenty-fourth, the Feast of St John, the fleet cast off. The nearer the time came for the expedition the more the Spanish ambassador expressed himself astonished at the scanty preparations with which it was undertaken.

'May it please God,' he wrote home to Philip II with hopeless irony, 'to blind or incapacitate the enemy, for on that depends entirely the well-being of this armada.'

Sunshine, music, cannon, rockets, flags and oriflammes. The next day the fleet arrayed itself off Belém, some seven hundred vessels. Glorious Portugal. On the twenty-sixth they sailed southwards down the coast, from Vasco da Gama's point of embarkation past his birthplace of Sines and wild coves with names such as 'Colour of the Man' and 'Belly', around Cape St Vincent and Henry the Navigator's town of Sagres, and eastwards for Lagos. Sebastião had made Lagos the capital of his kingdom of the Algarve, Arabic *Al-gharb* meaning 'the west'. It gave its name to a west African capital before it was razed to the ground in the 1755 earthquake.

Not far from the remains of its slave market I stared into an antiques shop looking for clues: candlesticks and saints, vigorous but dusty African sculptures, a huge pair of brass scales, one suit of armour, model ships and a whole wall-full of crucified Christs. In Lagos museum are the vessels used during the mass celebrated on the beach at Meia Praia to bless Sebastião's expedition. At night every 29 August, the Feast of John the Baptist's beheading, there's a mass baptism there, a rush into the sea after which there's no need to bathe for thirty days. You must keep your clothes on though, for Lagos town council recently rejected the Naturist Federation's proposal to reserve part of the Meia Praia for nudists. The town's most controversial figure is a statue of Sebastião, androgynous, baby-faced and rather pink with a helmet several sizes too large.

On the twenty-eighth the fleet reached Cádis, where Sebastião wasted a week in pageantry and bullfighting with his host the Duke of Medina-Sidonia. Did the duke foresee Sebastião's fate, or his own part in the Spanish occupation of Portugal? Did he dream that imminent events would gain Spain a fleet, called Spanish but really the Portuguese Armada, which in ten years' time he'd launch under protest against Elizabeth of England? Did he discuss her with Stucley? On 7 July Sebastião made African landfall at Tangier, a Portuguese garrison and mythical home of Antaeus whom Hercules could not defeat until he lifted him off the earth. If only Sebastião had kept his feet on the ground. His forces reached Arzila on the Moroccan coast by the twelfth and gathered themselves, or wasted their energies. Tom Stucley, with others in the council of war, railed openly against the king's plans. As they spoke Sebastião rang the bell for dinner. With God, he would strike inland across the hills to Larache whatever anyone said. Stucley had borne Edward VI's standard at Boulogne when younger than Sebastião, faced death in many battles and gallantly commanded three galleys at the pivotal defeat of the Turks at Lepanto. Now he flung out of the council and came close to deserting. But on the twenty-seventh the whole army set out for Larache into almost waterless terrain.

At last, all chance of surprise long gone, the Christian army marched in heat the last twenty-two miles towards Alcácer-Quibir, al-Ksar el-Kebir, 'the Great Fortress' on the road from Tangier to Rabat, a village enlarged and walled by Yakub al-Mansur at the end of the twelfth century. Now the town and its railway station are called Oued el-Makhazine. Nearby, on the banks of the Makhazine river, is the site of the Battle of the Three Kings. There the Portuguese army pitched up on Sunday 3 August, suffering hunger, thirst and heat. They took all day to ford the river. Before dawn next day the virgin-king Sebastião called his commanders to him. He was pale and sober. It was as if in the chill dark he suddenly understood where and to what he had brought them. Shall we fight or parley, he asked. No parleying, they agreed. To battle, at once. No, said Mulai Mohammed who knew the enemy they faced, first wait and recover your strength. So also said Lusty Tom Stucley, to jeers.

'Out of your inexperience and ignorance of war, you judge me cowardly,' he flashed. 'But this counsel would lead you safe to victory, and your haste to your overthrow. Yet, get on with it! You'll see that Englishmen are no cowards.'

The vanguard comprised the cream of Portugal's young nobility with three thousand German mercenaries to the right, Stucley's six hundred papal troops and two thousand Castilians to the left. On two sides, sixteen thousand infantry, mostly untrained conscripts, lined barricades of baggage wagons thinly interspersed with arquebusiers. The rearguard was formed by more Portuguese *Aventuros*. Within this square huddled clergy, slaves, camp-followers and children, Andalusian and German prostitutes, nine thousand in all, with mules and oxen. Some two thousand cavalry were deployed on the flanks, the Duke of Aveiro on the right wing and King Sebastião on the left.

They faced a crescent of thirty-five thousand cavalry, fresh and well-armed, with eleven thousand arquebusiers at least. But their Sultan Abd el-Malek was dying before the battle began. Poisoned, the post-mortem would reveal. At the Christians' first charge he tried to mount his horse. The exertion was too much and his men lifted him back to his litter. His finger was at his lips as he died: Keep my death secret until battle is over. What if Stucley's advice had been taken, if Sebastião had waited for his men to regain their strength and for life to drain from the sultan? But perhaps his haste, his bravery had been all too deliberate. Perhaps the king's gravity at dawn had been the gravity of a suicide who longs for the hand of the pale bride.

Sebastião would play the part, heroic medieval warlord, to the end. His steel armour, tooled and gilded, had been buckled on. The Tabard of St Louis covered his chest and back. The Sword of Afonso Henriques was at his side. He bore all, and his charger bore him, in August in Morocco under a maddening sun. Though, just before his crested helm was fitted and he mounted up, his men sluiced jugs of water into the neck of his armour, between steel and fair skin. After his first charge, white-robed horsemen rode against him and the crescent of raised dust swirled into a circle that engulfed Portugal's square.

It was crushed and thinned, full of screams, wounds, last rites, crazed animals. Once a Portuguese cavalry charge almost overwhelmed the enemy's superior numbers. Then once again.

'Believe me,' wrote the sultan's Jewish doctor, 'twice we thought to lose all!'

The Sultan of Fez, Abd el-Malek, was already dead in his litter. The pretender, Mulai Mohammed, drowned as he tried to flee, tangled in his horse's reins in the Wadi M'Hassan. Tom Stucley, Marquis of Leinster, was killed by his Italians whom he insulted just prior to the fight by deploying them amongst the Castilians. Or else he perished gallantly, gloriously with Portuguese nobles and prelates. At Hartland Abbey in Devon a mural shows him on one knee, beneath a tower in a desert-scape of palms and minarets wreathed by cannon-smoke, unhelmed and holding his banner aloft by the Makhazine river as villainous mussulmen take spears to him. In George Peele's play *The Tragical Battle of Alcazar in Barbary* (1594), towards the end of his long dying speech Tom Stucley philosophically sighs:

> Ah, sweet Sebastian, hadst thou been well advised,
> Thou mightst have managed arms successfully!
> But from our cradles we were markèd all
> And destinate to die in Afric here.

In Dryden's *Don Sebastian* (1690), the virgin-king says of his fall, if fate decrees that fall he must:

> It shall be like myself; a setting sun
> Should leave a track of glory in the skies.

247

About eight thousand of his men were slaughtered in four hours. Almost all the rest were captured and sold in the slave markets of Fez and Alcácer. Most accounts agree that fifty or so made it to Tangier. For three weeks no one knew where Sebastião was. He was taken prisoner and struck down by a Moorish general ignorant of his rank. Or, when the Duke of Aveiro showed the flag of truce, Sebastião rushed on the enemy in bad faith and was killed for his trouble. Or, he met Dom Luís de Brito with the consecrated banner wrapped around his body, and cried out: 'Let us seize the standard! Let us die embracing the banner!' But Brito and the banner were taken while the king rode away unpursued. Dom Luís de Lima got a glimpse of Dom Sebastião making off along the riverbank. He'd be back.

Meanwhile, the Black Sultan's brother sent one of Sebastião's gentlemen of the bedchamber to find his corpse. Soon, Uncle Philip II would urgently require it. That Spain needed him dead was all it took for Portugal to need him very much alive.

21

FOG

Colares and Cabo da Roca

IN A LETTER written soon after the battle of Alcácer-Quibir, a monk notes that 'to show the affection of the Portuguese for the *guitarra*, it is said that about ten thousand were found, among the debris of Dom Sebastião's camp, following the tragic day on which this king was routed by the Sultan of Fez and Morocco.' If the victor was dead even before he gained the victory, perhaps the vanquished lived even after he lost. If not, songs sung through the years to the accompaniment of another ten thousand *guitarras* would keep *saudades* alive for him. And *saudades*, as we know, are not just memories but hopes.

Fado, or fate, went to war concealed in soldiers' knapsacks. It returned as songs and ballads, from the stirring lament by one of the king's comrades-in-arms that ends:

> He seeks out death by spreading death
> Sebastião the Lusitanian
> Saying this is the hour
> That a beautiful death lends life honour,

to Quartetto 1111's pop song of the late 1960s, *A Lenda* (The Legend) *de El-Rei Dom Sebastião*. For a despairing, that is to say a hope-burdened people, a beautiful death is not enough.

Lusty Tom Stucley's fame didn't last. Ballads published in London between 1579 and 1600 soon faded. At Affeton Castle in Devon, above the lush valley of the Little Dart river, Sir Hugh Stucley told me how his family like to holiday in Morocco. However,

he assured me that they didn't go searching for Tom. Sixteenth-
century Stucleys could not be proud of him. Irish plots rumbled
on, but lacked that explosion of madness which Stucley and the
pope's troops would have detonated in Elizabeth's face.

The year after the battle, 1579, it was ordered that the doors of
the monastery of Santa Cruz in the ancient university town of
Coimbra be opened at five on the morning of the Feast of the Five
Martyrs of Morocco and not shut after mass because of the crush,
but kept open until compline be ended. In Santa Cruz are interred
the first two kings of Portugal, who between them reigned eighty-
three years. On the day of the blessed martyr St Sebastian, 20
January, people and clergy process to Santa Cruz 'in memory of the
great mercy and favour which the Kingdom of Portugal received
from our Lord God, through the intercession of that holy martyr,
in that he gave us on this day King Sebastião our Lord'. The desired
one, *o Desejado*, first appeared after his father's death. Desired once
more, he must reappear after his own and restore Portugal to
greatness.

I am walking, more humbly, on a track over the top of the Serra
de Sintra that leads to its end, its western scarp. It takes me from
the cork-lined Convento dos Capuchos to the heady chapel of Nossa
Senhora de Peninha high above Cabo da Roca and the Atlantic
Ocean. There at the Cape of the Rock, which is Europe's westernmost point, I am making for a meeting.

The views are intoxicating. To the south and west the Tagus,
and the river beneath the river, runs out into an ocean with the
sheen of grey hospital linoleum. But then, I am hardly seeing it.
My head is full of madness.

Below me at Colares they used to celebrate the *Festa do Imperador*
at which a sixteen-year-old virgin boy would be led into church
and crowned emperor for the day. More sensible, I think, than
ascribing power to a long bloodline and ending up dead in the
desert. But there's one strain they do preserve around Colares: the
oldest vines in Europe, brought from France in 1255. Each mother
root is planted ten feet deep, in the Mesozoic clay that underlies
the sand, by men wearing baskets on their heads. In case of sandfall
they can breathe. They don't plan to sleep under a dune.

One blistering day I'd struggled inland up the road from Azenhas do Mar, that tumbles down a cleft in high sea cliffs, to seek them out. At last, beyond picnic sites and pine forest, I'd found them. They looked good for their age, the only European vines to escape the 1870s' phylloxera plague. The aphid came from America. So did the resistant strains that restocked Bordeaux and the rest. All but these. In hope, I paid a lot for a bottle of red, but it was just seven years old, still too astringent to oxidise to any sort of kindliness. Its depth and richness suggested it might soften and strengthen to something fruity and briary, but I was disappointed. Ask for Colares Chita, the older the better, they said, like the one Fernando Pessoa drank at the Alcântara Mar nightclub in the first chapter of your book.

From Peninha I can see beyond Colares to the monastery palace of Mafra built by forty-five thousand workmen not long before the great earthquake. There, beneath carillon-towers like minarets, Manuel II and his mother spent their last night on Portuguese soil before embarking for exile in 1910. It was to Mafra, Dom Duarte told me, that the pope was destined to move, that is, to relocate the Holy See when Portugal realised its vocation as gateway between the old and the new worlds, when it ruled the fifth empire at last, when His Holiness presided over the empire of the Holy Spirit.

Up here, at the high convent of Our Lady of Peninha, tresses of women's hair hang in thanks for humbler miracles. Beside the ruined hermitage where holy men first lived eight centuries ago, Sebastião took refuge at Christmas 1977, planning to stay until 'the threatening month of August', the fourth centenary of Alcácer-Quibir. Almeida Faria tells us so in *O Conquistador*. On his twenty-fourth birthday Sebastião looked down upon Cabo da Roca and recalled how his grandmother Catarina 'used to tell me that, on a winter's day, in the early morning, despite the fog, João de Castro the lighthouse-keeper had gone down to Adraga beach to catch octopi when he came upon me inside an enormous egg, with my head, arms and legs sticking out'.

He keeps coming back. He makes landfall out of a sea fog that symbolises uncertainty and possibility. In Brazil, he is expected to descend from heaven to liberate the oppressed. In Morocco a group secretly waits for his return. Why, when his defeat there was so humiliating, so conclusive? His gentleman of the bedchamber found a corpse, tied his handkerchief around its neck and said, this is the king. But after four or five days in that heat some say Sebastião would have been unrecognisable. It was officially announced that his body had been interred under the governor of Alcácer's house.

Back home, at almost seventy, great-uncle Cardinal Henry took the throne and tried for papal dispensation to marry the thirteen-year-old daughter of the Braganças so that he could provide a legitimate successor where young Sebastião had failed. He spent his short reign raising ruinous ransoms for noble soldiers enslaved in Morocco. In 1579 plague hit Lisbon. Cardinal-King Henry died on 31 January 1580. Spanish armies entered Portugal on 18 June. The next day António, the prior of Crato who'd gone to Africa with Sebastião, was acclaimed king at Santarém. António was the bastard son of Sebastião's great-uncle Luís and had Elizabeth I's backing, but in August he was defeated by the Duke of Alba at the battle of Alcântara. Philip II of Spain made his entrance, as Philip I of Portugal, in December. He had tried to dissuade his nephew Sebastião from his Moroccan crusade and was in many ways pro-Portuguese. The first person he asked to see was Luís de Camões, but the poet was six months dead. In 1582, the year he paid a fortune for the remains of Sebastião, *si vera est fama*, Philip defeated a French expedition to establish António in the Açores.

Both Philip and António needed Sebastião dead. The desired one was now the hidden one, the king-so-longed-for, the once-and-future-king, object of a messianic cult that perfectly expressed the people's longing for the return of a strong leader. He was the icon for all who longed to live in not-Spain. Ten years after the revolution I asked after him.

'Now I suppose nobody thinks he's going to come,' a Lisbon friend told me then, 'but we are waiting for something, I don't know what, a kind of miracle perhaps.' She smiled sheepishly. 'More or less as the Jews wait for the Messiah we are waiting for I don't know whom, but something or someone who will give us a good life and all good things once more.'

There's waiting and waiting. There's living in vigorous expectation, or in suspended animation. A future or a blank. In the twenty years after Alcácer-Quibir four pseudo-Sebastiãos appeared.

A hermit of Penamacor was Sebastião in sackcloth and ashes; he spoke 'Arabic' gibberish and gathered a little court about him before he was condemned to the galleys. Sebastião of Ericeira mourned the battle, groaned at his country's fate and raised an army of peasants who resisted the authorities; two hundred-odd paid with their lives. It was Sebastião, a pastry-cook of Madrigal in Castile, who deceived John of Austria's illegitimate daughter in her nunnery there. It was a penitent Sebastião who reappeared at Venice in 1598, promoted by Portuguese expatriates. Later, it was Sebastião who stirred up trouble for Marshal Junot in 1813. And Sebastião, or the idea of him, who fomented riots in Brazil and spawned the Sebastianists whom Richard Burton met in São Paulo.

Now I have come down to earth at Cabo da Roca. Down to earth 460 feet above the ocean's frayed white fringe. Here, amongst abundant fleshy-leaved magenta-flowered politically-incorrect Hottentot figs, a rare thrift clings on, an endangered species whose very name seems uncertain of itself, *Armeria pseudoarmeria*. The pseudo-thrift has white flowers, not pink, as though it too made landfall out of a promising fog. My latitude is 38° 47' North, my longitude 9° 30' West. It says so on a plaque below a high cross. It also says, in Camões's words, 'Here . . . where the earth ends and the sea begins.' At the tourist post I could buy a certificate, if I so desired, to confirm my position. It would prove to my friends and business associates that I've ventured as far west as it's possible to go in Europe. Near the cross is a monument to the man who founded the local Rotary Club. Just to the north is the lighthouse where Almeida Faria's Sebastião grew up. It is the beacon that kills *saudade* in the homebound mariner's heart, though on a fog-free day he may first see what seems to be cloud, but hangs solid above the horizon and turns out to be the scarp of the Serra de Sintra that levitates until the light winks at its foot . . . and winks again on the cliff-top. As Sebastião is said to have come ashore at Cape St Vincent where ravens brought the saint's bones home, so too here we understand the end of that long ache of exile.

But why do we rush the other way? Why do we have to hurry to the edge and look over? As tourists we run to the beach, to headlands like this – Land's End, Finisterre, Fim do Mundo – following some atavistic instinct to see where our world finishes and where, beyond the horizon, possible worlds begin, in the hope of finding the best of them.

> Here is the end of all the ancient earth,
> Here begins the temptation of the sea.

Soon after Henry the Navigator set up his school of navigation near the *fim do mundo*, Portuguese sailors touched Madeira. That was in 1419. *Madeira* means 'wood'. The fire settlers lit to clear a few trees lasted seven years. Rich ash is the island's biggest asset. The first Portuguese boy and girl born there were christened Adão and Eva, Adam and Eve.

It must have been a charred and acrid Eden, but it was a beginning. Seed of the apocalypse. Slaves. Spices. Once we were so great. Alcácer-Quibir. Now we are so small. Brazilian gold. Lisbon earthquake. Once, but now. Great and small. *Aqui, aquém, além.* Here, on the brink of the beyond, I'm shuffling history like a Tarot pack: Caravel, Sphere, *Guitarra*, Perfect Prince, Tremor, Raven, Cross, Slave Girl, Hidden King, Poet, Rose of Winds, *Saudade*, Crescent, Fishwife, Deluge, Exile, Spanish Devil, Bull, Cinnamon, *Fadista*, Knight Templar, Gold, Saint, Gypsy, *Pega*, Castle, Carnation, Destiny, Joker.

Friends who have come to meet me here pick up their hands and try to read them. North, a pale ochre finger of rock. Next, a great grey stump. Beneath us, sea crumples and unfolds around stacks and rocks. South, the next headland is a shimmering silhouette. Westwards, haze muffles the horizon.

'The will to be far and far and far is very Portuguese,' Lídia Jorge remarked with biting lyricism. 'We have a taste for the very far without a name, not an empire but a metaphysical dream, without ground, always outside our time.'

'But after Sebastião's death we lost our independence', said Almeida Faria, 'our colonies started to be sold, our armada went away to fight Britain and was completely defeated, all because of Sebastião. But myths are irrational. Monstrous kings are always more appealing to our fantasy.'

'It's a paradox that, even at the height of decadence and Sebastianic longings, the Portuguese were busy building empires else-

254

where,' said Helder Macedo, 'and it's not with revivalist nonsense that empires are built. It was not King Sebastião who did it, it was the peasants from Tras-os-Montes and, alas, in its last few years, the soldiers from all over Portugal.'

I quoted Eça de Queirós at my friends. He defines Portuguese characteristics in *The Illustrious House of Ramires*, and concludes his list with 'underlying melancholy, vanity, desire to shine; everlasting hope for a miracle; attachment to the ancient family home, sudden departure for Africa'.

'This Portuguese identity that is this big myth, I really don't know what it is,' chuckled Luísa Costa Gomes, 'but people seem to be very fond of it. We are a country with eight hundred years of history, and only after 1974 are we so worried about this identity. What is it that we seemed to have and don't have any more? I think that what we have is ignorance. Ignorance of history, this very beautiful history of discoveries that we have, because we don't know what it was really about and we don't want to know.' Now she was angry. 'People are starting to talk about the shame of leaving Africa. We never cared about Africa in five hundred years, and this can be proven!'

'The way we are treating African and Brazilian people as foreigners is a stupidity,' said Ernesto Manuel de Melo e Castro.

'Every day people are being arrested at the airport and sent back to their civil wars to die,' said Luísa. 'Portugal the Gate of Heaven, and it's closed!'

The haze over the sea was thickening.

'So now you've turned your backs on the temptation of the sea,' I said. 'You've decided to face Brussels and Maastricht, it seems, to travel backwards out of the big world.'

'I think turning our back on the ocean is a fatal mistake,' said Ernesto. 'Maybe I don't belong to the Portugal of the nineties.' He shrugged. 'Because we joined the European Community we shouldn't stop being Portuguese. Our culture is much more Atlantic than Central European. As José Saramago says, this side of the Pyrenees it's quite a different thing.'

'Well, I hope that the European Union is the final nail in the coffin of dead King Sebastião,' said Helder. 'Rather than prophetic rhymes there are pragmatic EU regulations, roads.'

'So we don't have to stay in love with death?' I suggested.

'There's a morbid streak in all cultures. Some people like it, but with such a sense of loss, a traumatic accession to Spain, there was an almost necrophiliac element.'

'Brussels is prosaic,' Almeida Faria nodded, 'but millions come from Brussels every second. It's unfair to take the cash and attack it. I'm pro-Europe, not ignoring Brazil and Africa. When Portugal was an important country it was cosmopolitan, it had business with everybody; but the greatness of Portugal,' he grimaced, 'if that exists, is in its cultural life, in literature.'

'Our empire was not an empire of power over the sea like the English empire, or an empire of culture like the French. We are the empire of God.' Lídia Jorge laughed softly, 'It is something terrible, not material. We had the idea that we were very important and one day we discovered we were a little part of the Iberian Peninsula. Who are we? After the revolution we were alone. Which way to go? Europe, Brazil, Africa? Spain is changing but we are changing more deeply, more quickly.'

They used to say in Russia that only the past is unpredictable. But all our memories, our knowledge of what we once were, shift alarmingly. We tailor our past to fit the hopes we cling to, knowing that later we'll want to look back and make sense of life. Europe is busy doing that now. At its edge, Portugal too is suffering the same boring old mid-life crisis. I feel for it deeply, because I too am examining how my past – and the past of my family, my tribe, my people – dictates my future and how my future will continually shift my view of the past.

'Ah, now I see what happened.'

It's an equation we can read both ways. The present is the unspeakably brief now, simply a causal link, or the always and only moment of freedom we ever have. In adolescence we believe that the past can be left for dead. Forward is the only way to go, until we grow to understand that the equation runs backwards too. Belief in life after death is a way to prolong immaturity as long as possible. Of Portugal's most recent adolescence Maria Velho da Costa wrote this, in *Missa in Albis*: 'A 25 April in the year 1974 had to have been on its way. I too was helping it happen but it didn't touch my life. Unless puny insurrectionists become resurrectionists.'

Old-fashioned Marxists, as well as monarchists, would love to be Sebastianists. Some people still believe that the claimant who appeared in Venice in 1598 was the king. There they found him not guilty. It was in Naples, where Spain held sway, that they sentenced him to the galleys. But many who'd known him, including the Duke and Duchess of Medina Sidonia, were convinced he was the king.

'The documents of the trial have disappeared, they've never been found in the archives of the Vatican.' Maria Leonor Machado de Sousa looked sideways. 'An old monk who had lived with him in court since his childhood went to Venice with a list of the twenty-eight special signs he had – one arm longer than the other, one foot bigger, a different ear – and it's said he could recognise them all. There was a last one, I don't know what it was, a twenty-ninth, that would settle all doubts.'

'But didn't,' I said.

'There were a good half-a-dozen pseudo-Sebastiãos,' Helder pursed his lips, 'including that one who sounded credible, until it became quite apparent that he could not speak Portuguese. Sebastião was not a genius, but I think he spoke the language.'

'Yes, but that was after twenty years living in foreign countries,' argued Maria. 'Nowadays with Portuguese emigrants to France, after only two years they have mixed up Portuguese and French and can't remember words in their mother tongue. They have radio, TV, newspapers, and he had nothing.'

'You believe the case for that claimant is strong?' I asked.

'Yes,' she said, 'I think so.'

The thickened haze was lapping at the cliff-top. The ocean, the new oceanarium that is, lies on Lisbon's far side. To get to it from here you must turn round and go east, or upriver. If you want to reach the ocean from far Cape St Vincent you must now drive out of Algarve, through Alentejo and across the Vasco da Gama Bridge to the site of Expo '98. This is the route Sebastião will take. Seeing him, 'a little boy masked for some future carnival' in his niche on the façade of the Rossio station only recently, José Saramago was 'clear that the Awaited One will arrive by train, subject to delays', but I'm now convinced that he will let his ravens fly free at the world's end, shrug off his shroud of fog, step glitteringly arrayed

257

into his motorcade and sweep north and west flanked by raven-black motorcyclists, arriving from *o além* (the beyond), from *além do Tejo*, across the brand-new bridge to take the world by storm at Olivais.

My friends have left me. In the fog on the cape I still feel a little crazy. I think of the *avieiros*, those fishermen of Phoenician ancestry, who abandoned the sea and moved upriver. Almeida Garrett met them on the ferry. They argued that the sea was stronger than a bull, that they were more courageous than *campinos* fresh from the ring. But they'd already broken faith with the ocean. I met them, still bare-footed, at Caneiras. All their young seemed to want was motorcycles, cars, houses. As I've said, it's not a bad time, after a decade in Europe, to travel in Portugal with Almeida Garrett.

'Go on, money-grubbers, go on!' he raged in 1846. 'Reduce everything to figures, boil down all the world's considerations to equations of material interest: buy, sell, speculate. In the end, what profit will there have been for the human species? A few dozen more rich men. I ask the political economists and moralists if they've worked out the number of individuals who must be condemned to misery, overwork, depravity, criminality, wanton ignorance, insurmountable wretchedness, absolute poverty in order to produce one rich man.'

Nothing new in that equation. And now all Europe has turned its back on the sea to grapple with the minotaur at the heart of the EU labyrinth. Portugal no longer entrances itself in Camões's hall of mirrors, it checks the cut of its business suit in the long thin cheval glass. It reflects on its real size.

But I remember the screaming gypsy boy in the little encampment below Santarém who ran to his mother so that she might kiss his hurt better. She did it. I recall the sideshow on a Lisbon street, the vendor stamping on his toy man which levitated again, and again. I think of *Portugal* (1955) by Roy Campbell, the South African poet who fought for Franco in the Spanish Civil War. He ends his book by cherishing an illusion: 'Lisbon's Christian imperial mission (as it was then, and is again now) as restored and revived by the miracle of Fátima and the genius of Salazar.' You can waste a lifetime waiting for a strong man or woman to come back and pretend to kiss you better. Fernando Pessoa gave El-Rei Dom Sebastião a voice:

Mad, yes, mad, for I wanted majesty
such as Fate never allows.
My conviction did not fit within me;
that's why, where the desert lies,
my has-been self remained, not he who is.

My madness, let others take it from me
and all that went with it.
Without madness what can man be
other than a healthy brute,
a postponed corpse that procreates?

Pessoa had long been certain that the fifth empire, Portugal's future, was written down. Those who knew how could read it in the prophecies of the cobbler Bandarra and of Nostradamus. 'The future is to be universal.' But by the summer of 1935 he wrote a bleak 'Elegy in Shadow' which realises with a shock that:

The heroes shine at a distance
In a past impossible to see.

He reluctantly renounced mad dreams and in July 1935, four months before his death, wrote these four lines:

Now I am tranquil. Now I wait for nothing.
Now upon my vacant heart
Descended the blessed unconsciousness
Of not wanting an illusion.

The fog wraps me up. It is not swaddling comfort. It is not chill as death. It is fog. It rolls in. Beneath it the ocean mumbles invisibly. At my feet even the Hottentot fig and pseudo-thrift plants fade. But I'm on firm ground at Europe's edge. The frontier between hope and fear. The *now* between extravagant *saudades* for past and future. Cabo da Roca is not the end, but the beginning. Portugal the paradigm world power, so great, so small, has that at least to teach the rest of us.

SELECT BIBLIOGRAPHY

Hans Christian Andersen (trans. Grace Thornton), *A Visit to Portugal 1866* (London, 1972)

Mascarenhas Barreto (trans. George Dykes), *Fado: Lyrical Origins and Poetic Motivation* (Lisboa, n.d.)

Mascarenhas Barreto, *O Português Cristóvão Colombo Agente Secreto do Rei Dom João II* (Lisboa, 1988)

Martin C. Battestin with Ruthe R. Battestin, *Henry Fielding: A Life* (London, 1989)

Aubrey Bell, *In Portugal* (London, 1912)

V. de Bragança Cunha, *Eight Centuries of Portuguese Monarchy* (London, 1911)

Ann Bridge and Susan Lowndes, *The Selective Traveller in Portugal* (London, 1949)

Roy Campbell, *Portugal* (London, 1955)

John Dryden, *Don Sebastian* (London, 1690)

Almeida Faria, *O Conquistador* (Lisboa, 1990)

Henry Fielding, *Journal of a Voyage to Lisbon* (London, 1755)

Peter Fryer and Patricia McGowan Pinheiro, *Oldest Ally: A Portrait of Salazar's Portugal* (London, 1961)

Rodney Gallop, *Portugal: A Book of Folkways* (Cambridge, 1936)

Almeida Garrett (trans. John M. Parker), *Travels in my Homeland* (London, 1987)

Lawrence S. Graham and Douglas L. Wheeler (eds), *In Search of Modern Portugal: The Revolution and its Consequences* (Madison, Wisconsin, 1983)

Jonathan Griffin, *The Hidden King* (London, 1955)

Adam Hopkins, *Spanish Journeys* (London, 1992)

John Izon, *Sir Thomas Stucley: Traitor Extraordinary* (London, 1956)

Marion Kaplan, *The Portuguese: The Land and its People* (London, 1991)

Martin Kayman, *Revolution and Counter Revolution in Portugal* (London, 1987)

T.D. Kendrick, *The Lisbon Earthquake* (London, 1956)

Eugénio Lisboa with L.C. Taylor (eds), *A Centenary Pessoa* (Manchester, 1995)

H.V. Livermore, *A History of Portugal* (Cambridge, 1947)

H.V. Livermore, *Portugal: A Short History* (Edinburgh, 1973)

Rose Macaulay, *They Went to Portugal* (London, 1946)

Rose Macaulay (ed. L.C. Taylor), *They Went to Portugal Too* (Manchester, 1990)

Bernard McGuirk (ed.), *Three Persons on One* (Nottingham, 1988)

Kenneth Gordon McIntyre, *The Secret Discovery of Australia* (Sydney, 1977)

Maria Leonor Machado de Sousa (ed.), *D. Sebastião na Literatura Inglesa* (Lisboa, 1985)

Kenneth Maxwell, *Pombal: Paradox of the Enlightenment* (Cambridge, 1995)

George Peele, *The Tragical Battle of Alcazar in Barbary* (London, 1594)

Fernando Pessoa ('Bernardo Soares') (trans. Margaret Jull Costa), *The Book of Disquiet* (London, 1991)

Fernando Pessoa, *Mensagem* (Lisboa, 1934), translated (Jonathan Griffin) as *Message* (London, 1992)

Fernando Pessoa, *Lisboa: O que o Turista deve ver/What the Tourist Should See* (Lisboa, 1992)

V.S. Pritchett, *At Home and Abroad* (London, 1989)

Datus C. Proper, *The Last Old Place* (New York, 1992)

Alves Redol, *Os Avieiros* (Lisbon, 1945. 5th edition 1980)

Richard Robinson, *Contemporary Portugal* (London, 1979)

Dr António de Oliveira Salazar, *Doctrine and Action: Internal and Foreign Policy of the New Portugal 1928–1939* (London, 1939)

José Saramago (trans. Giovanni Pontiero), *The Year of the Death of Ricardo Reis* (London, 1992)

José Saramago (trans. Giovanni Pontiero), *The Stone Raft* (London, 1994)

Mario Soares, *Portugal's Struggle for Liberty* (London, 1975)

John Symonds, *The King of the Shadow Realm* (London, 1989)

Antonio Tabucchi (trans. Margaret Jull Costa), *Requiem* (London, 1994)

Padre José Teixeira, *The True History of the Late and Lamentable Adventures of Don Sebastian . . .* (London, 1602)

Padre José Teixeira, *A Continuation of the Lamentable and Admirable Adventures of Don Sebastian . . .* (London, 1603)

Miguel Torga, *Poemas Ibéricos* (Coimbra, 1965. 2nd edition 1982)

Miguel Torga, *Portugal* (Coimbra, 1950. 4th edition 1980)

Voltaire (François-Marie Arouet) (trans. Tobias Smollett et al), *Candide, or The Optimist* (London, 1762)

Richard Zenith (guest editor), *Translation*, vol. XXV: *Portugal* (New York, 1991)

INDEX

CENTRAL PORTUGAL

ATLANTIC OCEAN

- Pombal
- Praia de Vieira
- Marinha Grande
  - Leiria
- Batalha

Tomar

- Nazaré
- Alcobaça

FATIMA
Sa de Aire

Nila Nova da Barquinha
Entroncamento · Tancos
Golegã ·

Cast
de
Almourol
· Chamus

- Caldas
  da Rainha
- Peniche · Óbidos

- Santarém ·
- Vale de Santarem
  Cartaxo ·

- Alpiarça
- Almeirim
- Fazendas
  de Almeirim

c. de
finister

Coimbr

- Torres Vedras
- Azambuja ·
- Vila Nova da Rainha
- Ericeira
- Vila Franca
  de Xira
- Mafra
- Alhandra ·
- Alverca
  do Ribatejo
- Sacavem ·

- Salraterra de
  Magos

c.
Br

· L.

lagos
C. de
Vice

- Cabo
  da
  Roca
- Sintra
- Colares
- Ja de Sintra
- LISBON
- Cabo
  Raso
- ESTORIL
- Belém
- Cascais
- Carcavelos
- Boca
  do
  Inferno
- Costa
  da Caparica
- Almada
- Alcochete
- Montijo

Tagus

Alcaçer

- SETUBAL

- Cabo Espichel